# DUEL WITH THE DEVIL

# DUEL WITH THE DEVIL

*The True Story of How*
*Alexander Hamilton and Aaron Burr*
*Teamed Up to Take on America's First*
*Sensational Murder Mystery*

## PAUL COLLINS

CROWN PUBLISHERS
NEW YORK

Cataloging-in-Publication data is on file with the Library of Congress.

ISBN 978-0-307-95645-3
eISBN 978-0-307-95647-7

Printed in the United States of America

*Book design by Lauren Dong*
*Map by David Cain*
*Jacket design by Albert Tang*
*Jacket illustrations: [House of Representatives] Encyclopaedia Britannica/*
*Universal Images Group/Getty Images; [Burr] MPI/Stringer Collection/Archive*
*Photos/Getty Images; [Hamilton] Kean Collection/Archive Photos/Getty Images*

4 6 8 10 9 7 5 3

First Edition

*To my brother Peter,*
*whose room was my first library*

# [ CONTENTS ]

## [ A Note on the Text ]

The unusual court coverage of this affair—the first fully re-corded murder trial in U.S. history—allowed me to draw upon eyewitness testimony to a degree that is extremely rare for this era. Any dialogue in quotation marks comes directly from the conversations recorded in court, as well as from other contemporary firsthand accounts. While I have freely edited out verbiage, not a word has been added.

—P.C.

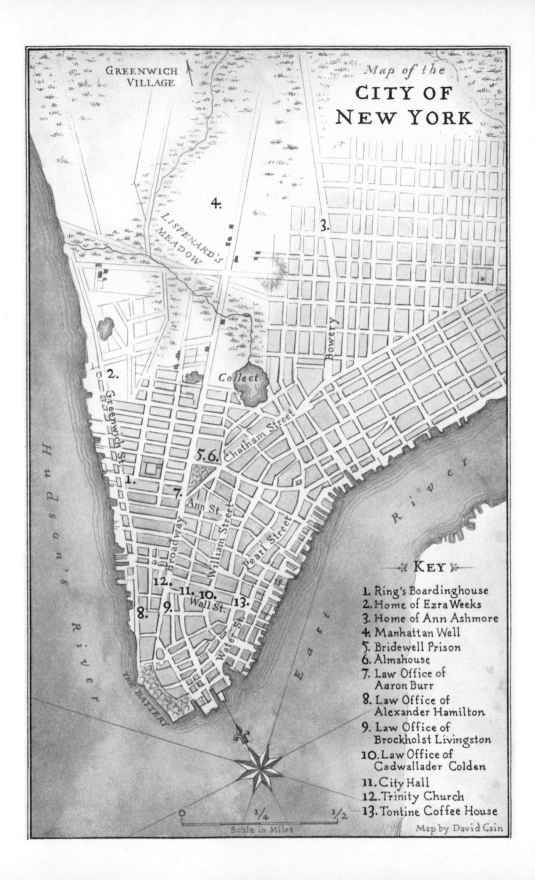

GREENWICH VILLAGE

Map of the
CITY OF
NEW YORK

LISPENARD'S MEADOW

4.

3.

Bowery

Collect

2.

Greenwich St.

Chatham Street

5.6.

1.

7.

Ann St.

Broadway

William Street

Pearl Street

12.

11. 10.

8. 9.

Wall St.

13.

Water St.

THE BATTERY

Hudson's River

East River

⊰ KEY ⊱

1. Ring's Boardinghouse
2. Home of Ezra Weeks
3. Home of Ann Ashmore
4. Manhattan Well
5. Bridewell Prison
6. Almshouse
7. Law Office of
   Aaron Burr
8. Law Office of
   Alexander Hamilton
9. Law Office of
   Brockholst Livingston
10. Law Office of
    Cadwallader Colden
11. City Hall
12. Trinity Church
13. Tontine Coffee House

Map by David Cain

0      1/4      1/2
Scale in Miles

# DUEL WITH THE DEVIL

# PROLOGUE

## [ *January 2, 1800* ]

ANDREW BLANCK HAD JUST BEEN SITTING DOWN TO LUNCH WITH a horsebreaker when Elias Ring and Joseph Watkins showed up and battered on his door. It was a bitterly cold day, and it took a fairly tough sort to live out in Lispenard's Meadow—but the boardinghouse owner and his neighbor, an ironmonger, were not to be trifled with.

*Where did you get it?*

*The well*, Blanck replied. One of Aaron Burr's new municipal wells was out in the meadow, and Blanck's son had found a muff, for covering the hands in cold weather, floating in there more than a week before. On Christmas Eve, in fact—just as the bells were tolling for the death of General Washington.

*I went to the well the next day and looked in*, he explained, *but I saw nothing.*

Joseph and Elias marched out to the meadow, followed by the horsebreaker. The men threw off the wooden cover and ran a long pole down into the dark hole. Mr. Ring could feel an object in the water, a heavy and inert mass, but he couldn't hook it. The local boys were now gathering to look, and one was sent back for some rope, with which they created a simple net. This time the mass came up.

There was a tangle of hair floating in the water—a wet shoulder—and a face looking upwards . . .

PART I

THE VICTIM

[ *Six Months Earlier* ]

# THE GREAT SICKNESS

IT WAS A FINE DAY FOR WONDERS. GIANT LOBSTER CLAWS, A LIT-
tle pagoda, some unburnable asbestos paper—these were the peculiar riches of a collection that the late Gardiner Baker had begun for
his museum nearly a decade earlier, during General Washington's
triumphant first term in office. But in July 1799 the museum wilted
in the drowsy Manhattan summer, its hush scarcely broken by the
arrival of two young women in plain Quaker dress. Accompanying
them was a strapping young man in the simple garb of a carpenter
on his day off.

*Elma?*

The younger of the two women fell all too readily into mor-
bid reverie, and sometimes her cousin Hope had to rouse her. But
in a such a place as this, how could one not stop to gaze in wonder? Towering above them was Gilbert Stuart's grand oil portrait
of Washington—the great man looked out over the museum, a reminder of when the country and the museum itself were both still
new and wondrous. Back then, Manhattan was the infant country's
capital, and Baker's Museum was still housed down on Wall Street
in a lovely sky-blue antechamber of the Stock Exchange. Customers paid two shillings to view an immense and intricate clock that
waltzed through an entire concert, get shocked by one of Baker's
splendid Electrical Machines, and stand in awe of a marvelous work
of glass sculpture—"a TRANSPARENT MONUMENT," the ads promised.
A figure of Christopher Columbus, it was lit to a fiery glow by a
cunning arrangement of lanterns and chandeliers.

But now the glow was fading.

The sounds of commerce from Greenwich Street filtered into the new quarters that the old curator's widow had been reduced to. Not so long ago, the museum had been wildly awake with Gardiner's latest scheme—a menagerie of "Living Animals"—including everything from a pair of wolves and a bald eagle to a monkey and a "Mongooz, a beautiful animal from the Island of Madagascar." Now they had lapsed into silence. Elma's cousin, Hope Sands, wandered past the nailed-shut storage boxes— filled, perhaps, with old Mr. Baker's hundreds of volumes of philosophy and natural history—and their fellow boarder Levi Weeks could pause before the wax figures of the great boxers Mendoza and Humphries, still posed as if ready to clobber each other. Nearby, a figure of Ben Franklin gazed impotently among waxworks of once-titillating feminine "beauties of New York, Annapolis, Salem, and New Haven."

*The famed Musical Concert Clock is for sale*, visitors were mournfully informed. *That is, should you wish to buy it.*

They did not: They were ready to leave. It was a shame, the passing of the old curator—but that summer in New York, deaths were no surprise at all.

SIGNS HUNG along the streets, creaking slightly whenever the breeze stirred, each proclaiming where its shopkeeper had come from:

STEPHEN DANDO,
FROM LONDON,
HATTER.

LAW AND BUTTE,
FROM GLASGOW,
BOOT MAKERS.

ANTOINE ARNEUX,
A LA PARIS,
MARCHAND TAILLEUR.

It was a tradition peculiar to Manhattan. Shopkeepers mentioned their hometowns in the hope of landing customers from their newly arrived countrymen; for everyone here, it seemed, hailed from somewhere else. Manhattan was where you went to reinvent yourself, whether you were slightly fractured nobility from Paris, a rabble-rousing radical from London—or, like Elma and Hope, young Quaker women from an upstate farm, simply looking to find better prospects in life.

The city swelled with such arrivals, and its population of sixty thousand made it the largest city in the young republic. Greenwich Street, once a rustic lane running through riverside meadows, was now sprouting fashionable brick houses and storefronts at a stunning rate. After a visit to widow Baker's museum, you could stop into William Maxwell's, Distiller & Tallow Chandler, for a good dose of his vaunted rum, and thus fortified, go to the next shop over for some godless tract such as Palmer's *Principles of Nature*. If you were feeling a bit testy, there were "well-finished Hair-Trigger Pistols" from gunsmith Joseph Finch, as he kept several cases on hand for Manhattan's querulous gentlemen. Or, if a quiet weekend indoors was what you had in mind, tinsmith Tom Eagles could supply a table's worth of "egg codlers," hammered teapots, and "coffee biggins"—the last being the latest fad from France, involving the *boiling* of coffee rather than merely drinking it as a dissolved powder.

Getting from one shop to the next was not the easiest task. Manhattan's muddy cobblestone streets were so badly paved that longtime residents acquired a cautious gait; Ben Franklin claimed you could spot visiting New Yorkers on Philadelphia's smooth streets by the way they shuffled. They had to, for old New York buildings were built in the Dutch style, with elevated first stories and stoops that jutted out into the street, ready to trip up the unwary on dark nights. Even the few streets with unobstructed brick sidewalks were comically narrow—just wide enough, as one chronicler put it, to accommodate "two lean men to walk abreast or one fat man alone."

Yet for the three museumgoers, it was still a pleasant afternoon's walk. It had not always been thus: Great swaths of the city had been destroyed by fire in the Revolution, and what wasn't burned out of spite was burned for survival. When he reconnoitered the British-occupied island in 1781, George Washington had found it "totally stripped of trees," with the old woods and orchards chopped down after a series of brutal winters. It was only now, a generation later, that the city had truly recovered.

Except, perhaps, in one matter: the water.

On a hot July day, water gushed from the shining brass pumps installed along the thoroughfare; the rills that splashed out were good for cooling off, as well as for putting out fires or washing up. But few people were foolish enough to *drink* from the public pumps. For Manhattanites, as it happened, boiling coffee in a tin biggin was an excellent idea—because otherwise, a cup of the stuff might kill you. The destruction and deforestation of the war had once nearly caused local wells to run dry, and the explosive growth of the recovering city had only made matters worse.

"The water is very bad to drink," lamented a teetotaling English traveler who unwisely quenched his thirst from Manhattan's public pumps—"before I found this out, and suffered sometimes sickness, with very severe pains in the bowels."

If you were walking down Greenwich on a hot summer day, you were far better off going into David Forrest's grocery for some of the local spruce beer—or better still, into the tavern on the corner. When a man in New York valued his health, he also valued a stiff drink.


The tavern wasn't the usual place for Hope, not if she were to follow Quaker principles of moderation. While her more free-spirited cousin Elma hadn't fully devoted herself to the sect yet, it was not quite a fit place for her, either. But for a young carpenter, on a hot day in July, the tavern near the corner of Greenwich and Barclay was a fine place to slake a thirst for drink or local news.

For the former there was cherry bounce, a sweet dram of cherry brandy spiked with extra sugar; or rum fruit punch; or blackstrap, a witches' brew of rum, molasses, and herbs; or the benign old favorite bogus, which was just rum mixed with beer.

Sooner or later, in any case, you'd be having some rum.

In newspapers, there was considerably more choice at hand: the literary-minded *New-York Weekly Museum*; Federalist broadsheets, including Noah Webster's *New-York Commercial Advertiser*; and Republican rags like *Greenleaf's New-York Journal*. Newspapers were still expensive enough that only the more respectable men in town had them delivered at home; others shared copies in local coffeehouses and taverns. The latest news was of the riotous mob who'd tried for three nights to pull down a local brothel just two blocks away, on the corner of Greenwich and Murray. Some in the tavern had, perhaps, firsthand knowledge of the shocking particulars of Mrs. Murphy's establishment, but what went on there was hardly enough to whip up a riot. No, it took a murder to stir this kind of anger—in this case, that of a man who'd disappeared into Mrs. Murphy's house of ill fame one night, only to be found the next day out by the docks—quite dead.

"We understand (for we resort to no such place) that the mob assembled again the night before last in considerable numbers," reported the *New-York Gazette*. At least a thousand rioters had tried to smash apart Mrs. Murphy's brothel, and Mayor Richard Varick had called out a regiment of mounted troops to disperse them. In the end, Mrs. Murphy proved the picture of fetchingly disheveled innocence. It seemed her customer had walked out of the brothel on his own and simply expired in the night—as young men sometimes did in Manhattan.

"The plea is, the necessity of *correcting* abuses, or *avenging* crimes," the *Gazette* warned the next day. "But what rectitude of judgment can be expected from a mob, composed of the lowest, most illiterate, ignorant, and inflammatory parts of a community? It acts upon *report*, commonly *false* reports—and vents its rage as frequently upon the innocent as the guilty—for, real innocence or guilt cannot generally be decided by them. If they strike the *culpable*, it is merely the effect of *chance*."

Levi Weeks, at least, could expect to work, make his name, and stay clear of these numberless mobs and snares of the city. The boardinghouse he lived in on Greenwich was a respectable one, and it had the pleasant distractions of his landlord's sister-in-law Hope and her cousin Elma. To be a carpenter and a foreman in his brother's upstanding construction firm—and a boarder in a respectable Quaker boardinghouse, with the chaste favor of two of the proprietor's unmarried relatives—it was a fine thing, really.

THE NEWSPAPERS were not as reassuring. There was the usual cacophony of notices, including an enigmatic dockside offer of "BRANDY Exchanged for PORK," and a ten-dollar reward for the return of "a Negro MAN, named Henry." But amid these ordinary items, a column in the *New-York Spectator* pierced like a needle: "A letter received in town yesterday by a reputable mercantile house, from Philadelphia, has the following painful sentence. 'The Fever is, we are sorry to say, now actually here, and has made some considerable progress.'"

Nobody needed to ask which fever it was. Along the Atlantic coast, there were two illness that everyone feared each year. In the winter it was the slow and crippling terror of smallpox, and in the summer, it was the swift-moving fire of yellow fever. The latter had plagued cities along the Atlantic seaboard for nearly a century, though for most of that time it had appeared only every decade or so. Since the end of the Revolution, however, the scourge had been returning with increasing frequency—and nobody was quite sure why.

Noah Webster had his own theory. He'd just published a new book, *A Brief History of Epidemic and Pestilential Diseases; with the Principal Phenomena of the Physical World, Which Precede and Accompany Them, and Observations Deduced from the Facts Stated*. After elaborately charting the occurrences of comets, earthquakes, volcanoes, and various plagues, the great grammarian was convinced: They were all somehow *connected*. Clearly some sort of invisible electrical fluid bound the earth to its inhabitants; to Webster, natural convulsions such as the eruptions of Mount Etna were like a tidal wave crashing through that electrical fluid. "Those periods, in general, have been most distinguished for sickness over the world, in which the fire of the earth has exhibited the most numerous and violent effects," he theorized. "It is probable that the invisible operations of the electrical fluid produce more effects than those which are seen."

That was one way to look at it: but another, and far more gratifying, was to blame foreigners. The first known outbreak of yellow fever had occurred in 1703, before its malignancy even had a name. It was simply called "the great sickness." The blame that first summer fell on a ship from St. Thomas that arrived in Manhattan peculiarly close to the beginning of the outbreak. Ever since, suspicion attached itself to these "vessels from one of the sickly ports of the West Indies." One epidemic was even blamed on a load of rotten coffee that an exotic trader had dumped unsold on a Philadelphia wharf. And for believers in contagion theories, this introduction of the fever to one city from the next had a logical conclusion: the need for a quarantine.

But others hazarded that there might be more local causes— "exhalations from the ground," as local scholar James Hardie put it. The origin of such exhalations was not hard to guess at; the prominent physician David Hosack later estimated that fully one-twelfth of Manhattan's inhabited area was occupied by privies. Down by the sunken elevations near the docks, stagnant pools of brackish water gathered in what one writer termed "an almost innumerable number of cellars and back yards . . . many of them stowed with large quantities of putrid beef, in the neighborhood of filthy sewers." Manhattan's rapid growth aggravated matters; one doctor complained that "in all the streets where buildings were going forward, the workmen were allowed to restrain the course of the water, in the gutters, by forming little dams, for their convenience in making mortar."

Curiously, one reader in Philadelphia had noticed something surely coincidental—mosquitoes appeared at about the same time as the fever did. "The late rains in the city will produce a great increase of mosquitoes in the city, distressing to the sick, and troublesome to those who are well," he wrote to the editor of Dunlap's *American Daily Advertiser*. "Whoever will take the trouble to examine their rain-water tubs, will find millions." The letter writer—who signed himself "A.B."—gave advice so modest that scarcely anyone even noticed it. Pour in "any common oil," he wrote, "which will diffuse over the whole surface, and by excluding the air, [it] will destroy the whole brood."

Back in Manhattan, New Yorkers like Levi Weeks and his fellow tavern idlers mused over A.B.'s letter, rolled up their newspapers to swat away the July mosquitoes, and wondered what on earth it could be that was killing Philadelphians.

BUT THE murmurs were getting louder. Unmarried young women like Elma and Hope who stayed in the city were, perhaps, courting death—and yet neither had the wherewithal to leave town. For a carpenter like Levi, there was simply too much work to be had during the summer months to leave—and, after all, the papers assured them that it was safe to stay.

"Idle tales," scoffed one newspaper at yellow fever reports. "Our citizens may rest easy about this fever at present."

And if they could not rest easy? Then, the editors suggested, they should at least keep a discreet silence. "A false report on that subject," they warned, "ought to be considered a calumny punishable by law." Yelling "Fire!" in a theater was nothing compared to yelling "Fever!" in a crowded city: It crippled trade for months. In its disastrous epidemic of 1793, when a tenth of its population had died, Philadelphia had misled other cities for weeks in a desperate bid to avoid quarantine. New York had done exactly the same in its own epidemics. And to stroll along Manhattan's docks that July in 1799 was to see just what was at stake: Wharves packed with cargo vessels, many named for the sturdy women the owners had left at home. In the dock at that moment there was a ship named *Sister*, the brig *Two Sisters*, and the schooner *Four Sisters*; there was also a *Louisa*, a *Bertha*—and *Betsey, Abigail, Lydia, Charlotte, Cornelia*, and *Prudence*—and not one but three ships christened *Mary*. You could haggle over everything from six-pound cannons to a rather perilously matched cargo of a hundred crates of Bursley crockery and three thousand Stourbridge bricks.

But as the month wore on, the news of yellow fever watches in other cities on the Atlantic seaboard grew ominously quiet. Philadelphia's board of health, it was said, had stopped issuing notices of the week's burials—and had stopped talking to New York at all about their mortality records. Over on Greenwich Street, a seventeen-year-old merchant's daughter, Elizabeth de Hart Bleecker, would be one of the first to find out why.

*There's a Negro man dying outside*, she told her sister one Friday.

Bearing water that the prostrate man was whispering for, they cautiously approached the shivering mass lying in their back alley. He was a sailor on the *Havannah*, he said, and had just landed a few days earlier. The girls quickly sent for a doctor, who immediately had the man borne off to quarantine on Staten Island. The symptoms were unmistakable and horrifying: As one of the fever's very first chroniclers described its victims with brutal directness, "they void and vomit blood."

These were the fever's stigmata: sores and blood, seeping from the ears and eyes and orifices—even from the pores of the skin itself—and a loathsome black vomit that resembled coffee grounds. They were the signs of almost certain death within days, if not hours. Victims became delirious with fever and bled from eyes stained a frightening yellow.

A few held out hope that the cases were isolated: The editor of the *New-York Mercantile Advertiser*, zealous as always on behalf of merchants, insisted that Philadelphia's mortality rate was "by no means alarming." Why should New York worry? But travelers arriving at the port told a different story: The yellow fever was now

in Providence, it was in Newburyport, and it was indeed in Philadelphia. Though Levi and Elma and Hope couldn't leave town, the
mistress of their boardinghouse could and did. By August, even the
*New-York Mercantile Advertiser* hardly blamed her or anyone else
with the means for fleeing the city. In fact, at that point the paper's
editor had nothing at all to say on the matter—for he himself was
dead from yellow fever.

# A Boardinghouse by
# Candlelight

By September 11, 1799, the deaths in Manhattan were getting to William Laight. He sat down that day to mark out his journal, a humble affair with columns lined in by his own hand, where each day, at 8 A.M., 3 P.M., and 8 P.M., the Greenwich Street merchant faithfully recorded the wind speed, direction, and temperature. It was a peculiar fascination, one that few others followed. But now the inexorable and mysterious cycle of fever stared back at him in those figures. On July 3, a clear day of 72 degrees and southerly winds, there'd been the first fateful hint: "Rumour of Yellow Fever at Philadelphia," he'd penned into a margin. Days after showers on July 9, the fever struck New York. Within a couple of weeks dry heat had set in—"Dog days begin," he'd written on the twenty-ninth—and within five days, the fever disappeared. Then, on August 10, "A shower in the night—Rumour of Yellow Fever." It was the same mysterious and deadly cycle every time: showers followed by warm weather, an ominous pause of a few days, and then . . .

September was the worst.

"Above ten have daily died of the Fever during this Month. . . . Oh, oh!!!!!!!!!!!!!," Laight wrote miserably in his journal.

The lucky ones had already left—"near 1/3 of the inhabitants have removed," he admitted in one annotation. Entire newspaper columns filled with notices of "Autumn Residences" of those "removed for the sickly season." One local observed, "As soon as this dreadful scourge makes its appearance in New York the inhabitants shut up their shops and fly from their houses into the country.

Those who cannot go far, on account of business, remove to Greenwich [Village]."

Manhattan was still small enough that Greenwich Village was indeed something of a separate village. Two miles north of City Hall, and reached only after passing through meadows and pasturage, it was still remote enough that residents addressed their letters from "Greenwich, NY." Its sandy soil had good drainage, which many suspected had something to do with its relative freedom from feverish miasma, though nobody was quite sure why.

William Laight lived farther south on Greenwich Street, in a neighborhood still deemed less hazardous than the docksides during the fever. But it was an uneasy compromise. No Manhattan street was entirely safe, not least because householders took to firing off muskets and cannons, in the desperate notion that the percussive shock would destroy the miasma. Guns didn't kill the fever, but—after one twelve-year-old boy wickedly loaded balls into a pistol—they did manage to kill a little girl as she stood in her father's shop.

Others reached in desperation for patent medicines. "Very efficacious in preventing the yellow fever," promised Lee's True and Genuine Bilious Pills—which, conveniently, were also a sovereign remedy "after a debauch by eating or drinking." For those who followed the fashions of Europe, there were Four Herb Pills by "Dr. Angelis, of Italy"—a place where "sometimes the same Malignant Fever prevails." More patriotic sorts had New York Anti-Bilious Pills, which also brashly promised to cure "asthma, gout, pains in the head, fainting, worms, excruciating pains, frequent vomiting, bloody flux, piles, palsey, apoplexy, and last of all consumption."

But among Manhattanites, the suspicion had formed that their many ills would not find true relief in pills or balms, and that any man who actually solved the problem might indeed deserve to be richly rewarded. Laight had closely allied himself to local political mastermind Aaron Burr, who was undertaking an ambitious project that would save the city—and, perhaps, their Republican Party.

The solution, they believed, was in running water.

LEVI WEEKS's landlady hadn't stayed around to find out if they were right. Instead, Mrs. Catharine Ring was being jarred and jostled, enduring the rutted path out of the city with all the patience her Quaker faith could muster. The coach's carriage seating literally used a suspension: It rested on leather belts strapped to the frame, sending every shock slamming through the compartment. More miserably, her sister Hope and her cousin Elma were not with her, even though they were some of her closest family; Hope Sands had grown up with her in upstate New York, and Elma Sands— the offspring of a single mother, her father long departed for South Carolina—had now been living with the Rings for three years, working in the family millinery when her precarious health allowed. The three women were all nearly the same age, in their early twenties, and Hope and Elma would have been welcome company for Mrs. Ring. But help was needed at the boardinghouse—and like so many others, Elma had been sickly a good part of that summer. It was possible that she simply couldn't withstand the slow, jolting carriage ride over rough roads into the countryside. And so, with the meadows and old Dutch farmsteads of Manhattan receding behind her, Mrs. Ring left Levi, Elma, and Hope in a city burning with fever.

The running of the boardinghouse, and the vital income that it produced for the Ring family, would be left to her husband, Elias. He was not the most practical man, it had to be admitted. First there was the flour mill he'd tried with his friend Caleb in upstate New York, a fifty-four-acre spread in Dutchess County on the worryingly named Murderer's Creek. That arrangement hadn't quite worked out. Next Elias had brought his wife, her sister, and her cousin to the city; he first tried to make a go of it as a mechanic and an inventor, then at running a general store, and then at running a millinery. Now he was stuck in the city, in charge of a boardinghouse that even his own wife didn't want to stay in anymore.

The Rings did not demand that the remaining boarders abide by their Quaker religion, but they expected them to remain dignified in their life and labors. And labor they did: Levi left the house each morning for his brother's work sites, trailed by his apprentice, William Anderson. Even with the yearly fever, the city was booming: The annexation of Loyalist property and the rebuilding of entire city blocks had made Manhattan a place of wild growth and speculation. The stock exchange that was run from the Tontine Coffee House ruled over the rise and fall of fortunes in shipbuilding, furs, and timber, and with this new wealth came new mansions.

Lagging behind the other workmen was the newest boarder, a recently immigrated English merchant named Richard David Croucher. Dapper and beginning to gray as he approached the age of forty, his tall and thin form could be seen on the streets as he set out to haggle over cloth and linens. Back at the boardinghouse, he'd talk animatedly to proprietor Elias Ring and the three unmarried ladies of the house—cousins Hope and Elma, and another boarder, named Margaret Clark. Croucher couldn't help but keep a watchful eye on them; as did, it seemed, the other men in the house.


WITH THE streets half-emptied by the fever, Croucher proceeded over to the market daily. He made frequent outings for food, having insisted on being a *roomer* but not a *boarder* at the Ring house: He paid each week for his room and fireplace but did not sit at meals in the dining room. When he was in the mood to spend, there was always roast joint at the tavern, or dubious local specialties like Humbert's bread and Aunt Roach's pies. For everything else, there were the city markets, where you could buy plate-sized oysters and leeks, and—if Hebraically inclined—could stop off at a kosher stall placarded JEW'S MEAT.

To a well-dressed Englishman like Croucher—an expert in cloth, and the kind of man who would keep his collars stayed and wig powdered even in the summertime—walking up Greenwich to the market was a sartorial nightmare. Americans didn't appear to *care* about clothing in the withering summer months. Girls went barefoot in the street, or kicked off their shoes and walked in stockings, perhaps inspired by the newly fashionable peasant wear of the French Revolution. Men stripped down to cotton frocks, like sleepwalkers in their nightclothes; that some still donned their powdered wigs made it more of a travesty. But worst of all was the alarming appearance of vagrants—dirty, disheveled, even worse dressed than the servants, and peering hungrily into vacant homes.

"Our streets are filled with straggling fellows," the *New-York Daily Advertiser* complained on September 19, 1799, right after Croucher had moved in. "Under the pretence of begging, [they] are no doubt making observations on houses and stores, to commit nightly depredations on those that are left unoccupied."

It was true: Neither wealth nor piety shielded residents. That week no less than Willett Hicks, a rotund merchant nicknamed "the Bishop of the Quaker Church," found his Pearl Street shop broken into, and a iron chest carried off. Inside was a gold watch and dozens of pieces of his monogrammed silver—everything from spoons and tongs to teapots and milk pitchers. Then the nearby Flood and Tracy grocery shop was raided. Another local burgher, John Sickles, happened to walk past his darkened clothing store at midnight and out of habit tried each of its three doors; the third unexpectedly swung open to reveal thieves robbing him of fifty vests, and he was promptly stabbed in the face for his trouble. When the thieves were pursued back to a hideout, confederates were found melting silver into crude ingots that still had bits of stolen spoons sticking out.

As each night fell and the city burned with fever outside, residents barred their doors to thieves and waited. The wakeful boarders of 208 Greenwich could hear . . . *something*. Unable to sleep in the humid evening air, Levi's apprentice might have been the first to notice the hushed movements across the creaking wooden floors, the bedroom doors locked in the night, the stirrings in the very frame of the building. *Something* could be discerned through the

walls. Not the rifling of any thief. It was the sound of two people—
and not the sound of Quaker chastity.

But who?

*COME BACK SOON,* Elias Ring wrote to his wife in the first days of
October. *I miss you.*

It was a hopeless request: The city was still far too dangerous. Yellow fever deaths were marching up even the formerly safe
environs of Greenwich Street; William Laight had interrupted
his weather log's tally of deaths to ominously note by one entry:
"Cassie, our neighbor." A laborer a few houses farther up came next,
and then a cart driver. By October 7, 1799, when a tenant died at a
boardinghouse on 189 Greenwich, the inhabitants of 208 could feel
death closing in. Hiding inside and peering out the window hardly
brought any comfort: Pigeons with strange gangrenous sores had
started appearing on the city streets.

"In this pestilential period," one local paper mused grimly,
"scarcely a species of animal escapes a portion of evil."

Doctors scrambled to find a treatment. The eminent David Hosack confidently presented a sweating cure; and then, as his patients
died writhing in perspiration, he quietly withdrew it. Then again,
he could hardly compete with the cure promoted by the most popular physician in the country, Elisha Perkins. The inventor of "metal-
lic tractors"—three-inch alloy rods that could "draw off the noxious
electrical fluid that lay at the root of suffering"—Dr. Perkins had
moved into the city and promptly set up shop over on John Street.
Perkins had sold thousand of metal tractors, and his customers for
the magic rods included George Washington; now Manhattanites
would be blessed by this same doctor's genius.

"Having obtained from various experiments satisfactory evidence
that the Yellow Fever is within control," Dr. Perkins advertised, "it
is his intention, if he finds suitable encouragement, to continue his
residence in this city." Alas, he found neither. Within weeks, he

was bundled into a winding sheet and sent back to Connecticut, as lifeless as his wonder-working chunks of metal.

Nothing seemed to work.

"To pour buckets of cold water on the head of a man . . . Three years ago this experiment was the vogue!!!" complained Noah Webster. "Copious bleeding has had its day. But [now] mercury seems to be the favorite. . . . Where one patient survives its effect, ten proved fatal."

The only real relief, in this as in every other outbreak for the past century, would come from the heavens. "First frost," noted William Laight in his logbook on October 18, 1799. Those two simple words held a vast sense of relief; for now, as the fall leaves turned bright, the fever surely would end. Word spread out into the countryside, and within a week the city's residents had begun to reappear, hale and rested from their months away. "General movement back," Laight dutifully wrote down in his logbook.

The summer's refugees discovered a city that was now rather the worse for wear. Merchants found their cellars smashed into, and trunks of merchandise opened and stolen. An abandoned flock of sheep, their owner likely dead, milled around by New Street. In front of the Tontine Coffee House, two cannons were simply dropped on the ground, perhaps by a fleeing homeowner unable to blast the miasma out of his backyard.

But there were hopeful signs, too. Full columns of notices in the newspaper ran under the heading RETURNS. Mr. Fontbonne posted his yearly announcement of trees for sale for fall planting—PEACHES, PLUMBS, GREEN GAGES &C.—and John Street burbled with the sound of girls being sent back to Mr. Reed's tutorials in English and geography. The city swelled back to life; soon the autumn harvest poured into the market squares, and Long Island cod landed heavily on the docks.

The frosty morning air also hinted at the coming winter. After a summer of gouging dying families on the price of coffins and nails, speculators were now buying up local supplies of wood and sticking residents for an extortionate six dollars a cord. Back at the board-inghouse, Richard Croucher prepared for the winter fabric buying season, while Elma, ailing some days but not others, often remained curled up in her bed on the second floor. Drops of laudanum helped with her pain, though not enough—"I should not be afraid to drink it full," she'd tease after taking a few ineffectual drops from the medicine vial. Levi looked in on Elma when he could, but he was putting in long hours at his brother's work sites, knowing the build-ing season would soon slow.

The humbler folk of the city were already stopping work to cele-brate the season. The end of the pestilence had come just in time for the city's Irish immigrants to indulge in their peculiar love of Hal-loween. Living down by the muddy docks, they'd been hit worst of all by the fever. Toasting loudly and singing lilting airs, they gath-ered that evening to roast nuts and apples over open fires, and drank whiskey in the graveyard as the autumn night of All Hallow's Eve closed over them and their fellow Manhattanites.

They had survived.

# 3

# The Young Quaker

THE CITY'S RECOVERY WAS FAST—A LITTLE TOO FAST, SOME worried.

"But a few days ago our city was covered with sack-cloth and ashes," wrote one *New-York Mercantile Advertiser* correspondent. "Scarcely a carriage was to be seen but the black and dismal hearse; nothing was to be heard in habitations but the expiring groans of victims, and the lamentations of surviving friends. Thank God the scene has changed; business and bustle, joy and gladness have taken place of Death and his sickly band of diseases." But now, he fretted, youth with "their bottles, their billiards, and their brothels" were roaming the streets. Where, he demanded, was "he who convinces giddy youth that wisdom does not consist in the thickness of his pudding neck-cloth, the breadth of his whiskers, or the spindle straw size of his rat tail queue?" And what better way to save the young men of the city from such foolishness, the correspondent wondered, than by occupying them with an intellectual puzzle?

"I therefore humbly hint," he proposed, "that a certain premium be offered, say a hundred guineas, to any one who shall produce the best solution to any philosophical or mathematical problem."

In fact, some of Manhattan's greatest minds had already spent the previous year grappling with a deadly serious puzzle: what to do about the city's foul and brackish water. Potable water was supplied by just one well, the Tea-Water Pump, a couple of blocks north of the site being considered for a new city hall. Some residents made pilgrimages there, like a thirsty urban herd to an oasis: The proprietors would let you fill up a large barrel for threepence. Everyone else waited for the Tea-Water Men, a small army of deliverymen who carted massive wooden 140-gallon hogshead casks around the city, selling water by the bucket to subscribing households.

But everyone knew the stuff was terrible.

"They pretend their water is pure and nice; it is no such thing," one of Noah Webster's correspondents charged. The local pond not far from the well, known as the Collect, had become "a very sink and common sewer"—a frothing brew of effluence from tanneries and furnaces. "Dead dogs, cats, etc, [are] thrown in daily," one resident grumbled, "and no doubt, many buckets from that quarter of town." As to what was in those buckets, another proclaimed, it was "all of leaking, scrapings, scourings, p——s——gs, & ——gs, for a great distance around."

Schemes for clean running water had been bubbling up for as long as most residents could remember; after a plan to pipe Manhattan with hollowed-out logs was proposed in 1774, a well was even dug and a crude steam engine erected before British invaders interrupted the project. Its engineer, the ingenious Irish émigré Christopher Colles, was held at bayonet point by British troops but managed to escape through the tall grass of Trinity Church's graveyard; returning after the war, he found occupying troops had cruelly wrecked his work. It proved to be the only project that the hapless genius had ever come close to seeing through.

"Had I been brought up a hatter," he sighed, "people would have come into the world without heads."

After the great fever in 1798, the calls for a solution had grown louder. "The health of a city," warned physician Joseph Browne, "depends more on its water, than on all the rest of its eatables and drinkables together." Browne's own ambitious proposal for driving yellow fever out of Manhattan was to pipe in clean water from miles away, via an elaborate series of dams and reservoirs by the Harlem River. If the scale of Browne's idea was a bit grand, the basic notion behind it was entirely sensible, and in the spring of 1799 the state assembly passed a bill to charter a corporation that would provide the city with clean water.

Dubbed the Manhattan Company, its board of thirteen local worthies had received five proposal bids in short order; nearly all came from recognized contractors and inventors, men already well-known to the committee members. But the first to arrive bore a return address that led back to a boardinghouse, of all places. It read: *208 Greenwich Street.*

Behind the archaic dress and the careful *thee* and *thou* of his manner, Elias Ring possessed the restless mind of a modern inventor. The young patriarch had mulled the mechanics of water for years since operating a mill upstate. Along with tending the boardinghouse with his wife, Elias had painstakingly designed and built a patent model of his own contrivance, and for the past two years had run an ad in Philadelphia and New York newspapers for this grand invention:

## NEW PATENT WATER WHEEL

> The subscriber has taken this method to inform the public that he has invented a new WATER WHEEL to work in the TIDE or other CURRENT, which may be fixed at the end of any dock, where there be a good tide so as to go. . . . If it were necessary, he could produce sufficient proof of its efficacy from the best characters in the States, whose judgment may be relied upon as having seen it tried on a small scale were convinced that a wheel built on this principle, and fixed in a good tide, would go with any force sufficient to drive any works. This wheel may likewise be of great use in raising water out of large rivers and or for the use of watering Towns and Cities.

But the city to be watered by his inventions, he now realized, was his own. And unlike the rather fanciful proposals of Joseph

Browne to bring in water from Harlem, Elias made an astoundingly practical proposition: The supply they needed, he claimed, was the much-abused and fouled waters of the meadows nearby.

"The Collect has been unjustly stigmatized with the name of a filthy stagnated pond," Ring began, "but the Collect proceeds from a collection of springs. [It] is rendered in some measure filthy by throwing dead carcasses into it." The solution was simply to fill in clay over the more putrid banks and erect a high fence to bar tanneries and butchers from using the Collect anymore. Refilled with sweet new water by its springs, and pumped out by a steam engine, "the Collect will supply a daily sufficient quantity of water for the consumption of the City." It could be done, he estimated, for the pleasingly round sum of $100,000.

That some of that windfall might come to him had been his dream back in the spring. But it had not quite turned out the way he imagined.

AT THE boardinghouse, Richard Croucher could be seen returning from his final evening rounds, having bothered the local household-ers to buy stockings. There was far worse work to be had than his: Staggering along some of those same rounds were the milk mer-chants. It wasn't even *good* milk that they were selling—it always stank of Long Island meadow garlic—but New Yorkers drank it anyway, and so the merchants barged over from Brooklyn and made deliveries with two heavy pails hung over their shoulders by a rod. Everyone on these streets had their own burden, but for Croucher it was this peculiar one: Something about him kept the occasional prospect from buying his fabric. It was hard to say *what* was off-putting about his sales manner. Yet he doggedly made his rounds, never entirely giving up.

Levi Weeks, lounging at the boardinghouse between carpentry jobs, was not so easily discouraged, either.

*Do you wish to accompany me to my brother's?* he asked Hope.

It wasn't far—Ezra Weeks kept his contracting business and

lumberyard just eight blocks away, over on the corner of Greenwich and Harrison—but Levi was making a social call, not reporting to work.

Hope was taken aback; then she demurred. It had been some time since Levi had shown her much in the way of attention, and besides, she really couldn't go today. And even if she could—well, answering to the handsome young carpenter's first request for an outing was perhaps unwise.

Elma, passing through the room, felt no such restraint.

"Why don't you ask me?" she asked pointedly.

"I know," Levi replied, "that you would not go if I did."

He was right, of course: Elma did not go to Ezra's with him. She never would, these days. She was always claiming illness, and she'd turn moody about it, then strangely weak—almost glassy-eyed. But whenever he was home from his work at Ezra's job sites, Levi still took pains to attend to her, even nudging the other boarders and family aside: *You will not attend to her as carefully as I will*, he'd insist.

And so Levi went to his brother's without either woman by his side. A visit to Ezra's house—where the contractor lived a steady married existence, building manors in the day and returning home to the hearth in the evening—was like a glimpse into a possible future for young Levi. And a prosperous future, at that, for his older brother had landed one of the most desirable contracts in the city.

To see it, one needed only to stand outside and look northward. Just a block away, at what would come to be called Leonard Street, the road and the city gave way to a marshy wilderness. This was the northern border of the city: Lispenard's Meadow, an untrammeled and swampy tract of mud, gnarled wild apples and brambles, with Manhattan on one side and the enclave of Greenwich Village on the other. Crossing it was a fine trip for courting couples; on the Manhattan side lay a popular theater and a saloon, while on the other lay the route to Turtle Bay, where parties of dozens of young men and women would go with hampers for a "turtle feast."

For urbane dandies, the meadow in between was a trackless

waste so ill thought of that, one resident recalled, "when one man offered to present the Lutheran Church with a plot of six acres . . . the gift was coldly declined because the land was not considered worth fencing in." Those fond of the flintlock fowling piece and the pin-hook fishing rod were happy to let their fellow city dwellers hold such notions; they knew better. A small creek, Minetta Brook, burbled through much of the length of Lispenard's Meadow; there were fine trout to be had from it, and fat pheasants to be flushed out from the stands of goldenrod that leaned over the streamside.

But the real catch in the meadow was in wood and water: namely, in the bored-out logs that Ezra Weeks dragged there to carry the city's new water supply. The Manhattan Company's board had quickly decided they wanted wooden pipes—because iron ones were seven times as expensive. "Two wooden Cylinders, of five and six inches caliber, will be amply sufficient for the mains down Broadway," they explained. These pipes, they assured themselves, would last twenty years before they needed replacing. But that still meant thousands of logs needed to be bored out and laid in a matter of months, before the ground froze. There was not much question as to who was up for that job: Ezra Weeks had the contract from the Manhattan Company for some three miles of buried wooden piping, and he'd also secured the immense pile of white and yellow pine logs needed for it. New Yorkers who complained the previous month when wood was six dollars a cord now found it going even more dearly.

"People are paying the enormous fee of sixteen dollars for a single cord of hickory wood," one local noted in amazement.

If they wanted to know where the timber had gone, they needed to look no farther than under their feet.


IT WAS a fine time to be in the Weeks clan, but after visits with his brother, Levi still found himself a bachelor living alone at Elias Ring's boardinghouse.

*Do you want to go the Charity Sermon?* he finally asked Hope one day.

A charity sermon by the Bishop Prevoost had been announced for St. Paul's Chapel on December 8, 1799—for the benefit, it was said, of a local school. Everyone knew that a charity sermon by the bishop was one of the highlights of the year at St. Paul's; until moving back to Virginia a few years before, George Washington himself had been a regular presence at them.

This time, Hope said yes.

They stopped off first at Ezra's, where the theater up the block had been displaying a double bill: THE YOUNG QUAKER, read the first listing; THE AGREEABLE SURPRISE, added the second. Even with its bone-chilling lack of heat and its rather makeshift orchestra of fiddles and drums, the theater was a fine place to sit back, buy some oranges from concessions, and then eat them lasciviously until the women in the next gallery box blushed and snapped their fans open.

If the play was no good, the audience would entertain themselves by singing gibberish back at the stage:

*Ditherum doodle,*
*Adgety Nadgety,*
*Gooseterum foodle,*
*Fidgety nidgety nadgety mum!*

There would be no such base entertainments for Levi or Hope, though. They instead made their way over to St. Paul's Chapel on Broadway and Fulton. Looking about a church darkened in the coming winter evening, its shadows cast long by candlelight, Levi observed an overflowing collection plate passed around, for St. Paul's that evening was, one observer wrote, "one of the most crowded churches we ever witnessed." He gazed upon the assembled great and the good of the city of Manhattan, dressed in the rich modesty of stiff brocades and satin linings; next to him on the bench, he could see Hope, her garb plain but dignified by her Quaker dictates. But alas, no Elma; he'd asked her to come, too, of course—and, naturally, she had begged off on account of physical strain.

"A father of the fatherless," intoned the bishop, "and a judge of the widows, is God in his holy habitation."

The city had plenty of both now. Just a few weeks ago, a fellow carpenter had fallen off a scaffold on Water Street and died, leaving a widow and two children behind. Days later, some live wolves on exhibit in the museum—the very one just up Greenwich Street, where they'd gone with Elma—had broken out of their pens and fallen upon a young boy, nearly killing him before the patrons' eyes. But above all, mortality this year meant the fever. Announcements had been made by nearly all the city's major congregations that the following week would have a day of Thanksgiving, in gratitude to God for surviving "the destructive Disease with which we were visited the last season."

The city felt more bountiful and generous now, and the evening had been a fine one for charity: As Levi and Hope left, it was found that $138 had been collected. The air outside was cold and filled with the crunch of boots through the first snow of the year, which had fallen just days earlier. For children, that meant the joyful pelting of the house at Garden and Broad, an abode blessed with a crotchety owner who burst out like a jack-in-the-box, shaking his fist as boys fled. For courting couples, the snow meant sleigh rides northward through Lispenard's Meadow, across what was known as the Kissing Bridge.

Hope's and Levi's breaths were barely visible; on moonlit nights like this, the city saved whale oil by not lighting the streetlamps. The streets bore the spectral cast of the moon and the snow, and the sounds about them were curiously muffled as they walked the block north from the chapel. But had they cleared away the drifts of snow on Broadway and set an ear to the ground, they might have been able to make out a new and unaccustomed sound beneath them, one running counter to their direction—a rush flowing south—the sound, three and a half feet underground, of piped water coursing down from the northerly meadows.

NOTICES HAD been appearing for days, signed by the board of the Manhattan Company:

> NOTWITHSTANDING THE INTERVENTION OF A MALIGNANT FEVER, WHICH OCCASIONED SO GREAT AND LARGE A DESERTION OF THE CITY . . . THE DIRECTORS ARE HAPPY IN ANNOUNCING TO THEIR FELLOW CITIZENS THAT CONDUIT PIPES ARE LAID IN SEVERAL OF THE PRINCIPAL STREETS, AND THAT WATER IS NOW READY TO BE FURNISHED TO MANY OF THE INHABITANTS AND TO ALL OF THE SHIPPING IN THE HARBOR.

The last point was a welcome one: Near the harbor was where the fever was always at its worst, and there was hope that—as one resident put it—the Manhattan Company might fulfill "the wish of every citizen, to have the water conveyed, in the first instance, to those parts of the city most exposed to autumnal fevers."

But for prosperous residents on the more fashionable interior streets, the water would be a boon as well. It was, the directors proclaimed, "of a quality excellent for drinking and good for every culinary purpose"—and there was enough of it, they claimed, that every subscribing household could positively gorge itself on fifty gallons' worth a day. And this, of course, was just the beginning: As soon as the frost came out of the ground, the service was to be expanded another twofold across Manhattan. Ezra Weeks and his younger brother would have a busy new year indeed.

But as Hope and Levi returned to the boardinghouse that evening, one person there was not sharing in the Weeks brothers' good fortune. For back in the springtime, the board had not adopted

Elias Ring's plan—no, they'd gone with hollow logs carrying water out of a well in the meadow, and a primitive pump supplied by one Nicholas Roosevelt. Curiously, the water board's president *knew* Roosevelt—he'd sold Roosevelt thousands of acres in a rather scandalous land deal years earlier. And for the plum $1,500-a-year position of water superintendent, the board had hired not Elias Ring or Christopher Colles, but none other than Joseph Browne—the engineering dilettante who had lobbied for the system to be built in the first place. That was quite a coincidence, too, for Dr. Browne happened to be a business partner from years earlier with one of the board members. He *also* happened to be the brother-in-law of the board's president.

Elias Ring never stood a chance.

Hope and Levi, arriving home that night, could be forgiven if they didn't notice a curious absence in any stray issue of that day's *Greenleaf's New-York Journal*. Elias Ring's hopeful ad promoting the New Patent Water Wheel, after running for some two years, had quietly been withdrawn—and it was never to return.

## 4

# THE BLACK VEIL

THE INCOMING MAIL CARRIAGES FOR DECEMBER 19, 1799, ARRIVED
to a slumbering and sodden city. As it was a day of prayer for delivery from recent fevers, many of the shops would stay closed that
day. At the Merchants' Coffee House, however, where deals were
struck amid tables of appraisers, stockbrokers, and lingering Chamber of Commerce board members, it was an ordinary Thursday for
the more determined men of business. But one newly arrived letter from Virginia, when carefully sliced open, contained a shocking
announcement:

> *Alexandria, 15th Dec. 1799*
>
> *Dear Sir,*
> *This is a day of mourning to us, and will be so to the*
> *United States, when the cause is known—*
> GENERAL GEORGE WASHINGTON IS NO MORE.

Word raced down Wall Street as another letter from Alexandria
was opened to reveal the same stunning news about the sixty-seven-
year-old statesman: "He made his exit last night between the hours
of 11 and 12 after a short but painful illness of 23 hours. . . . We are
all to close our houses, and act as if we should do if one of our own
family had departed."

One man felt distinctly unmoved as he bustled about his business in the Insurance Room of the Merchants' Coffee House. John

Shaw had a busy wine shop down on Pearl Street, and he was not about to waste time mourning the rebel whose war had stripped so many old gentry of land and business.

"It is a pity General Washington had not died five and twenty years ago," he snapped.

The country was still sharply politically divided. Tradesmen and farmers naturally gravitated toward the party of Aaron Burr and Thomas Jefferson in their tavern talk, while their merchants and masters just as naturally took to John Adams and Alexander Hamilton's moneyed Federalists. After all, Federalist control of the banks meant that if they wanted a line of credit for business, they had to back the party of Adams and Hamilton. But among some merchants that supported Hamilton and his Federalists, there remained a hangover of Loyalism from the war—and while the past decade had nurtured a vociferous American nationalism, they still retained warm feelings toward the old country. For a few coffeehouse patrons such as Shaw, it went beyond that: A couple of years earlier, one of them had indignantly raised a British flag over the Merchants' before it got ripped down by an equally indignant patriot.

*I said*, Shaw repeated, *it's a pity General Washington didn't die five and twenty years ago.*

No one rose to the provocation. Not everyone had loved the man, true, but he had led America through its darkest days. Now, after three years of bitter partisan battles under Adams, doubts were all that remained—and it was with a certain foreboding that publisher Charles Snowden hurried over to his *New-York Daily Advertiser* print shop to compose an elegy on the spot for his evening edition. "WASHINGTON was our pride, our guardian, and our defense," he quickly wrote. "Amidst threatening storms of some violence, amidst the more dangerous convulsions of party rage, it was still our consolation that WASHINGTON lived."

Now the country's great unifier was gone. It seemed as if the partisans of Jefferson and Adams might crack the fragile republic apart by the following year's election. For the British-leaning Federalists, there was the spectacle of France's new democracy spinning into frightening anarchy and ruin—while to French-leaning Republicans, the roundly condemned censorship of the Alien and Sedition Acts smacked of monarchy. And there were more subtle moral fissures slowly forming in this new country as well, the kind that could be seen right next to Washington's death notice in the *New-York Gazette*, where there ran an ad headlined A NEGRO MAN TO BE SOLD CHEAP.

But for now, at least, the city voiced a singular grief. Out on Wall Street, John Shaw ran into one of Washington's old soldiers, Colonel Mansfield, who repeated what he'd heard Shaw say in the Insurance Room. The wine merchant quickly realized he was in trouble: He'd never said those words in the coffeehouse, he insisted.

"It's a damned lie!" he blustered.

The old colonel did not like hearing his general spoken ill of, but he liked being called a liar even less. He promptly flogged the wine merchant in the middle of Wall Street, and Shaw did not find any defenders. Some New Yorkers, it seemed, still approved of swift justice.

"WHAT MEANS this melancholy sound of Bells, which daily strikes our ears?" the Reverend Linn's voice rang over the pews of the North Dutch Church. "What means this sorrow which marks the face of every Citizen?"

The city that Sunday was swathed in black, from the veils hung over women's faces to the armbands worn by the men. In the distance muffled bells rang from every church; by order of the city council, the bells had been wrapped so as to toll in a ghostly, mournful chorus.

"What mean these sable ensigns that hang in our Churches?" the elderly minister called out, motioning at the black crepe newly hung over the pews. "We are witnesses this day that no character, however exalted, that no services however long continued and extensive, can save from the stroke of *Death*."

Nearly all the city had gathered in melancholy masses—all,

that is, except for Levi Weeks. After breakfasting in the boarding-house, he trooped over to his brother's lumberyard for a day of hard work. Even Ezra Weeks himself hadn't stayed home, but Levi was young and ambitious; in any case, he had to make doors for the new house of Mr. Cummings, and the planes and saws wouldn't work themselves.

Levi had a good deal of labor ahead of him. Cummings was a wealthy merchant with a growing business on Broadway and a new two-story home, and Levi had been handed an order for eight doors, all of different sizes. As ten o'clock approached, the sun was shining fully on the low wooden houses by the corner of Greenwich and Harrison, and it was turning out to be a fine day outside—as good as any that week for tackling the job.

*Damn it.*

Levi sprawled onto the ground, his boot caught—he'd torn a gash in his knee, the bright red blood oozing in the cold morning air.

His brother was still out at the church; straightening himself, Levi hobbled back down Greenwich to the boardinghouse by the corner of Barclay Street. Inside, he ran into another boarder, Sylva-nus Russel, who was certain the carpenter wouldn't make it back out to one of the later church meetings that Sunday.

"Levi, you won't be able to go out today," he said, peering at his bloody knee.

"I am determined to," Levi insisted, before allowing, "tonight."

Elma fussed over him; as ill as she had been much of the fall, and for all the moodiness she had about her, it was the rare chance for her to tend to someone else. She followed him upstairs and plas-tered his knee, and he rested awhile in his room. Illness and injury were common enough plights that boardinghouse beds, coarsely built of poplar and painted green, were always constructed low to the ground, the better to crawl into and out of when sick or dying. By the afternoon, though, he and Elma were back downstairs and sitting by the fire in the common room while he nursed his banged-up knee. It was proving a sleepy Sunday indeed: The theater had even canceled the day's performance of *Lover's Vows* out of deference to the late president. Eventually, Elma's company could no longer quiet the carpenter's restlessness. As the sun set, Levi plowed through a large dinner, intent on going back to the lumberyard to finish the day's work.

Elma disappeared back upstairs and dressed to go out for the evening as well.

"Which looks best?" she asked Mrs. Ring. She'd picked out a calico gown and a white dimity petticoat, and long white ribbons—though such choices would matter little until she found another muff. She was missing hers, and the thick, pillowlike mittens were a necessity on a night like this.

Levi stepped in with his coat still on his arm—and though nearly dressed, Elma vanished behind a curtain.

"Where's Elma?" he asked absently.

"She is hid behind the bed," Mrs. Ring said primly.

"Don't mind me," the carpenter scoffed. "I want you to tie my hair."

His long hair secured and coat arranged, Levi stepped out into the falling darkness of Greenwich Street.

As Mrs. Ring lit the candles in the common room, the front door groaned with her husband's return from the Friends meeting. For an inventor, Elias was curiously slow to fix their cockeyed door; but then again, so were the carpenter, apprentice, and shipwright who lived in the boardinghouse. Elias settled into the commons room with his boarders Sylvanus and Lacey—all while Elma dithered over her dress and looked impatiently outside.

She had just gotten around to borrowing a muff from a neighbor when Levi stepped back in.

He wasn't staying long. His brother had been entertaining guests, it seemed, and so now he'd need to go over yet a third time—to finally get the day's work done.

"The clock has just struck eight," Mrs. Ring marveled.

He'd be putting in a late Sunday indeed, but it couldn't be helped. The boarders and the Rings went off to bed, and after a brief respite in his room, Levi departed once again, his footsteps coming heavily down the boardinghouse staircase. Mrs. Ring, being in a ground-floor bedroom, couldn't help but put her ear to the door.

*What are you doing?* asked Elias drowsily.

*Shh.*

She could hear—she thought—another person following Levi, and then a whispering in the hallway. The hushed voice stopped, cut off by a loud groan from the half-broken front door—and then, nothing more.

Mrs. Ring blew out her candle, and the heavy silence of a long, dark winter's night descended.


Levi's apprentice paced the parlor and tended to the fire, passing the time. He shared a room with the carpenter, but as keys were expensive and carefully protected, it was only Levi who could unlock its door. And now, after returning home for the evening, the boy was locked out; even Mrs. Ring couldn't get him in.

It was ten o'clock when Levi got back, tired from his work.

"Go to bed," he sighed to his young apprentice, fishing the key out of his pocket. He spotted Mrs. Ring, up in her bedclothes, lingering by the edge of the parlor.

"Is Hope got home?" Levi asked.

"No," she replied. There was the Friends meeting, and Hope—unlike her cousin Elma—was the kind of convert who would stay late. But that, at least, left someone else for him to pass the time with before turning in.

"Is Elma gone to bed?"

"No," Mrs. Ring said, fussing about the room a bit. "She is gone out. At least, I think I saw her ready to go, and have good reason to think she went."

Elias was up now as well, and Mrs. Ring shooed him away.

"I'm surprised she should go out so late at night—and alone," the carpenter mused.

"I've no reason to think she went alone," Mrs. Ring said primly.

Levi, sitting by the fire, considered this thoughtfully for a moment, and then rested his head heavily against his hand. He wasn't going to bother asking who she might have gone out with. Except for Croucher, the boardinghouse residents were young— even the Rings themselves were still in their twenties—and for a hardworking carpenter, the subtle currents of courtships could be too much trouble to work out.

Dawn broke the next morning over a cold and cloudy sky, and Levi readied himself for the usual breakfast. You could expect bread, cheese, preserved apples, eggs, and a solid draft of warm beer. Tea and coffee were only slowly taking hold at breakfast in the finer houses, and the city's old Dutch families still drank cocoa at breakfast—but for a kitchen full of groggy apprentices and artisans, warm beer remained the drink of choice in the morning. With the new water service installed in only a few households, warm beer was the best way to start the day's work without being seized by dysentery.

Not everyone was at breakfast, of course—Croucher, living cheaply as he did, refused to pay for a home-cooked meal, and Elma hadn't gotten up either, though she was enough of a layabout that it was hardly worth noting. When Levi got back to the boarding-house for lunch, though, he still did not find her at the table.

"Is Elma got home?" he asked as he came in.

"I have not seen her," Mrs. Ring said plainly. "I expect she is upstairs."

"She's not in the second story," he called back down in a puz-zled tone, and then headed back out to work again. If the weather had been a bit rough, Elma might well have simply stopped off and turned in at the boardinghouse of Henry Clement, up by Lispe-nard's Meadow; and yet, as hours passed, and as the other boarders returned home, there remained a curious silence from Elma's un-touched room.

*Have you the muff that Elma borrowed last night?* asked her neigh-bor Elizabeth.

Mrs. Ring sat Elizabeth by the fire and sent over to Clement's for it; surely it was still there with Elma.

"I guess she has gone to be married," sighed Elizabeth. A rather scandalous theory, to be sure, but young women were known to resort to running off—particularly when decency demanded that they do so.

These were things little spoken of, and even less written of. Oh, there was the occasional gossip during a trial—just recently, when eighty-two-year-old Gideon Washburn got caught in sin with his horse, and both were sentenced to death—*that* got talked about. And there were the books, never shown openly but purchased surreptitiously from a pharmacist or printer, or obtained by asking around down by the docks—guides such as *Aristotle's Master-Piece*, which amid its painstaking explanations of generative organs and medieval humors, promised forbidden knowledge. A new illicit local edition was circulating around the city, cheekily attributed on the title page to "The Company of Flying Stationers." Hiding on page 85 was a recipe of chamomile, fennel, and mallow roots that promised to induce abortion. For more fortunate readers, it reminded them that "the action of the clytoris in women is like that of a penis to man," and the key to "brifk and vigorous" enjoyments—especially with "cares and thoughts of business drowned in a glafs of rofy wine."

Such things might be done—but not spoken of aloud in a decent boardinghouse. Marriage, particularly when Elma was an illegitimate child herself, was perhaps the least scandalous reason that she might have left. And what else could account for a girl borrowing nice clothes and running off like this?

"Married or not," Mrs. Ring clucked over Elma and the missing garment, "I think it very ungenerous not to return it."

But then word arrived back from Henry Clement himself, and the ladies were almost startled out of their sitting-room chairs.

*Elma hadn't been over there at all last night.*

As the day passed, the two women continued their searching looks at the carpenter. Had *he* gone out that evening with Elma? *I have looked into her room some fifty times waiting for her,* Mrs. Ring snapped at him. *I looked more than fifty,* he replied sorrowfully. Little more was spoken that day: Little more needed to be. If she had not gone out with him, or with anyone else in the boardinghouse, then the reasonable supposition was that she had needed to resort to a procedure—one of a hidden birth, or the quelling of a new pregnancy. And the longer she was gone, the more likely it was that something had gone very wrong.

Night fell, and she had still not returned.

THE NEXT morning's *New-York Daily Advertiser* ran a new notice pleading for the help of its readers at solving a mysterious disappearance:

### STOLEN

Twelve Silver tea SPOONS, marked on the handles with the initials S.B. in cyphers. The spoons are large and plain, and have been but little used. Any information respecting them will be thankfully received, and if the spoons, or any of them, can be recovered, a handsome reward will be given, and no questions asked. No. 112 Chatham Street, two doors above the tea water pump.

There was not, however, any word of Elma. One might advertise for missing spoons, but not a missing woman—for unlike cutlery, a woman may *want* to be lost. But if Elma had not quietly gone to a midwife, then where was she? Some kind women in Boston had recently started a Female Humane Society for those who found themselves in a delicate situation, but such help was not so readily found in Manhattan.

Breakfast passed uneasily; the worry could now be read on Mrs. Ring's face. One by one, the boarders stood up and departed for work, until only Levi and the landlady were left at the table. She then paced back and forth across the parlor, over and again, until Levi stood and took her arm.

"Mrs. Ring, don't grieve so. . . . Things will turn out better than you expect."

She looked at him in a long, painful silence: What did he know that would give her hope? But he had nothing to add. Gently releasing her arm, the carpenter pulled on his hat and—awkwardly, without another word—shook open the stubborn front door and stepped outside.

It was a busy day, with scarcely any token at all that Christmas was approaching. While German settlers down in Pennsylvania made much of hoisting a pine tree in honor of St. Nicholas, in Manhattan the old Dutch traditions merely regarded December 25 as a rather subdued holy day. This one, though, was looking like it might be particularly joyless. The hours stretched into afternoon and then evening at the Ring household, with still no trace of Elma; their neighbor Elizabeth was growing a good deal less concerned about her missing muff than about the girl who had borrowed it.

*Where had she gone?*

The passing of another evening brought no answer. Christmas, as ever in Manhattan, passed with so little notice that many shops didn't even close for the day; the theater stayed open, and the new issue of the *New-York Spectator* arrived at coffeehouses, ready to fuel the day's latest arguments. A snowfall that week had made for a white Christmas, though the only man much interested in that was Noah Webster, who hobbled clubfooted along the frozen streets. Dr. Webster was not one for sentimental nonsense about snow on Christmas—he was, a local mused, of "passionless immoveable countenance, sarcastic and malicious even with children"—but he was a great believer in hard winters warding off pestilence.

"A green Christmas makes a fat Church-yard," he snapped.

But for the few people who felt festive enough to struggle through the snow, there was still the old Christmas tradition of slogging out into the swamps and meadows to go fowling. The sport had become rather more refined with the arrival of French refugees from the Revolution; the exiled gentry were fine marksmen at shooting on the wing, and had started a new fashion in Manhattan for beautifully carved double-barreled shotguns. The reports of fowling pieces could be heard cracking over Lispenard's Meadow, where turkeys and pheasant fell from the sky and bled into the snow. The city had tried every once in a while to end these hunts, but the meadows retained a little of the wildness of old times; and so, for that matter, did some of the hard-bitten old Dutch and new Scotch families living on its borders.

But watching the festive slaughter, one might have spotted a peculiar detail on one of these tough and impassive women dwelling by the meadow: On her hands, she wore a scuffed and curiously familiar quilted muff.

# 5

# THE MYSTERY IN THE
# MEADOW

CAPTAIN RUTGERS WAS ACCUSTOMED TO HEARING STRANGE IM-
portuning requests as he took his strolls up Greenwich Street. As
warden of the port, he wielded a certain power over all the incoming and outgoing merchant vessels, and could make life difficult indeed for any captain or wholesaler who neglected to pay the right
dock fees or file the correct papers. But while Elias Ring was not
quite an unknown fellow, the boardinghouse keeper was not the
usual sort to stop him in the street.

*Have you heard of a muff turning up anywhere?* Ring asked.

Today, of all Sundays, should have been a respite from what
would be a busy week—and certainly from interruptions like this.
New Year's was just three days away, with all the new regulations
that the turn of both the year and the century would bring, and
there were new traders coming into port from New Orleans and
outward bound for St. Thomas to deal with. Captain Rutgers sized
up his inquirer.

"It's an *odd* question," he finally said.

Ring's high-pitched voice turned confidential; he explained that
he was not so much looking for the missing garment but its wearer.

"A young woman," he explained hesitantly—a relation of his
wife's. "Gone a week."

"What became of her?"

Well, that was just why he'd come to Captain Rutgers; Elias
thought that one of the merchants or dockworkers might have

spotted the muff. He had reason to believe—impious as the notion was—that the young girl might have drowned herself.

"A love fit," he added mournfully. In the muttered opinion of some in the boardinghouse, the fit was over Levi. Rutgers considered the matter for a moment, his breath hanging in the cold and still December air.

"Employ Mr. George Wallgrove," the captain said finally. "An expert at sweeping the river on—such occasions."

The need for such services arose often enough that the captain did not need to elaborate. It had not been so long since port workers by Norton's Wharf found a despairing man floating facedown in the Hudson, his hat and shoes left quietly on a nearby rock, awaiting an owner who would never return. Such acts of self-destruction were, at least, somewhat less alarming than the gentleman who had recently stood in Bowery Lane and applied a pair of pistols to his own head.

But where in the river were they to start looking?

"The nearest dock," Mr. Ring reasoned, and he considered Greenwich Street carefully. There was a dock within a couple blocks of the boardinghouse—right down their cross street of Barclay, in fact. The girl might have almost walked a straight line from his front door and into the freezing river itself.

"Rhinelander's Battery," he mused grimly. "The handiest place—the most likely."

Wallgrove was fetched and set to work. Grizzled by his years of work around the docks, George was a jack of all trades; though trained as a cooper, he'd risen through the ranks to the appointed office of Culler of staves and hoops, a wood inspector whose oath of office left no doubt as to his importance in a port's economy. And when he wasn't making inspections around the docks, George was just as ready to man the local fire pumps whenever the alarm was sounded. His fearlessness would serve him well that day: Dragging the river at this time of year was hard and dangerous work that few could handle well. The heavy load of a recovered body meant that capsizing or falling in was always a danger. Most men couldn't last long in the Hudson's waters even on the best of days, let alone a freezing one like this—for swimming was still so little taught that even many sailors scarcely knew a single stroke.

Ice was forming in the river, and it bumped at the sides of Wallgrove's launch as he made his way around the foot of Rhinelander's Wharf; the decrepit old fortifications at the dock gave the search an even more melancholy air. Long, rakelike tongs served like hands in the chilly water, as did a "creeper," a line dragging a claw of four hooks fastened together. In shallower water, Wallgrove might have even been able to resort to a favorite tool of river men: a long tube with a glass bulb on the end, which served as a sort of telescope under the surface of the water. It was a fine instrument in the shadier pursuits of the sea, when recovery men were hired by smugglers to recover the loads tossed overboard when revenue cutters bore down upon them. But the deep and freezing currents of the Hudson would require painstaking and bone-numbing work with drag lines.

Hours later, George came ashore in defeat: He was no closer to an answer.

Elias Ring morosely made his way back to the boardinghouse, where a gloom was settling more deeply over his wife. Despite some whispers that perhaps Elma *had* gone out with Levi that night, he still insisted that she hadn't and that he didn't know where she was now.

"Levi," his wife asked their boarder, "give me thy firm opinion from the bottom of thy heart. Tell me the truth—what thee thinks has become of her."

The young carpenter regarded a city still so deeply in mourning for the loss of a president that it seemed almost entirely unaware of the young woman vanished from its midst.

"Mrs. Ring," he finally replied, "it's my firm belief that she's now in eternity."

THE NEXT morning they awoke to the sound of gunfire. It was the report of sixteen rifles, marking the dawn of New Year's Eve, and the shots were to ring out every half hour until sunset, echoing over the empty streets. Most businesses were closing early or not opening at all, and carriages had been barred altogether, so that residents might journey through the snowy streets to one of the greatest spectacles the city had ever seen: a memorial parade for General Washington. Even with the gloomy spirits inside the boardinghouse, Levi could hardly ignore what was to happen outside.

"Hope," he asked between the cannonades. "Will you accompany me to the procession?"

She had little desire to stroll through a city that could indulge in extravagant grief for an aged president, and yet scarcely stir itself to find her cousin.

"I have seen processions enough," she replied bitterly.

He would go without her, then—but he would not go alone, for it seemed as if everyone else in the city was attending that morning. As ten o'clock approached, the streets thronged with thousands of New Yorkers, all lining a route that proceeded by City Hall and down Wall Street, and along Broadway to St. Paul's Chapel. In the park by the almshouse, marchers congregated and took their assigned formations for the grand funeral of the late president.

It was not the actual funeral for Washington, of course—that had been held in Virginia days earlier, with its details covered minutely in newspapers across the land, right down to woodcut diagrams of the positions of Washington's pallbearers. Here, though, America's largest city would give the new country's most solemn and impressive expression of national grief.

At ten o'clock, the muffled bells struck and rifles crackled, and a grand column moved forward in a dead march through the snow. Leading the grand procession were regiments of dragoons pulling prize pieces of artillery seized from the redcoats—a minor slight to the British consul in attendance, perhaps, but forgivable at an old general's funeral. They were followed by cavalry and militia, and ranks of aging war veterans—many now in their forties and fifties, their uniforms fraying but dignified. Walking behind them, accompanied by his aides, strode the familiar form of a fellow veteran and political giant newly appointed as head of the army: Alexander Hamilton.

The erstwhile lawyer was resplendent in his major general's uniform, made somber by the black crepe tied around his arm. It had been on his orders, issued on the occasion of "this great national calamity," that the procession was organized—Hamilton had planned the whole thing, every step and flourish, right down to the rifle shots and banners. Deeply trusted by Washington and grudgingly accepted by President Adams, Hamilton walked at the symbolic midway point in the procession: Here was the man who united its military vanguard and the civilian ranks that followed.

Behind him, in their peculiarly martial formations, marched the city's fraternal organizations. There was the Tammany Society, with its political elite dressed in black as sachems and warriors, with bucktails pinned to their caps; the Mechanics Society, marching en masse for the first time since the funeral of "our late brother mechanic" Ben Franklin; and most impressive of all, the city's Freemasons. The old president had been a member from his youth, reaching the rank of master mason, and lodges now marched the streets in formation, headed by the ambitious young assistant attorney general Cadwallader Colden. In his hands, Colden gripped a Masonic black-and-white banner that bore the emblem of an emptied hourglass and sickle, its words snapping in the frigid wind:

**BROTHER WASHINGTON—THE GREAT—**
**THE WISE—THE VIRTUOUS.**

Behind the lodge brothers came the city's own great and wise: the boards of its banks, insurance companies, and chamber of commerce. At their head walked the principals of the newly formed Manhattan Company, led by the one man who could draw as many whispers as Major General Hamilton. More than just the person in charge of newly dug wells and water lines, he was a lawyer and politico constructing a Republican network in the city—one aimed squarely at Hamilton and his reigning Federalists. The company chairman was none other than Hamilton's fellow war veteran, brother lawyer, and political opposite: Colonel Aaron Burr, Esq.

There would be no debate today, no fiery rhetoric, no ripostes delivered from atop a hogshead in the square: just the slow, inexorable march of mourning. The procession turned onto Broadway, revealing a final great mass of the city's professionals: the city council, the students and faculty of Columbia in full academic dress, and the assembled lawyers, surgeons, and doctors of Manhattan. Of the latter, the great personage was the brilliant young Dr. David Hosack—both the leading physician and leading professor of medicine in the city. At thirty, he had not one fleck of gray in his dark and wavy locks, and yet had in just four years already risen to chair of materia medica at Columbia. He could only bow his head before that inexorable defeat of his profession: Sometimes even a president could not be saved.

With the mournful clamp of soldiers' boots, an empty symbolic urn for General George Washington arrived. Borne on the shoulders of the mayor and seven veterans of the Revolution, it shone atop a burnished symbolic bier, surmounted by an eagle of gilt and black lacquered wood. Among the pallbearers walking stiffly beneath it was Henry Brockholst Livingston, once the aide-de-camp to Benedict Arnold and now a great courtroom rival to Hamilton and Burr. Having come of age just as the Revolution began—in 1799, Hamilton and Livingston were both forty-two years old, and Burr was forty-three—these three men belonged to a group of Americans peculiarly marked out for history, and they now faced the passing of their mentors among wise generals and elder statesmen.

The crowd and ranks of marchers parted as Livingston and the other pallbearers pressed forward through the opened doors of St. Paul's. Before them scampered twenty-four children—girls dressed in white robes—clutching baskets and dropping laurel leaves in their path. Their small voices sang out into the echoing chapel:

*Bring the laurels, strew the bays;*
*Strew his hearse, and strew the ways.*

"Its appearance was really splendid," one judge in the crowd noted approvingly. If the day was a final tolling of the bell for General Washington, it might as well have also been a mighty salute to General Hamilton. The procession he'd arranged had brought out the entire city—from the mayor to majors, from bankers to mechanics, from callow students to aged doctors—the present and future of the city alike. Hamilton, Burr, and Livingston were all veterans of the war and part of a generation that had firmly consolidated its influence in the newly born government, while Dr. Hosack and Cadwallader Colden were part of the rising next generation. Nearly born during the war itself, they were the nation's younger cousins among these founding fathers.

Levi Weeks had worked at times on contracting projects for Hamilton and Burr; such great men were not unknown to him. New York was still small enough that any citizen could easily cross paths with the founders of the young nation. But watching them all gravely walking in procession was to behold the assembled might of the reborn city and nation before one's eyes. These were ambitious and brilliant men—powerful men—the sort who might hold a simpler man's life in their hands.

INSIDE THE confectioner's shop on Pine Street the next morning was a grand spread: platters of gilt gingerbread stamped with the figures of King Louis XVI and Marie Antoinette; blancmange molded in bas-relief of French officers dueling each other in cocked hats; and marzipan modeled into a grand and beautiful facade of the Palais des Tuileries. The proprietor, in his former life as a French nobleman, had barely escaped the guillotine; forced to learn a trade after arriving penniless in New York, he'd discovered an almost magical skill at conjuring sweets. Monsieur Singeron outdid himself with his New Year's plum cake, rich with candied oranges and mace and lashings of brandy, topped with a frosting unaccountably patterned into Cupids hiding among rosebushes and hearts shot through with arrows. To begin the year with such romantic sentiment was so unexpected and delightful that Singeron had turned it into a Manhattan fashion.

The rather more tiresome New Year's traditions, of course, remained unchanged.

"Some think it is the first year in the Nineteenth century," one local reported of January 1, 1800. "And others, the last year of the Eighteenth."

But along with the passing of the century, the memorials to Washington had become impossible to avoid, and relentless. It wasn't enough that a Mr. Greenwood had advertised himself as "Dentist to the Late President"—now there were also ads for mourning jewelry, and subscription announcements for everything from a portrait of Washington (guaranteed to "afford peculiar satisfaction") to a portrait of Washington's *urn* ("executed by the original designer of this much admired ornament") to fancy-dress-ball tickets that promised the debut of "the Washington Minuet."

But New Year's Day, for Manhattanites, was always a respite from such cares, and it began, like any grand affair in the city should, in Mayor Varick's house, as locals filed in at noon from the church service. "There," recounted Mr. Thorburn, the local nail maker, "they broke the first cookie and sipped the first glass of cherry bounce of the season. From thence they went from house to house and broke their bread with merry hearts."

This was a much-loved tradition from the Dutch. Local gentlemen made a circuit around the blocks, catching up on all the family news of the previous year while the women of the houses laid out the riches of the city—tureens of oysters pickled in white wine, cold jellied lamb, plates of macaroons, and glass after glass of brandy. Men staggered from one house to the next well into the night to pay increasingly merry tidings of the new century, the groups picking up revelers from each house and growing in mass and hilarity. "Before the moon sunk behind the blue hills of the Jerseys," Thorburn marveled, "you might see twoscore of these happy mortals in one company."

As the cold winter evening set in, a few households could sober up with coffee brewed from the wooden pipes that fed clear, cold water from the freshly dug well out by Lispenard's Meadow. It was on the meadow, in fact, that local resident Mrs. Blanck heard the curiously offhanded piece of news that had been making the rounds that day: A young Quaker girl had disappeared almost without a word, and maybe the last to see her was the neighbor girl who had lent her a muff.

Mrs. Blanck reached among her winter clothing, and the eyes of her listeners widened.

*This one?* she asked.

ELIAS RING and his neighbor Joseph Watkins marched up to Andrew Blanck's house on the Bowery the next day.

*The muff,* they demanded. *Where did your wife find it?*

Blanck was surprised: He'd just settled down to lunch with James Lent and a fellow named Page, men he'd brought to help him break a horse. Living on the fringes of Lispenard's Meadow, there were always such matters to attend to: a horse—a good black trotter—had been stolen nearby back in the fall, while an ownerless steer had just turned up in an enclosure a few weeks ago.

*Where did she find it?*

*The well,* Blanck blurted out.

Nearby, about midway between Broadway and Bowery, in the valley between the sandy hills at the top and bottom of the meadow, there was a well newly dug by the Manhattan Company. The grandly named Manhattan Well hadn't been found suitable for the pipeline, though; another had been chosen, and this earlier attempt was now covered up with wooden planks. Ring and Watkins hoisted up poles to sound the disused well, and set off across the snowy meadow with Blanck and his guests alongside them.

His young son William had found the muff floating in the water more than a week ago, the cartman added—on Christmas Eve, in fact—and had brought it home and presented it to his mother.

"I went to the well the next day and looked in," Blanck would later explain, "but I saw nothing."

The men reached the well and tossed aside the snow-covered planks. Inside, the brick-lined walls descended into darkness, as clots of snow and pebbles trickled in from the surface above. Page gingerly lowered the tip of his pole into the well. The bottom was sandy and dark, and the frigid water that had once been meant for the city's kitchens had risen unattended to nearly six feet in depth. He gripped the wooden rod and swept it gently through the water, then suddenly stopped.

*There's something down there.*

James Lent tried it as well, and nodded—there was a mass deep in the water, but it was too big and heavy for the wooden pole to hook around. Elias Ring looked grimly on as his neighbor grabbed a set of nails and a hammer; the ironmonger banged irons into the wooden poles, preparing a crude set of grappling hooks. James tried levering the object out with just one, but it was simply too heavy; for a moment, though, a flash of calico cloth floated up near the surface—and then vanished back underneath.

James kept his weight on the pole, holding the burden in place just below the surface, and the men turned to a boy who had sauntered up.

*Go fetch some ropes,* they told him.

Thick coils of hemp were hurriedly procured from the nearest house, and another man now joined in—Lawrence Myer, a fellow teamster of Mr. Blanck's. With a half dozen men gathered around the hole, the poles and ropes were rigged into a makeshift net and lowered to gently snag the inert mass in the water.

*Ready—one, two, three—lift.* Even with the muscle of two teamsters and an ironmonger among those pulling, the mass was sodden and heavy; it rose slowly under the cradling ropes, breaching the surface and ascending into the cold winter air, streaming water back into the dark well.

A body.

The sickening sag of weight tightened against the ropes as the corpse rolled over, as if inexorably drawn back to its hiding place within the earth. The men righted it and then hauled it up, laying the lifeless form out on one of the well's planks. This had been a woman, once: Her head lolled to the side, and her hair hung in her face; her feet were bare and her dress torn. A comb and a white ribbon still hung in the disheveled mass of her wet hair.

The horsebreaker paused to stare at the terrible unblinking face—and then, turning away, strode purposefully across the meadow to find a constable.

# PART II

## THE ACCUSED

# 6

# SOME PERSON OR PERSONS AS YET
# UNKNOWN

THE CONSTABLE ARRIVED TO FIND A CROWD MILLING ABOUT THE supine figure laid out on a plank. *Levi Weeks is to blame,* one man insisted to the growing crowd, and the mutterings passed among the gathering citizenry—*he's who she was last with.*

Determining the claim's truth was hardly the business of a constable, or indeed of any officer of the law. Policing largely existed to guard property along the docks, and to maintain a night watch on the poorly lit streets. The watchmen, known as Leatherheads for the leather helmets that they varnished to ironlike hardness, spent their nights manning guard boxes. If a Leatherhead was unwise enough to doze off, drunk students amused themselves by tipping the boxes over.

Their daytime counterparts were even less prepossessing. The city's seven wards generally had only two constables apiece for waking hours, and they neither walked a beat nor stirred themselves for much of anything else unless a crime victim came to City Hall and asked them. Even then, they were only to fetch or search whoever the victim accused. Constables were not to investigate anything on their own or even ask a suspect any questions; that was a magistrate's job.

But murder was different. There was no living victim to lodge a complaint, after all, and there was the added danger of a suspect fleeing such a heinous crime. Communication between authorities across the states remained so crude that a murderer allowed to slip away might reinvent himself altogether in another city. So the constable had to act, even on mere hearsay and reasonable suspicion. He set off for Levi's workshop with a few men from the crowd in tow. When the group reached the shop, Weeks didn't even notice their arrival; indeed, the constable walked right up behind him and tapped the carpenter on the shoulder.

*Yes?*

Weeks hardly seemed violent. In fact, he appeared surprised to see an officer of the law. And yet he was the one person—the only one—to have any rumors attached to him, claiming that he'd gone out with Elma when she was last seen. But to James Lent, it was hard to believe that the fellow before them might be a murder suspect.

"Is *this* the young man?" he asked the constable.

"Yes," said the officer, nodding.

The horsebreaker ventured closer and peered at him.

*Well*, he finally said—*I am very sorry for you.*

Levi looked at the men gathering about, and read the expressions in their faces.

"It is very hard to accuse—" he began indignantly, and then stopped. He dropped his head. "Is it the Manhattan Well she was found in?"

*Come with us*, they told him.

The streets were busy; the city was again open for business after one day of mourning and a second day of merriment. The carpenter followed the constable down the snow-covered streets in silence, and then northward across the meadows. Levi was led to the front of the gathering crowd.

"Weeks," Lent demanded, "do you know that young woman that lies there a corpse?"

Levi gazed upon the body: It was in a horrible state, with sodden stockings fallen about the ankles, and scratches over the hands and feet. The arms and legs had gone stiff, but the head still lolled to one side, its reddened face half glancing skyward—"like a person walking against the wind," one member of the crowd mused.

"I think I know the gown," Weeks replied quietly.

"My young friend, that is not the question I ask you," Lent said, pressing closer. The horsebreaker guided Levi's gaze back to the body that lay upon the ground, where well water was now freezing stiffly into the folds of her dress.

"Is there no mark in the countenance that you know?" he asked.

*Yes*, the carpenter finally nodded.

"There is," he said.


ACROSS THE street from the jail, the cries had been ringing out in the cold air that day.

*Port wine! Cognac!* auctioneer Jimmy Smith yelled. *Capers and olives! Herring and shad!*

Along with the business from the horse sales and stables on his stretch of Broadway, Smith had an impressive array of food and drink on offer that Thursday afternoon. There were twenty boxes of capers to get rid of, 252 gallons of fortified brandy to unload, and heavy crates of earthenware to move.

*Mackerel!*—he called to bidders, for he had ten pungent barrels of the stuff—*Mackerel!*

Across the street, a group of men walked onward, unmoved by the auctioneer's calls. The great door of Bridewell swung open to them, and constables led their suspect in. Manhattan's jail was a looming, cheerless building of gray stone, whose feints toward architectural pretension somehow made it all the more gloomy. Bridewell had been designed just before the war by Theophilus Hardenbrook, an architect more at home creating country manors; this might have explained why he'd included an ornate wooden cupola atop the middle of its three towers, but neglected to provide an open yard for the prisoners. The unfortunate inmates of his building could be seen pacing the dizzying parapets around the cupola at all hours of the day, desperate for air and sunshine. Its one saving grace was that the prisoners, perpetually staring out over the city rooftops, were almost always the first to spot fires; they'd even been given a bell in the cupola to sound warnings.

*This way.*

They passed through the central tower of the building—where the jail keeper, Alexander Lamb, kept his family and maintained a watch over a commons and booking area. This keeper's tower was flanked on either side by the wings where the prisoners were quartered. When new arrivals mounted the stairs into the prisoners' wing, the history of the place pressed down upon them. Soon after opening, it had been seized by the occupying British, who promptly starved American prisoners to death—and, some even claimed, dosed inmates with poison. The infamous place hadn't been dismantled after the war, because it was simply too useful. On any given day one could find a hundred men within its walls, and perhaps half as many women.

*Get in.*

The key turned in the lock, and the footsteps receded.


BEFORE LEVI stretched a dark and bitterly cold room, its dirty straw floors crowded with the wretched of the city: pickpockets, shoplifters, prostitutes. His jail mates included Bib and Gilbert, two young black men in for petty larceny—which meant they'd stolen less than $12.50 in goods. They were a typical pair. Bridewell was always the home of the drunken and pathetically scheming of the island, the ones in for pocketed silverware and filched handkerchiefs, or for drunkenness and vagrancy. Scattered among them one could also find newly captured runaway slaves and apprentices. In such a crowd, a promising and respectable young artisan like Levi Weeks stood out.

He might have been unique, were it not for one other young man staring out from Bridewell's barred windows that afternoon. David Frothingham was neither a drunkard nor a thief. The son of an upstanding Massachusetts family, he'd established himself as one of the first printers on Long Island, and as a promisingly fiery voice among Republicans. *Frothingham's Long-Island Herald* decried slave auctions as a "disgrace to humanity," and issued one of the island's first books—a forward-looking address titled *The Rights of Animals*. Aaron Burr shrewdly recruited him as the print foreman at his strongest political ally in the city, *Greenleaf's New Daily Advertiser*. The job required that Frothingham move into Manhattan, and it paid a mere eight dollars a week; he had to mortgage the Long Island newspaper and leave behind his wife and six children. But to serve alongside the most inspiring and dashing Republican in the city—how could he say no?

Perhaps he should have.

Frothingham's troubles began on November 6, 1799, when *Greenleaf's* reprinted a report about the *Aurora*, a zealously Republican newspaper in Philadelphia. "An effort was recently made to suppress the AURORA," the article claimed, "and Alexander Hamilton was at the bottom of it. Mrs. Bache was offered 6,000 dollars down, in the presence of several persons." And where might Hamilton have gotten the kind of cash to buy off his opponents? "British secret service money," the writer helpfully suggested.

The article had already run in other cities, of course. To accuse Hamilton of suppressing the opposition press, or of being in the pocket of the British, was all typical mudslinging. And to be fair, the Federalists *had* tried to shut down the *Aurora* before, and *Greenleaf's* as well—in fact, an indictment of Thomas Greenleaf under the Alien and Sedition Acts was interrupted only by the fellow's inconsiderate death from yellow fever. Frothingham himself had shrugged off personal attacks by Federalists, who called him "a vile sans-culotte"—a disreputable Republican lover of all things French and anarchistic.

But Hamilton would not treat this particular accusation so lightly. "I have long been the object of the most malignant calumnies of the faction opposed to our government," he complained to the attorney general. "In so flagrant a case, the force of the laws must be tried."

Assistant Attorney General Cadwallader Colden soon marched

into the newspaper offices to question the owner. But Thomas's widow, Anne Greenleaf, claimed to have no authority over *Green-leaf's* at all—and, when asked who did, produced David Frothingham. The bewildered foreman now found himself hauled into Bridewell for an article that he did not write, reprinted in a newspaper that he did not own. He was being made an example of—as a warning, perhaps, to any other mere underlings of Burr's. And although he was given the defense counsel of Burr's old friend Brockholst Livingston—a man he could never have afforded otherwise—when they faced the grim visages of a judge, the mayor, and Major General Hamilton himself, the case looked hopeless indeed.

"This is not a question that concerned the liberties of the press," warned the judge, "but only its *licentiousness.*" Were these Republican papers, the judge asked Hamilton, in fact hostile to the United States government?

*Affirmative!* the major general's voice rang out.

Livingston was reduced to pleading for the welfare of Frothingham's wife and children back in Long Island. That hadn't worked, either.

"He ought to have thought of them before he violated the laws of his country," the judge snapped, and gaveled them off. Frothingham was sentenced to four months in Bridewell, in cold and dark cells scarcely yards from City Hall itself. But unlike Levi, at least he knew when he might be free again.


The young carpenter miserably regarded his fellow inmates. Some had been confined for so long that nobody even knew why they were there anymore. One wild-looking blind and insane man known as "Paul from New Jersey" snored quietly on the floor, with only a block of wood as his pillow. When awake, he wandered around naked and filthy. An appalled visitor, asking why the man had been left naked, found the staff unconcerned: "The keeper explained that when furnished with a shirt, the rats soon eat it off."

An inmate's supper was hardly better than what the rats ate. The jail had managed to get the cost of feeding prisoners down to what it cost to feed horses in the auction stables across Broadway—about five or six cents a day. Keepers lugged in a tub of mush and set it down on the floor with a heavy thud: The cornmeal slop, darkened with a few dribbles of molasses, was a prisoner's sustenance. Only a fortunate few had actual plates or utensils to eat it with; the rest used their fingers. Levi was arriving late enough in the day that he'd missed lunch, which was just as well. That meal was more mush and molasses; breakfast was even more molasses still, albeit with a hunk of rye bread and a draft of boiled cocoa shells—the latter being a sort of brewed warehouse sweepings. It was, one unfortunate recipient recalled, "a mean, insipid, and musty drink."

A lucky few managed to get let out by their jailers to cross the street to Grenzeback's grocery, where they picked up desperately needed rum. The laxity about booze runs led to the occasional embarrassment, as in the previous spring when a prisoner named Stagg was spotted near a polling station with money and a ballot in his hand. A Republican poll watcher charged that the jail keeper at the time, Mr. Michaels, was paying off prisoners to cast illegal Federalist votes in the local elections. Michaels shot back that it was the "French Bullies"—Burr's Republican henchmen—who'd given Stagg a ballot, and that he'd been heroically pulling it *out* of the prisoner's hands.

The money in Stagg's hands, the jail keeper admitted, was for a rum run.

Michaels did not last much longer at Bridewell. Nor did his accuser emerge unscathed: Michaels crowed that the fellow was a deserter during the Revolution, and announced the man's business address for anyone who wanted to harass him. Like Frothingham and so many others in the city, they were just bit players to be tossed about in the great partisan melee over the young country's uncertain future.

It was Levi's own future that concerned him now, though—and whether he might have any at all. He huddled against the cold as darkness fell outside, the shadow of his first evening in jail passing over him. The cell windows were barred but without glass, leaving him exposed to the elements. It was impossible to escape the cold. But as they shivered and stared out the darkened windows, the prisoners of Bridewell could discern a light in a building next door to the jail. Almost within sight of the suspect himself, a room was being prepared for the dissection and autopsy of Miss Elma Sands.

THE FOLLOWING morning, January 3, 1800, Benjamin Prince was making his way toward Broadway when he saw his colleague. *Good morning, Dr. McIntosh!*

The two physicians fell into step together. Prince and McIntosh had both been summoned from their practices by Charles Dickinson, the local coroner. Dickinson was no doctor himself; his post was a political one, a holdover from the days when it simply meant a "representative of the crown." The inexperience of these coroners meant that municipal records were replete with such unhelpful causes of death as "horseshoe-head," "twisting of the guts," and the not particularly informative entry "bed-ridden." But Dickinson, at least, knew that he was out of his depth on this case.

The two doctors made for a curious pair. Druggist and physician Benjamin Prince was growing into a leader among Aaron Burr's faction around City Hall. He'd visited homes to battle sudden epidemics, and witnessed the ravages that yellow fever and smallpox could inflict on even the mightiest citizens in just a matter of days. For his part, William McIntosh was experienced in the ailments of poverty and neglect—the slow grind of consumption, alcoholism, untreated infections, and hunger. Born to a pauper family in the Bridewell almshouse, the young McIntosh proved to be a medical prodigy and was pressed into assisting in its infirmary as a child. The city council had been so impressed by the boy that they paid for his medical education. He was now the appointed almshouse physician to the very paupers whom he'd grown up among.

The men passed Grenzeback's grocery and the livestock auction, where just recently a tamed deer had sprung free from its pen and trotted off down the street; they walked past the windows of Bride-well, where freedom was not so easily attained. At the almshouse, a coroner's jury sat waiting for them, as the law decreed for the in-quest; and on the operating table before them was spread the body.

*Gulielma Sands,* officials quietly noted in their records.

The external examination would come first. The whiteness of Elma's skin would highlight any injuries, or at least any visible to the naked eye and to the magnifying glass. The inquest jury, em-powered to interrupt and ask questions during the dissection, leaned in and watched with interest.

*Is her neck broken?* one of them asked.

Dr. McIntosh examined Elma's head and neck, gingerly han-dling them for the telltale droop of broken vertebrae.

*It is not,* he replied.

There was a deeper suspicion, though, that always attended the death of a beautiful young woman—and rumors had been circulat-ing about Miss Sands ever since her body had been found.

*Is she with child?* a juror called out.

It was the kind of question that haunted the entire field of medi-cal jurisprudence. Criminal forensics scarcely existed yet: The first two books in English on the subject, barely adding up to two hun-dred generously margined pages, had only just been issued in the past few years. But both were overwhelmingly about infanticide and abortion, a subject that all too often verged into death for the mother as well. "It is murder in fact," insisted one text, "and often a complicated crime of murder and suicide."

Even among those intending no suicide at all, resorting to abor-tifacients like oil of tansy sometimes led to poisonings; doctors dissecting these perished women duly recorded irritated stomach linings, doughy and flaccid uteruses, and the unmistakable herbal aroma of tansy wafting over the room as the corpses were opened up. Other women, who instead chanced piercing a fetus with a cro-chet hook, ran even more serious risks from hemorrhage and peri-tonitis. Medical texts insisted such women could not claim rape as an excuse for having risked the procedure: Pregnancy was seen as a proof of willingness, for a number of doctors persisted in believing that a rape could not produce a child. Other jurists and doctors, perhaps wiser in the ways of the world, had long and pointedly disagreed with this notion.

But whether Miss Sands had kept her virginity, and willingly or not, was not of particular concern to Dr. Prince and Dr. McIntosh. The signs of virginity that their texts relied upon had been obliterated by long immersion in water. Yet the presence of a fetus could suggest a clear motive, either for suicide by the mother or murder by the father. It might explain her death away with a single line in the coroner's rolls. And so Dr. McIntosh carefully sliced into the uterus, opening it to the unsteady light of his laboratory's lanterns and windows. He was looking for a white and pink pulpy mass inside, a sign of life sometimes scarcely identifiable to the untrained eye. The jury stared intently at the body on the table as the two doctors examined and then puzzled over what they found.

The mystery of Elma's death, it seemed, was about to deepen.

"A report prevailed injurious to her honor," the new editor of *Greenleaf's New Daily Advertiser* reported dryly of the autopsy. "For the satisfaction of lovers of virtue it is mentioned that this appeared totally groundless."

So there was no fetus. But if seduction was not the reason behind her death, then what was? As prisoners and their keepers alike warmed themselves with rum against another freezing evening, the coroner's jury solemnly departed from the almshouse. Elma's family and neighbors at last received the coroner's assessment.

"A verdict of WILFUL MURDER," one newspaper printed, "by some person or persons as yet unknown."

# 7

# THE GLOOMS OF CONSCIOUS NIGHT

THE WAGON MADE ITS WAY WESTWARD TOWARD GREENWICH Street, the jostle of each rut and cobble passing unnoticed through the lifeless body of its passenger. For anyone who watched it roll by, the body laid out inside was well-known indeed—and the identity of her killer was no mystery at all.

HORRID MURDER! announced one paper, BY HANDS OF A LOVER!

The story ricocheted across the city, and then beyond the mere bounds of the island in outbound carriages and mail; in a matter of days it would be up and down the Eastern Seaboard. Elma Sands seized the imagination of writers, who conjured a forbidden romance: The beautiful young girl dressed in bridal clothes, taken by a fatal love into the fields beyond the snowy streets of the city; the muff, found floating in the water by an innocent child and given as a gift; the body, hidden mere feet beneath Lispenard's Meadow, suspended in the cold and dark well that was to have brought new life to New York.

"She was that evening to be privately married to Mr. Weeks," *Claypoole's American Daily Advertiser* breathlessly related to Philadelphians. "The young Lady dressed as a bride; but alas! Little did she expect, that the arrangements she had been making with so much care, instead of conveying her to the Temple of Hymen, would direct her 'to pass that bourne, from which no traveller returns.'"

Levi had been wise to surrender to the constable; had the young carpenter sought refuge in his brother's home, the place might have come as near to being torn down by crowds as Mrs. Murphy's house

had the summer before. "The city," one local judge warned a relative in Albany, "is much agitated." So agitated, in fact, that one of
the great writers of the Revolution, Philip Freneau, was moved to
write something that in recent days only the death of George Washington had coaxed from other Americans: tragic poetry.

> *Could beauty, virtue, innocence, and love*
> *Some spirits soften, or some bosoms move.*
> *If native worth, with every charm combined,*
> *Had power to melt the savage in mind,*
> *Thou, injured ELMA, had not fallen a prey*
> *To fierce revenge, that seized thy life away;*
> *Not through the glooms of conscious night been led*
> *To find a funeral for a nuptial bed,*
> *When by the power of midnight fiends you fell,*
> *Plunged in the abyss of Manhattan-well . . .*

But now her body was being moved more gently among the
mourning men and women of the boardinghouse. The front door of
208 Greenwich, still creaking unevenly, groaned open: Her coffin
bearers carried her in and set the body down upon the cold plank
floors. Elias Ring and Richard Croucher gazed at the cold and ashen
features that would not be hidden beneath a nailed-down wooden
lid for another two days. The warm glow of lantern light in the sitting room hinted at the life that she had left behind—the living presence that had disappeared just thirteen days before through that very
same front door.

Elma had finally come home.


A STRANGE business to be attending to, a murder mystery: strange,
at least, along the mercantile stretch of brokers and brick stables in
the neighborhood. Before Cadwallader Colden had set up offices at
47 Wall Street, the building had served as a coffee merchant. On one
side of his office was a shop selling hogsheads of rum and porter. On

the other side, Major Leonard Bleecker—a distinguished patriot who'd witnessed Cornwallis surrendering at Yorktown—was busily opening a stockbroker office.

Amid the bustle of old soldiers and new business, Colden cut a curious figure. The namesake grandson of a much-respected but Loyalist former governor, and scarcely seven years old when the Revolution broke out, Cadwallader had been spirited off to London for his education; upon his return, he'd wisely dispensed with the old man's politics, but kept the elder Colden's scientific and philosophical curiosity. At the founding meeting of the local Tammany Society—a salon that Aaron Burr was now commandeering into a political brotherhood—the young Colden had raised a startling question for the debate portion of the evening. Were people, he wondered, inherently barbaric or noble?

"Is there implanted in the human breast by the Supreme Being," he wondered aloud, "such a thing as *innate affection*?"

Colden's job of late had certainly given him reason to consider the alternate possibility of innate depravity. His law practice, first set up a few years earlier, had involved fairly ordinary jobs of conveyancing and notarizing. But soon the new attorney shared office space with the attorney general—his own brother-in-law—and when the post of assistant attorney general came up in 1798, young Cadwallader got the nod. Instead of scrutinizing property lines and wills, he was now confronted with prosecuting every variety of thieving, banditry, dishonesty, and depravity that New Yorkers could offer.

They had certainly kept him busy that winter. After some "tolerably well executed" counterfeit ten-dollar notes had been found in circulation—the coarser quality of the paper was the tip-off—forgers had raised the stakes by circulating genuine five-dollar bills altered to look like twenties. Some miscreants preferred acquiring goods without any cash at all; a respectable-looking shoplifting duo had been hitting fabric merchants along Pearl Street, usually by entering shops separately at nightfall, with one man distracting the merchant while the other stuffed chintz and cambric under his cloak. When the two were finally seized—they made the mistake of hitting the same store twice in one week—they proved to be an incorrigible pair known as Rap and Baker.

Others were harder to catch: A swindler named Jacob Weiser had been making the rounds, leaving his marks sputtering that he was "a monster in human form." The pugnacious French proprietor of the finest bookshop on Broadway promised a five-dollar bounty for "the damn'd villain guilty of the theft . . . of a double-barrelled GUN" from behind his counter. Even Brockholst Livingston paused from arguing cases to advertise a reward for over $1,200 worth of stock certificates that he had stashed in a trunk of clothes—a trunk which, alas, was then burgled from a house in Brooklyn.

It was the murder cases, though, that haunted Colden. Days before he and Livingston had faced off over the libel claim against David Frothingham, there'd been another legal battle between the lawyer and the attorney general's office—this one over what anyone would once have assumed to be the most appalling homicide case of the winter. In that same courtroom in City Hall, a bewildered-looking Portuguese immigrant was brought shuffling up to the docket, under the gaze of an immense crowd that filled the court and street outside to watch him. John Pastano, the jury was informed, had been a boarder in the home of Benjamin and Mary Castro, a pair of Portuguese cigar makers, only a few blocks away at 190 William Street. The two had taken him in for free, pitying their penniless fellow countryman. His time there went reasonably well, at first; thanks to the recommendation of a local pastor, the young man was set up in a job with a Broadway wine merchant. But soon Pastano got it into his head that Mr. and Mrs. Castro were whispering things about him, bad things—that he was a thief, a robber, that he was no good. He yelled at the frightened couple over dinner, where their denials only enraged him more: He *knew* they were out to get him.

At about three o'clock on the afternoon of October 1, 1799, while Mr. Castro was out of the house, John Pastano crept up behind Mrs. Castro in her kitchen and stabbed her three times in the neck.

The case seemed a straightforward one: The prosecutor brought forward just four witnesses and read Sir William Blackstone's definition of murder to the jury. Livingston tried rather harder: Because Pastano spoke little English, the attorney had as an interpreter Rabbi Seixas, himself the native-born son of a Portuguese family. Like Livingston, Rabbi Seixas carried the quiet advantage of being considered a great patriot—one so dedicated that he'd moved his entire synagogue out of occupied Manhattan and down to rebel-held Philadelphia for the Revolution. For witnesses, Livingston called a respectable merchant and a local priest; both testified that Pastano behaved erratically. The man, Livingston argued, could not be held responsible for his actions.

The jury deliberated for just minutes—so quickly, in fact, that they did not even leave their benches: *guilty*. In the first week of January 1800, Cadwallader Colden could assure himself that Pastano was to die—to be hanged that coming Tuesday, in fact—sentenced, in the judge's declaration to the packed courtroom, to hanging and dissection.

*Corpo pendurado*, Rabbi Seixas had patiently explained to the defendant. *Anatomização*.

And yet something unsettling remained about the notion of John Pastano as a willful murderer: the recollection, perhaps, that after murdering Mary Castro, he had filled his hat with her blood and wandered out into the street with it. When he was collared over by the Tea-Water Pump, broken English had spilled out from the man.

"Why you catch me?" he asked innocently. "Me not do it."


HAD JANUARY 5, 1800, been a normal day, the morning's gossip would have been about the conflagration that Greenwich Street narrowly avoided the night before, after a servant had placed a scorching hot brick in her bed to warm herself against the bitter cold. But it was Elma that the neighbors thought of that Sunday. Her body had been on display in the boardinghouse the entire day; the house residents could hardly avoid her sightless stare even if they had wanted to. Nor, it seemed, could anybody else in the neighborhood:

Elias Ring had been simmering with anger, and steering passersby into the house to see what had been done to his cousin. Her breasts, where chastely exposed, showed dark bruises.

"Her fingers appear to have been scratched from the knuckles down," one visitor observed. "There were many dislocations."

To the crowd, it looked like Elma Sands had put up a fight. But with whom?

If Mr. Ring ever became too overcome to talk, an equally enraged Richard Croucher was ready to. *This is young Levi's doing*, the cloth merchant hissed to visitors, his graying locks shaking in indignation. And as the proprietor of the boardinghouse brooded nearby, the gentle teachings of his Quaker faith gave way to a bottomless despair.

*If I should meet Levi Weeks in the dark*, he muttered—*I should not think it wrong to use a loaded pistol—if I should not be found out in it.*

As bad as Bridewell was, Levi was safer with Assistant Attorney General Colden keeping him in jail. Dueling had stubbornly remained a menace to Manhattanites ever since Colden had taken office. It was now far from its origins in the European "field of honor"—where noble swordplay had served to ward off the more ancient plague of chaotic revenge and honor killings—and transplanted to the brawling wilderness of America, where more deadly pistols had replaced rapiers. The very first duel in America, fought within a year of the *Mayflower*'s arrival, had been between two servants. But now dueling was largely practiced by those members of society most likely to give or take offense: journalists, politicians, and military officers.

It hardly took avenging a murder to set a duel in motion. One mocking newspaper letter that year proposing a "dueling club"—it was jocularly signed by a Mr. William Blood and Charles Bullet—listed an only half-joking set of fatal offenses: "any interruption of conversation—differing from any opinion given in the club—refusing to drink a toast—not taking off a heel tap—not clapping a song—a glum look—indifference while one is speaking—treading on the toe—accidentally brushing against one in the dark . . ."

In fact, dueling had long been notorious for its pettiness. One chronicler marveled at a fight that began when "two French nobles could not agree whether a certain letter on some embroidery was an X, or a Y." In another infamous case, an army colonel and a navy captain dueled after their dogs became entangled in a park. The dogs survived that quarrel; the naval officer did not. It was not even unknown for the two referees in a duel—the "seconds"—to *also* take offense with each other and arrange themselves into a firing line perpendicular to the primary combatants.

Such madness was strictly prohibited in New York, but not in New Jersey. Quietly arranged barge trips across the river provided a legal cover for dueling. Within the last few months of 1799, a pair of French immigrants—who still preferred the traditional choice of swords—had met in the storied dueling ground of Hoboken. The fight ended when one fatally ran the other through. Soon afterward, a local merchant had dueled with pistols not once but twice in a single week; but not before none other than Aaron Burr himself had dueled with John Barker Church, a member of his own Manhattan Company water board. The only casualty was a button shot off Burr's coat.

Were Levi Weeks to be let out of jail at that moment, virtually any New Yorker could take it upon himself to gun him down and quite possibly get away with it. Colden could hardly prosecute such fights, even if he wanted to—not when, scarcely a month earlier, a prominent man had publicly taken bullets in both legs during a duel in Paulus Hook, a field in what was coming to be known as Jersey City. The wounded party in the duel was Colden's namesake cousin, the gentleman horse breeder Cadwallader R. Colden. And the victor? John Provost—the assistant attorney general's other brother-in-law.


THAT MONDAY afternoon, Elma began her final journey through Manhattan. Any Quaker coffin was a plain one; local carpenters found they could keep their brass fittings and fine rubbed mahogany aside, for orders from Friends were rarely for much more than a raw pine box with iron handles. Elma was dressed in the same clothes she wore in life, as were the mourners—Friends considered all funeral garb to be just another form of vanity. Such simplicity was almost provoking in Manhattan, a place where elder burghers were still known to show off silver coins as coat buttons, and where any fashionable youngster would sooner walk into street posts than wear spectacles. In such a vain city, the Quakers' plain life was never more evident than in how they met death.

The unsteady front door of the boardinghouse creaked open, and the coffin slid out under the guidance of many hands on both ends. And then—the cold air hitting them, and a crowd gathering in Greenwich Street—the Ring family had a notion.

*Open the coffin*, they ordered.

It was common for Quakers to keep a body within a parlor or bedroom for viewing by family and friends, but the Rings had decided the frozen sidewalks of Greenwich Street were their parlor, and the city the outraged and grieving family. The coffin was laid down and the lid removed to reveal the lifeless visage: Elma Sands, staring upward toward the cold and clouded sky; the curious eyes of Manhattan staring down upon her corpse. This was hardly part of any Quaker ceremony. A dead body displayed on a Manhattan street in this age was like nothing any New Yorker had ever seen, an act so plaintive and primitive as to be shocking. Dozens of onlookers came—then hundreds—and then more.

With her battered body before their eyes, the crowd seethed.

"Mr. Weeks will no doubt speedily meet the rewards of his demerits," snapped one correspondent—a reward that would be found on the scaffold.

Amid the bluster and anger, a young man strode up to the roiling scene, his demeanor more dispassionate than the rest. James Snedeker was a surgeon and physician, not yet out of his twenties, his practice still newly established in town. He'd been Elma's doctor, helping to nurse her through her many complaints in her final months; in passing by Greenwich Street that day, he found himself confronted by her corpse for the first time. The young woman he had once helped keep alive now lay before him, utterly lost to his arts. But as her physician, Dr. Snedeker had one last dispensation to look more closely and searchingly than most, and so, amid the stares of onlookers, he carefully turned her head and examined her neck and chest. The skin that had been pale and warm was now cold and in the strange second flush of incipient decay; and yet he could still make out markings on it. He then placed his thumbs on her chest and, moving them forward in tandem, pressed down firmly.

*Click.* A dislocated clavicle: He could feel a bone, pressed down on one end by his thumb, rise up against his other finger from under her skin. Anyone in the crowd could make out what looked to be her final wounds: There were, one witness reported, "blows on her brow, chin, and breast." But there were, her doctor mused, other mysteries here as well—ones hidden beneath the skin itself. The eminent Dr. Hosack, pressing to the front of the crowd, confirmed the grim finding. He deemed her death "a sudden extinction of life" caused by "violent pressure upon the neck."

The bitter cold of the January afternoon was stiffening Elma's dead body as it lay by the busy avenue. Thousands had gathered to view her remains; the scene was one of such shock and disarray that onlookers hardly knew what to think. One hour of the appalling affair passed, and then another—and another still—before the Rings lifted Elma's coffin for its final journey.

The Friends Burying Ground was eight blocks away on Little Green Street, in the shadow of the Friends Meeting House itself. To see a funeral in that building was one of the most peculiarly affecting experiences in Manhattan. Friends and family might lay the coffin on a simple table with a white linen sheet upon it, the lid opened, and then sit in profound silence—sometimes for five or ten minutes, sometimes for the hour altogether—unbroken by speech or music. When a member felt moved to speak, they would stand, but mostly they sat in deep and penetrating silence. It was a silence that extended right up to the edge of the grave itself. With little but quiet weeping as accompaniment, the coffin would be lowered into the ground. The plot of a Friend was unmarked with any headstone, nor selected with much thought of being near family; for that, too, would speak of an overweening self-regard. All Friends were to be equal in death.

But this death was not like others.

As the final spadefuls of dirt settled over the grave and the sun set upon the city, an indictment was being drawn up in the attorney general's office. Levi Weeks stood accused of murder—"being moved," the charge read, "and seduced by the instigation of the Devil."

# 8

## WHATEVER IS BOLDLY

## ASSERTED

THAT THURSDAY, A SINGLE VOICE OF REASON IN THE *New-York Daily Advertiser* sought to calm Manhattan's fury.

"The public are desired to suspend their opinion respecting the cause of the death of a young woman whose body was lately found in a well," an editorial pleaded. Yes, there had been "horrid imputations" cast upon "a certain young man"—but he was "sober, industrious, amiable. . . . He has no conceivable temptation to perform such an atrocious action." The victim, on the other hand, most certainly did: "She had several times been heard to utter expressions of melancholy, and throw out threats of self-destruction, particularly the afternoon before."

This was news to most in the city, though scarcely any other theory on the case had gone unheard by now; pamphlets were even circulating accounts of ghosts and "dancing devils" around the Manhattan Well. The handbills were anonymous, but their target was not, for they claimed that the wraith of the victim—incorporeal, lonely, terrified—had been spotted hovering in Levi's bedroom.

"Handbills were generally distributed throughout the city," marveled one local of the campaign against Levi, "either by the industry of those bent on his destruction; or, perhaps, by some unprincipled scribbler who could conjure up thousands of ghosts and goblins for the sake of raising a few pence to purchase a dinner."

New Yorkers could still entertain such fanciful notions: The coldly rational and the wildly wondrous mingled together in the columns of their papers. In the same week that it gave notice of Elma's burial, the *New York Weekly Museum* pointedly ran a New Jersey coroner's claim that a murderer touching a dead man's face caused blood to trickle accusingly from the corpse's nose. Jostling with the announcement of a live "Beautiful African LION" exhibited on Broadway with "legs and tail as thick as a common size ox," and a notice proclaiming THE NEWTONIAN SYSTEM OF ASTRONOMY REFUTED, one could also read of the splendid achievement of a pair of coin counterfeiters in an upstate jail. The public was informed that, working with nothing but a penknife and chunks of cedar, these enterprising gentlemen had a built a perpetual motion engine consisting of "30 cogs and spur wheels of various dimensions, and set in motion by various weights." Instead of the crude horse-driven pumps the Manhattan Company relied upon, now "water might be brought into this city with trifling expense." The public merely needed to let this pair of great benefactors out of jail.

It was not too difficult to fathom the motives behind the counterfeiters and their perpetual motion claim. As to who had been rash enough to rise to the defense of the infamous Levi Weeks, the answer—like the mysterious death itself—was likely hidden among the wilds of Lispenard's Meadow. For while the editorial defending him was unsigned, a savvy reader might spot the masterful hand of Aaron Burr.


PERHAPS IT was inevitable that the top lawyer in Manhattan would become entangled in the case: Circumstances had almost guaranteed it. Levi Weeks's brother Ezra was a leading architect and contractor with a finger in nearly every major construction project in the city—including, as it happened, the plumbing for the Manhattan Well. Burr, of course, was the chair of the Manhattan Company. With a body in his own water company's well, and his contractor mixed up in the alibi, Aaron Burr could hardly avoid this case even if he had wanted to. Yet anyone looking for the founding father after the ad ran would have encountered yet another mystery: He'd quite suddenly left town.

His Richmond Hill mansion still bustled with the presence of his longtime slaves Harry and Peggy, who remained at the call of Colonel Burr's daughter, Theodosia. At seventeen, Theo was something of an intellectual debutante; she was so at ease with classical languages that in time she would ponder composing a book of mythology rewritten "in the form of amusing tales for children." There was even gossip that the young Washington Irving was nurturing some affection for his fellow prodigy. If Irving had recognized a kindred intellect, it was little wonder: Since Burr had become a widower in 1794, his familial attentions had been devoted to educating his daughter. The late Mrs. Burr's intellect was, one observer noted, "the equal of her husband"—and, having stayed up all night to read Mary Wollstonecraft's *Vindication of the Rights of Woman*, he promised his ailing wife that their daughter would be as learned and accomplished as any male scion in the city.

"I yet hope, by her," he pledged, "to convince the world what neither sex appear to believe—that women have souls!"

Theodosia had grown into a young woman capable of hosting visitors during her father's long absences on business and legislation. Even at fourteen, with her father away, she had charmed a Mohawk chief who had unexpectedly arrived at the house with an entourage of clergy and politicians. But on quieter days like these, humbler visitors were still welcomed into the great reception hall, where they passed through the side door to the right, and ascended the grand staircase with its mahogany railings to the equally grand dining room on the second floor.

Through the Venetian windows and out on the balcony, they could see Burr's dominion: Sweeping down several hundred feet from the mansion, there stretched a broad lawn, ranks of ancient oaks and basswood, and the wintry outline of a fine flower garden enclosed by hedges; beyond that lay Lispenard's Meadow. On a clear and cold winter's day, one could see out to the Hudson River.

The more modest creek curling around the north side of the hill, Minetta Brook, was an ancient boundary line that Dutch settlers had dubbed Bestaver's Killetje. For grounds that still appeared un-spoiled, Richmond Hill looked over a long history indeed.

Colonel Burr had his own past with this mansion, long before he'd purchased it. He'd first set foot in Richmond Hill as a liberat-ing soldier, scarcely twenty years old. Once the estate of a Loyalist, it was seized in 1776 as Washington's headquarters for the New York campaign—and in it, an impetuous young Burr served alongside Alexander Hamilton as one of Washington's aides-de-camp. Like Hamilton's, Burr's promise as an officer was immediately apparent. The orphaned grandson of powerful revival preacher Jonathan Ed-wards, he'd inherited the old man's fierce intelligence and magne-tism, and he arrived at Richmond Hill already a war hero. He made his name at just nineteen in the doomed Battle of Quebec; before the war was over he would winter at Valley Forge with Washing-ton and have his horse shot out from under him at the Battle of Monmouth. In the years since, he'd risen to great prominence, able to buy the mansion that he'd once so admired as a young soldier. It was at Richmond Hill that young Burr and Hamilton first sur-veyed the great expanse of Manhattan and wondered how to wrest control of the country from the British. Now—as rival lawyers and politicians—they wondered how they might wrest that control from each other.

Burr seemed curiously preoccupied that year, though, with the prosaic question of municipal water—with the very creeks and wells that his mansion overlooked.

"Pipes for the conveyance of Water have been laid in different streets to the extent of a Mile & upwards," he explained to one stockholder. As chair of the Manhattan Company, Burr oversaw the efforts back in the summer to find a usable spring. The Man-hattan Well had been a promising candidate—until they tried to use it. "The Machine for raising Water performs perfectly what was promised," he explained, "but we are embarrassed with quick sand which is drawn up in such quantities as to choak the pumps every hour."

They'd turned to the old Colles Well nearby instead, and the Manhattan Well quietly disappeared into obscurity. To have any of his wells associated with a murder was the last thing Burr needed for his new company, or as a respectable squire of the meadows. He had trouble enough already. While his home was a magnificently bombastic Ionic marvel from the outside—"one of those Grecian temples built of two-inch pine planks," as one visitor put it—all was not well within.

Just a few months earlier, the colonel had quietly inserted a notice into *Greenleaf's New Daily Advertiser*:

### RICHMOND HILL.

TO BE LET, and immediate possession, the House and Farm, adjoining Lispenards, formerly the property of Mr. Abraham Mortier; any quantity of land, from five to fifty acres, will be let with the house. The Garden is in complete order, and great forwardness, and the 16 room house well filled. Enquire at 221, Broadway.

A. BURR.

He found no takers. It was not for lack of prestige: Between Washington's and Burr's tenancy, the house had been occupied by then–vice president Adams; his wife, Abigail, adored the home, calling it "a situation where the hand of nature has so lavishly displayed her beauties that she has left scarcely anything for her handmaid, art, to perform." Yet for all of Abigail's praise and the promise of Burr's newspaper ad, any visitors coming to view the mansion found it rather less richly appointed than in years past: Gone were the Brussels rugs, the pianoforte, the fine china service, and the costly silvered mirrors that had once graced the halls.

There was something else they could not see, and that was the letters crowding the absent colonel's desk. When Burr was away, his slave Peggy was careful to observe two tasks: to retrieve the ink bottles so that they would not freeze in his unheated office and to lock up his papers. Left in open view, they would have raised the eyebrows of any visitor. "The extreme wrong I have suffer'd from a person in whose candour & integrity I had placed implicit confidence, and by much art and management have been basely defrauded by him, is a lesson of care and caution in my future steppings," accused Henry Drinker, a Philadelphia correspondent. The letter was now nearly a year old and still unanswered. Instead, there was a note in Burr's hand to an impatient uncle: "I do not as yet perceive any resource from which I can raise a Dollar. . . . You constantly address me as if it required only an exertion of Will on my part to raise money." What money he had raised was of the worst sort: In late November 1799 he'd written out a promissory note for $1,500 to a pair of local merchants.

No, what a casual visitor to this fine mansion could not see was what a great many creditors and business partners had come to suspect about their old comrade and founding father: Aaron Burr was broke.


THAT SUNDAY in Philadelphia, the Drinker household received a sharp knock at the front door of 110 North Front Street.

*Burr?*

The statesman was waiting outside on the cold stone steps, brisk and desirous of meeting the master of the house. It could not exactly be called an impromptu visit, for the two-day journey from New York down to Philadelphia entailed taking a ferry past the perilous chunks of ice in the East River, and then coach service from Paulus Hook, all while limited by the coach company to a paltry fourteen pounds of luggage. The timing of his arrival was not good: Henry Drinker was one of the most prominent local Quaker merchants and a longstanding clerk of the local meetinghouse; Sunday afternoon was hardly a fit time for him to be conducting business. But

Burr had been avoiding Drinker for months—and now urgently wished to speak to him.

The colonel was ushered inside and warmed his hands as he admired the house. Where New York homes were wooden and Dutch, Philadelphia's were brick and British—and this one was a splendid three-story mansion on a double lot, placed squarely amid the new fortunes and lively mercantile activity of North Front Street. A few doors down, at the back of a chocolatier's shop, horses walked in endless circles to drive the mill wheels for grinding cocoa; beyond that, there were the lathes and lumber piles of a cabinet workshop. Henry's own home was fittingly known among the locals as "Drinker's Big House," the monument of a lifetime of canny trading and debt collection by the old man.

As his guest settled in, Henry Drinker walked in gingerly on his corns, showing some of the frailty of a man of sixty-five. Yet his rectitude and crisp manner remained, and he bore the plain clothes and the double chin of a successful Quaker merchant. Burr, a generation younger at forty-three, was as small and wiry as the merchant was portly; with his warm brown eyes and tousle of black hair just beginning to gray, the colonel still possessed the energy and quick bearing of a field officer.

There were pleasantries to observe and news to exchange— terrible case up in New York, was it not? Burr remained an old and honored guest in Drinker's house. As a new widower some six years before, he'd even brought his young Theodosia for a visit once. But this particular call was still a shock.

*So what is to be done?*

Surely the colonel could see the difficult position he placed Mr. Drinker in—how could he not? Burr had signed a contract back in '94 to purchase some eighty thousand acres of Pennsylvania land from Drinker, and—well, matters had gone awry from there. The land was nearly a fifth of Drinker's holdings in Pennsylvania and New York, and yet the Quaker merchant was still without his promised money. His papers overflowed with five years' worth of apologetic letters, all filled with delays and excuses from Burr. "The

Purchase if made will be made with a View to Settlement in the Spring," read one from 1795, adding: "Payment uncertain."

It simply had to stop.

What was more, state property taxes had been accumulating on the land—taxes that Drinker initially refused to pay, as they were rightly owed by Burr. He had been mailing Burr for months, years now, to have this matter resolved—rarely with any satisfactory response from Richmond Hill. Surely Burr could see that he must honor the contract.

Drinker was accustomed to bargaining hard: He still underwrote cargo ships from Britain and ran a busy iron mill. He was a canny enough businessman that he'd managed to support the Revolutionary patriots in one early boycott campaign, and then turned around to secure a commission to sell British tea during another. Even if those business instincts sometimes backfired—at one point in the Revolution his vague allegiances earned him an exile from the state—they'd served him well enough that he now controlled some half-million acres of land in New York and Pennsylvania.

Burr considered Drinker's requests carefully.

*No.*

It was simply impossible. Burr had been under terrible burdens for years now: After a 1796 land speculation had gone bad, a business partner left him holding the bag for immense debts. Burr did not like to talk numbers, for he was a gentleman, but those knowledgeable of such matters said that he was on the hook for at least $80,000. It was an *astounding* sum. But if Drinker wished to continue his pursuit—why, then—what Burr no longer possessed in money, he still possessed in wile. And it would be a shame for the good merchant to expose his business interests to legal difficulties.

The damnable truth dawned on Drinker: He was trying to get money out of a lawyer.

"I am not aware of any cause of litigation subsisting between us," he assured his visitor. "Save one."

That hardly mattered to Burr. The justness of the old merchant's complaint was irrelevant: He could tie up Drinker in endless

litigation anyway. Burr had a reputation for harrying foes with blizzards of appeals and motions, and when the occasion called for it,
the colonel's attitude toward legal processes could possess a marvelous flexibility. The law, he once explained, "is whatever is boldly
asserted and plausibly maintained."

Burr pressed the merchant relentlessly through the day, wearing
the old man down. *We must come to an agreement*, he insisted.

By the time they adjourned, the elderly merchant had missed his
Sunday meeting at the Friends meetinghouse, an almost unheard-of
lapse for him. And as darkness fell, the old man miserably contem-
plated another face-to-face stalemate with Burr scheduled for the
very next day.

On January 14, 1800, Drinker wearily informed one of his business partners of what had happened next.

"I have had to pay a large demand made on me by Aaron Burr
Esq.," he wrote, chagrined. *"And tho' it was directly opposite to what
of right should have been my situation with him* . . . I foresaw he was
disposed to perplex & spin out the matter to considerable length."

Colonel Burr, returning to Richmond Hill with some $12,000
in bonds and bills strong-armed from his own creditor, promptly
talked yet another $1,500 out of his local merchants. His creditors
staved off—however briefly—Aaron Burr was now ready to get
down to business.

He had a man to save from the gallows.


ELMA'S FAMILY and friends had not suffered in silence while Burr
was away. The defense's whispering campaign had prompted an unsigned counterattack in the *New-York Mercantile Advertiser*:

> To insinuate suspicion that the ill-fated girl was herself
> the perpetrator, is such an outrage on probability, that
> all who are acquainted with the circumstances must hear
> the remark with indignation. Miss Sands, so far from
> shewing signs of melancholy, was uniformly cheerful and

> serene; and, on the day previous to the murder, was re-
> markably so. Her expectation of becoming a bride on the
> morrow was the natural cause of her liveliness. Alas! How
> soon the gay prospect blackened with the shades of death!
> Her murderer yet lives; but let him tremble with horror at
> the vengeance that inevitably awaits him.

Perhaps. Burr had his own suspicions about the case and about the motives of those who had raised the loudest fuss over it. As a cryptic anonymous notice in the *New York Weekly Museum* shot back, "Those who are incapable of great crimes won't readily suspect others of them."

For Burr understood murder well. True, his earliest legal work was of the dreariest commercial variety: Like his old war comrades Hamilton and Brockholst Livingston, he'd leaped into the profession in 1782, when much of the state's legal talent was disbarred for Loyalism. Burr and Hamilton set up law offices on Wall Street within months of each other; the instant demand for new lawyers hit just as the upheavals of the Revolution created a bonanza in property dispute cases. Their clientele tended to follow their political inclinations, with Burr representing the radical and ascendant Whigs and Hamilton often defending the now much-abused Tories.

But soon Burr had his eye on higher offices: In 1789 he accepted the job of New York's state attorney general, where his dockets included prosecuting a slave named Pompey for robbery, pursuing a rape suspect called Titus, and indicting the hot-tempered proprietor of a glassworks for murder. Though he left the office to serve terms in the state assembly and the state senate, his private law practice continued to thrive throughout the decade. Dealing with judges was like addressing family to him—quite literally, as his brother-in-law and an uncle both sat on the bench. Burr thoroughly understood lawyering, and he probably knew Cadwallader Colden's job even better than the prosecutor himself did.

Aaron Burr was not modest about his abilities. In the previous few months, New Yorkers had been circulating a fine example of lawyer humor, which imagined an irate tailor hitting his attorney with a monstrously itemized bill, spelled out in pounds, shillings, and pence:

| | | | |
|---|---|---|---|
| Measuring and taking orders for a full suit of clothes | £0 | 6 | 8 |
| Warrant and instructions to my foreman for executing same | £0 | 6 | 8 |
| Going three times to the woolen draper | £4 | 4 | 0 |
| Writing to the button merchant | £0 | 6 | 8 |
| Filing his declaration of 16 sheets | £0 | 16 | 0 |
| Fees to button merchant | £0 | 18 | 0 |

And so on, for dozens of line items. The jest might as well have been at Burr: His clients were left with no doubt that they'd received the services of New York's finest attorney, because he promptly and enthusiastically billed them for it. As part of the defense team behind a huge settlement that he was now litigating for the French trader Louis Le Guen, he even billed his client twice as much as had fellow top counsel Alexander Hamilton.

Burr was one of the finest lawyers in town, and he knew it. But as to his being one of the finest men—on this, there was far less agreement.

# 9

# A Perfect Monster

ALONG THE LOWER REACHES OF GREENWICH STREET, SOME FIVE or six blocks from the Ring boardinghouse, the buildings turned more mercantile and oriented toward the shipping businesses on the Battery. By Number 40 you reached the office of Nicholas Cruger, one of the city's wealthiest West Indies merchants. It abutted an ice-house, where thirsty sailors and clerks would stop by for ice cream, milk punch, and "syrup of raspberries."

At the next building, a passerby in the aftermath of the murder case might well have spotted Cruger's most famous import from the West Indies: Major General Alexander Hamilton, Esq. Cruger had personally hired this illegitimate son of a St. Croix merchant as his clerk, and shipped the promising young boy off to America for an education; three decades and one revolution later, Hamilton could be seen through the windows of 36 Greenwich Street, sometimes late into the night, writing court briefs by candlelight.

It was the kindest light in which to view Hamilton's law of-fice: His own son described the place as "rather a shabby affair." But then, the major general always treated his offices as a sort of glorified field tent. With his weapon of choice, a quill honed by slices of his penknife, Hamilton would come to draw sharply slashing lines of attack into the sheet of Britannia stationery be-fore him:

*These things are to be admitted, and indeed cannot be denied, that*
*he is a man of extreme and irregular ambition; that he is selfish*

*to a degree which excludes all social affections; and he is decidedly* <u>*profligate*</u>*.*

The spartan furnishings of the law office stood in mute rebuke to such men: Hamilton was prone to furnishing a space with a plain pine desk and chair, and kept his files stored on planks laid over blocks. Among his papers was a case for which, after receiving a generous fee from his client, he sent the check back with a simple notation: "Returned as being more than is proper."

Hamilton took up the quill again and kept writing.

*He is far more* <u>*cunning*</u> *than* <u>*wise*</u>*—far more* <u>*dexterous*</u> *than* <u>*able*</u>*.*

He had to steady himself: his angry underlining and cross-outs could pierce straight through the paper. But he felt compelled to keep writing, page after page.

*The truth is, with great apparent coldness he is the most sanguine man in the world. He thinks every thing possible to adventure and perseverance: although I believe he will fail, I think it almost certain he will attempt usurpation, and the attempt will involve great mischief.*

After a few more pages of invective, he would set his quill down. He had other work to attend to, and he could not spend any longer on his political grievances. Yet he could hardly help it, for the most curious legal case ever to pass through his office was the defense of Mr. Levi Weeks, and his fellow counsel was Mr. Aaron Burr, Esq.—the very man about whom he had just written.

IT WAS not always thus between them. Hamilton and Burr still dined together on occasion, as did their wives and daughters. But they were the worst of friends—or, perhaps, the best of enemies.

"Little Burr," Hamilton once mused. "We have always been

opposed on politics but always on good terms. Burr beckoned me to follow him, and I advised him to come with me; we could not agree."

Ruddy and red-haired, vocal where his rival was reserved, Hamilton was as easy to distinguish from Burr in person as he was in print. Where Burr exercised a near-surreptitious magnetic influence over idealistic young liberals, Hamilton was a loud advocate for the propertied classes; as the author of most of the *Federalist Papers*, he'd argued for ratifying the stronger central government of the U.S. Constitution, but against the Bill of Rights. Both men had known each other from the Revolution, when Hamilton left his staff work with General Washington to lead a bayonet charge at Yorktown. But after the war, with a family to support, he'd taken to—as he drolly put it—"rocking the cradle and studying the art of fleecing my neighbors."

It was difficult for him to maintain his law practice. As Washington's trusted protégé, he served as the new nation's first secretary of the Treasury—a job that, ironically, paid rather poorly, even as Hamilton almost single-handedly founded the U.S. Mint and the First Bank of the United States. He continued serving in the embattled Adams administration as a major general, charged with preparing for a brewing war with France—all the while battling insurance companies from his law office over French privateer raids on merchant vessels. He was immensely proud of his government service, but he needed the scruffy law office to pay his bills.

Their profession meant that Hamilton and Burr couldn't avoid each other even if they had wanted to. As the best lawyers in Manhattan, they were on one side or the other of the leading cases of the city. On Monday they might be on opposite sides of a property line dispute, and on Wednesday on the same side of an insurance settlement for lost crew and cargo. On Friday they'd be on opposite sides again over a *different* lost ship.

But a murder case?

It was not Hamilton's usual line of work at all. His reputation was as a mighty courtroom orator in commercial law cases; his criminal defenses could be counted on his fingers. His first such case was representing a client accused in 1786 of dueling, and had ended inauspiciously in defeat. In two decades at the bar, he'd defended a single murder case, one rape case, and a few shoplifting charges. But Hamilton owed the Weeks family—quite literally.

During fever season, the major general and his family had rented a home in the sylvan uptown hinterlands of Harlem Heights; charmed by the views over the river, he was now planning on building a family manor there. The thought pleasantly occupied him in his travels: "I remark as I go along everything that can be adopted for the embellishment of our little retreat," Hamilton told his wife, "where I hope for a pure unalloyed happiness with my excellent wife and sweet children."

He envisioned the Grange, as he dubbed it, as a handsome edifice of classical columns and balconies, with fashionable octagonal dining and parlor rooms, and surrounded by ornamental beds of tulips. It would, at last, be a mansion worthy of their social station—one, not coincidentally, just as fine as Aaron Burr's. While building it, Hamilton plunged tens of thousands of dollars into debt—and had hired none other than Ezra Weeks as his contractor.

"My country estate, though costly, promises, by the progressive rise of property on this island and the felicity of its situation, to become more and more valuable," he reasoned.

If it was a distinctly optimistic line of reasoning, a paper debt was still of less concern to him than the good home he owed to his long-suffering wife, Elizabeth. When not fishing on the Harlem River or hunting with his dog Peggy, the major general had been known for his rather less sporting pursuits. Nobody needed to ask why Martha Washington had nicknamed her house's tomcat Hamilton. Later, when he was caught in some questionable transactions with an embezzler, Hamilton had to resort to a closed cabinet meeting and an audit of the Treasury's books to explain the payments. It was his own money being paid out to the fellow for blackmail, and not part of any fraud, he explained—"My real crime is an amorous connection with his wife." The revelations were leaked, and it was a mark of Hamilton's formidable reputation as a patriot, and his equally formidable reputation as a cad, that even his political opponents found adultery an entirely believable explanation.

It was hard to say what was more galling in the aftermath: Aaron Burr's decision to serve as the mistress's divorce lawyer, or that very same Colonel Burr intervening to save Hamilton from dueling with James Monroe over the scandal. To owe Burr both his life and his worst public humiliation was grating—but Burr's new utility scheme was worse still. The much-vaunted waterworks had been a scandal even before the murder, for the Manhattan Company itself was not at all what it appeared to be. Hamilton scratched down a final angry note into the margins of his letter on Burr. "He has lately by a trick established a *bank*," the major general wrote, "*—a perfect monster.*"

THE WELL that Elma Sands was found in belonged to no ordinary water company: It was part of the most shadowy and roundly vilified business in all of Manhattan. To Hamilton and other Federalists, perhaps the only real surprise of the case was that a murder *hadn't* been discovered on Manhattan Company property before.

Granted, the board of respectable gentlemen who assembled every Monday and Thursday at 23 Wall Street saw nothing sinister in their duties. The body in the Manhattan Well was a shocking matter, of course. But the water had to keep running, as indeed it would continue to do, with shifts of team horses turning endless circles to power the pumps that fed Manhattan homes. Piped water was now to be a part of the city's life; New York's first commercial plumbing-supply outfit, situated on the aptly named Water Street, had even begun placing ads in the newspaper to trumpet its selection of "Lead Pipes to convey the Water from the logs in the street, into the houses . . . fixed in such a manner, as not to freeze on the coldest days."

The decision to pipe this water from around the Collect, though, was controversial. Stirring up the "five acres of putrid mud," one critic charged in the *New-York Commercial Advertiser*, was "an idea most monstrous, and capable of producing effects the most pernicious . . . the death of thousands of useful citizens might arraign their carelessness." And the danger, he charged, was hardly justified by the desire to quickly head off summer epidemics.

"The yellow fever may possibly be prevented by such a measure, but I am afraid it would be by substituting in its place the plague itself," fretted the correspondent. "It is like a person eating garlic to take away the taste of onions."

To the Manhattan Company, these were the mere quibbles of the small-minded. Founding board member Aaron Burr already had bigger ideas on his mind. As water reports were dutifully read and filed, the colonel was pondering splendid plans for the betterment of his fellow citizens in Manhattan. Plans that might, say, involve some highly inventive financing schemes. Why not build a toll bridge? Why not indeed: They had already begun building one across Lake Cayuga. And, he suggested, they might sell "a Tontine for raising Capital by small quarterly subscriptions to be divided among the survivors at the expiration of seven Years"—with his company, of course, taking its fee first. And insurance! Ads would be placed with the local newspapers for life insurance, with premium tables going all the way down to one year of age; between the annuity it would pay out on their survival, or the takings from other insured siblings dying—"suicide and the hands of justice always being excluded"—one might plan quite sensibly for the far-off adulthood of one's offspring.

"Parents," their ad copy explained, "by assuring the lives of their children from infants, until they attain a given age, may secure for them such sums of money as may be required to secure them apprenticeships . . . or to marry." With rates starting at an annual payment of $2.57, it seemed a fair enough deal.

But why was a water company selling bridges, tontines, and infant insurance?

It was a question that nettled Hamilton to no end. Initially promoted as a great public good by Aaron Burr, just a year earlier the
private water company had won the support of no less than Major
General Hamilton himself. Burr, in his final months of a one-term
stint in the state assembly, had gone out of his way to secure his
rival's backing, for Hamilton knew the awful privations of yellow
fever well—"We die reasonably fast," he wrote drolly to a friend
during one outbreak. The notion of a private company running the
effort, rather than the government, also flattered Hamilton's Federalist ideals; though he often lobbied for more defense funding, he
tended to regard other government projects with suspicion.

Hamilton's support for any Burr plan would come at a price, of
course: namely, a key role for the Federalist-dominated city government, through a board of six appointed by the city; a permanent
spot for the city recorder; and one-third of the company's shares
going to the city. Also, surely by coincidence, Hamilton's undistin-
guished brother-in-law John Church was now to have a seat on the
water board. With these assurances in hand, Burr left with a powerful endorsement for his bill.

Curiously, however, this was not the bill Burr presented to the
state legislature.

Passed in the wee hours of the session—Colonel Burr had can-
nily waited until many lawmakers had already left to journey home
from Albany—Burr's final bill provided for an astounding $2 mil-
lion in capitalization, a board twice as large as originally planned
and to be dominated by Republicans, and a piddling one-tenth of
the stock to be owned by the city. One friend of Hamilton's snorted
that Burr had "begotten it on the body of the Legislature when it
was lulled into a profound sleep by his arts and misrepresentations."
Exactly what they sleepwalked into was hidden deep inside the bill:
a perpetual clause that empowered the Manhattan Company to use
any "surplus funds" however it saw fit. For anyone who did not
understand what that meant—and few did, at first—a member of
Burr's entourage was happy to later elucidate.

"His object," he explained, "was a bank."

Digging the Manhattan Well never had anything to do with water at all, and everything to do with politics. And now the curious thriftiness of all the company's projects—digging out a half-soured old well, employing horses instead of steam power, using hollowed logs instead of iron pipes—began to make sense. *Burr was hoarding the money to buy the next election.*

It was a tactic Hamilton understood all too well. He had clinched Federalist power in years past with the long-exclusive charter of the Bank of New York—the party was almost printing its own money. But with a Republican-run bank, not only could the disenfranchised acquire property and qualify to vote, but previously reliable Federalist merchants could now switch parties without fear of financial retribution.

The power of Federalist banks, a Burr aide happily reported, "is now *totally* destroyed."

Federalists were apoplectic, and with good reason. The electoral college members to be chosen in the April state elections meant that Burr's bank was no local matter. New York was the swing state in the upcoming presidential election—and Manhattan was the swing district in New York State. Control the city, and you controlled the 1800 presidential race.

"All will depend on the city election," Thomas Jefferson confided bluntly to his fellow Virginia politician James Monroe.

In this, if nothing else, the Federalists were in full agreement with him. To them, the venture was nothing less than Burr's own Trojan horse for enriching himself and spreading his rabble-rousing populism. "The Collect is made the foundation of a Bank—the Bank is to overflow you with a deluge of notes . . . to make the fortune of Mr. Burr," charged one editorial. The writer conjured a Burrite landscape of godless French radicalism, with "Jacobin fish women" jeering at the wealthy, or worse: "Your lives and properties will be the sport of licentious foreign tyrants and ferocious mobs."

At the center of it all was a water company—and the murder that now haunted it.

BROCKHOLST LIVINGSTON sat through the water board meetings, taking in the pleasant march of progress being made by their company. He was an unmistakable presence in any gathering: Balding and cerebral in appearance, he had a prominent nose that one contemporary deemed "a regular Roman triumph." Livingston had duly considered all the old Federalist complaints about their water company, and he wasn't much bothered, not least because he was a founding board member and a close ally of Burr's, as well as a probable Republican candidate in the upcoming state elections.

More improbably, though, he'd *also* been hired by the Weeks family to defend Levi.

For a criminal case to command the talents of the city's top three lawyers was unheard of, and yet Livingston had much in common with his two fellow counselors. He'd gone to school with Hamilton, and to college with Burr; like Hamilton, he'd also been a wartime aide-de-camp to George Washington—and like Burr, he was the scion of a powerful New York family. In the years since the war he'd built a law practice the equal of Hamilton's and Burr's, and become a trustee of Columbia College. But for all his respectable trappings, Livingston had always been known for an explosive sense of humor and an equally unpredictable temper. The two had combined disastrously a year earlier, when an editorial of his made a mild if careless jest about a local Federalist figure, James Jones. Incensed, Jones assaulted Livingston—beat him with a cane, in fact, while the lawyer was out promenading with his wife and children—and then grabbed him by his famous nose and yanked. It was the worst insult to the man's vanity possible. Livingston immediately challenged Jones to a duel, in which he killed him with a single shot to the groin. A fuss was raised in the Federalist newspapers, but who would try a man publicly assaulted in front of his family—and who would dare to prosecute a Livingston? The constable had refused even to arrest him.

The duel with Jones haunted the lawyer, though. "His best friends cannot lament his death more than Mr. Livingston does," one acquaintance reported.

Perhaps it was regret over the killing of Jones, or maybe it was that during the war Livingston had been held in the miserable prison ships the British kept in New York Harbor, but whatever the reason, and despite his formidable record in commercial law, Livingston had been more ready than his fellow lawyers to serve on some of the most clearly hopeless criminal cases on the docket. Just within the previous couple of months, he had defended Frothingham against the merciless libel charge by Hamilton, and represented the crazed John Pastano over the murder of his landlady.

Livingston knew better than anyone that even with the best defense lawyers, the state could exact swift and terrible retribution. Two years earlier, there'd been the case of John Young, a bassoonist from the local theater's orchestra pit. Young had run up some debts, and when a deputy sheriff came to arrest him for it, the musician panicked and shot the man dead. Livingston tried to get Young's charge knocked down to manslaughter, but the trial did not go well: The gallery was packed with a hostile crowd, and when the judge's sentence of hanging and dissection was pronounced, the spectators broke into victorious jeers—"an indecency," one newspaper decried afterward, "which ought never to be tolerated before a tribunal." Three weeks later, human body parts were found bobbing up against one of the local market piers in the East River. They proved to be the remains of Livingston's late and very recent client.

"This shameful exposure was not through the wantonness of the surgeons, as supposed," reported the *New-York Journal*, "but of the porters employed to sink them, being contained in a bag, with weights for that purpose; it seems the porters conceived the bag was of value, and by this means the parts were set afloat."

In a state so hard in its justice, it was little wonder that the Weeks family had hired the city's best lawyers to defend the bewildered young carpenter. Together, they would be greatest criminal defense team New York had ever seen. And they'd need to be, for the noose around their new client was now drawing even tighter.

# ⇥ 10 ⇤

# THE SILENT SLEIGH

AT ABOUT NINE O'CLOCK THAT FRIDAY, AN ELECTRIFYING YELL broke the night.

"Fire! *Fire!* FIRE!"

Bridewell's fire alarm clanged madly, and churches took up the alert as citizens scrambled to their upper windows and rooftops to find the source. Some began running northward, while others ran south, and it took some confused minutes to figure out why. On that winter's night *two* fires had broken out simultaneously: one at a house in the northern reaches of the city, and the other down at the docks. The house was soon "entirely consumed," but the docks augured even worse. When fire crews raced down to the Battery, they found "the heavens illuminated from fierce devouring flames"—columns of fire shooting skyward from the *Admiral Duncan,* a British trader set to sail to Liverpool the next morning fully loaded with $70,000 worth of cargo. It had gunpowder below decks, and as flames climbed up its masts and belched out from its portholes, another ship—the *Olive*—went up as well. The crew of the *Admiral Duncan,* out for one last night on the town, returned to find their vessel being desperately cut loose, and the burning hulk drifting into the East River. By the next morning, all that was left was smoke, and the smell of charred timber lingered in the air: the work, it was murmured, of an arsonist.

But across the city, the defense team and the city's recorder were pondering another, much more quietly mysterious evening. The recorder carefully dated a document—"Sworn, 18th day of January, 1800"—and listened as Levi's sister-in-law made a sworn statement.

*On Sunday, the twenty-second of December last, my husband and I were at home,* she began.

They'd been lucky to get Elizabeth Weeks to make this affidavit at all: It had not been long since she'd borne Ezra a daughter, and these were perilous days for the health of a young mother. She was ready to testify, though, that John McComb, Jr.—Hamilton's choice of an architect for his new Grange mansion—had come with Mrs. McComb to visit them on the night of Elma's disappearance. And, crucially, there had been another visitor for that evening: Levi Weeks.

*About candle light,* she continued, *or a little while after, Mr. John McComb and his wife came in. Levi Weeks was then in the room, and remained with the company till after the clock struck eight, and then went away. The McCombs left about twenty or twenty-five after; Levi Weeks came in, and remained.*

Had she seen anything unusual in his countenance?

*No,* she replied. *He appeared cheerful—ate a hearty meal—and went off to his lodgings, about ten o'clock.*

It sounded like an entirely unremarkable evening, which was exactly what the defense team needed to hear. With respectable friends and family ready to testify to Levi's alibi, and his bond easily backed by a powerful brother, the young carpenter was released. A generation earlier Levi would not have been so fortunate, but bail laws had been considerably loosened after the war.

Ironically, the still-unreformed severity of debtor laws had likely helped to secure a fine defense team in the first place. Burr and Hamilton were both in the habit of running up the kind of debts that could put them at Ezra's mercy, and debtor laws meant a contractor or architect could have them thrown into jail for any inability to pay a past-due debt. It was a threat that prominence gave little protection from: A few years earlier, even New York's attorney general had been confined for a debt while still serving in office.

Wisely, neither Hamilton nor Burr entered any fee into their ledgers for defending Levi Weeks.

But if bond money and the debts of prominent lawyers could keep Levi safe from the Bridewell jail, Elias Ring's talk of shooting him meant that he was still well-advised to lie low. For that matter, his other witnesses and supporters needed to keep quiet as well. "Those who dared to suppose him innocent," one local observed, "were very generally considered as partakers in his guilt."

Some hinted that Ezra Weeks himself was also involved in Elma's death. In the newspapers, even the McCombs suddenly found themselves under scrutiny. "Directly in the rear of Mr. McComb's houses," warned the New York *Commercial Advertiser*, "the lower beams of a very extensive wooden building have just been laid"— one so tall and close to the property lines, in fact, that it violated city fire codes, which the builder had outrageously circumvented by paying off some paltry fines. "Should an accident happen, the whole of Broadway would be endangered," the paper complained. It was a stinging attack to make, especially after the devastating local fires of the previous week.

Ezra knew that he had to remain patient. He had his eye on the local City Hotel; its builder was teetering on the verge of selling the $100,000 behemoth at an immense loss, and Ezra had money ready to snap it up cheaply. And McComb, along with his Grange commission for Hamilton, had another and even greater project on the horizon: that of building a new City Hall.

Things were going quite well for the builders, save for one problem: a prosecutor utterly determined to get their foreman executed.


Soon snow was falling over the city, covering the charred piers on the East River, filling the hollows of Lispenard's Meadow, and slowing Greenwich Street to a stately, muffled march. One figure could still be found stamping doggedly through the winter weather, his mind occupied in deep thought.

Cadwallader Colden was thinking about a squeaky door hinge.

*Mark that noise*, the Rings informed him. With both Levi and Elma now gone from their quarters, the Rings' boardinghouse sat in doleful silence: a stillness occasionally broken by the creak of their poorly hung front door. *There's the staircase, and our bedroom—mark that as well.*

From their bedroom on the first floor, Elias and Catherine Ring explained, they could hear the door creaking as Elma departed the house on the evening of December 22, 1799. And it was here that they heard her whispering with—well, with someone, some other boarder—as she prepared to leave. Mrs. Ring had few doubts as to who that other person was.

*That very day, Elma told me that they were to be married*, Mrs. Ring insisted.

*It's true*, Mr. Ring added. *He had affections for her.*

William Anderson, Levi's apprentice, came forward with even more damning evidence: *I saw something*, he admitted.

He shared a room with Levi and had been locked out the night of the disappearance—he'd waited and waited in the parlor for Levi to come home with the key. What stuck in Billy's memory, though, happened well before that evening.

*One night, Levi waited until he thought I was asleep. Then I saw him depart from the room dressed only in his shirt. I heard him creeping upon the stairs*, he recalled. Levi did not come back until morning.

A modest Quaker couple running a boardinghouse, a roommate who could implicate Levi in an affair with the deceased— these were the sorts of people who would make for good testimony. Colden considered the other possible witnesses from the boardinghouse, too: Mrs. Ring's unmarried sister, Hope Sands; artisans such as Sylvanus Russel; and the peculiar London cloth merchant, Richard Croucher. True, boarders generally made a point of attending to their own business, because it was the only way to tolerate close quarters. But to one boarder, the quarters had been a little too close.

*I saw Elma and Levi in an indecent act*, he hissed.

This was the kind of information Colden was waiting for—

information he desperately needed. His office's handling of Manhattan's previous two murders had not inspired much confidence, not least because one bore disturbing similarities to this new case. Two weeks before Elma's disappearance, *another* murdered woman was found hidden in a cistern, this one mere blocks from City Hall in the narrow alley of Hague Street. The unfortunate victim was Rose Malone, a widow who had remarried a week earlier. Her new husband, William, was immediately suspected, and bundled off to jail under blaring headlines of HORRID MURDER! But there the headlines ended: The attorney general's office had quietly dropped the case. The fact that Colden was only the assistant attorney general was not much cover: Since Attorney General Josiah Hoffman was Colden's brother-in-law, he could hardly distance himself from the unsolved murder.

Even when all the evidence was on their side, affairs were not going well for state law enforcement. Snapping open a newspaper brought this thunderbolt of news from Albany: AN ACT TO PARDON JOHN PASTANO FOR MURDER. "It appears satisfactorily to the Legislature," the act read, "that at the time of the commission of the act aforesaid he was insane, and is therefore a proper object of mercy." Both the New York State Legislature and Governor John Jay had personally reversed the state attorney general's office's highest profile case ever: Pastano's death sentence was commuted, and the killer of Mary Ann de Castro was now to be repatriated to his home island of Madeira.

The attorney general's quick and ruthlessly straightforward conviction of Pastano was, it emerged, anything but. True, another boarder had caught Pastano in the middle of stabbing Mrs. Castro and was then stabbed himself, and numerous witnesses saw Pastano out in the street covered in blood. But while the attorney general and his assistant were both young and hasty to convict, the defense of Pastano by Brockholst Livingston—older, shrewder, and all too worldly in the ambiguities of violence—had completely undone their prosecution.

In a deft legal feint, Livingston had allowed the attorney general

to win the trial virtually uncontested. All of the testimony mar-
shaled by Livingston instead concerned Pastano's insanity. This
seemed an odd choice: Under New York State law, there was no
legal defense of insanity for a murder charge. Only the legislature had the authority for reversing a murder conviction on those
grounds, an event that had never occurred in Colden's or Hoffman's
lifetime—and, they felt they could quite safely assume, never would.

They were wrong. Even in the hard-hearted world of New
York justice, the prosecution of Pastano went too far. *They never
should have indicted him in the first place*, for the man was obviously
insane—and that, state law made clear, should have made his case a
matter for the justice of the peace. Had Pastano merely been jailed
indefinitely or deported in heavy chains, nobody would have taken
much notice. But under criminal prosecution, Pastano had drawn a
penalty of execution and dissection—an appalling fate to visit upon
a helplessly mad wretch. It was an immense blunder for the ambitious young prosecutors to have made. To have its reversal publicly
approved by Governor Jay—a fellow law-and-order Federalist, no
less—was perhaps the greatest humiliation to the attorney general's
office in a generation.

If Colden's career was to recover, he needed to win this
next case.

INVESTIGATING A murder was a thankless task in New York: The
local police were essentially watchmen, and beyond the immediate
pursuit of a fleeing miscreant, actual crime investigation was largely
left to the prosecutor himself. With Weeks bailed out and one local
worthy already supporting his alibi, that would not be easy. If he
was going to snare his killer, the assistant attorney general would
have to figure out just where the carpenter really spent that fateful
December evening.

Other New Yorkers, though, were beginning to wonder where
the defense team itself had disappeared to.

"Where is the magnanimous General Hamilton?" snapped

*Greenleaf's New Daily Advertiser.* Still smarting from Hamilton's jailing of its foreman David Frothingham, the Republican paper was not above reminding New Yorkers of the general's peccadilloes: "Is he rioting in the pleasure which the imprisonment of a poor printer affords him? Or is he employed in relieving the wants of some tender *amiable creature*?"

In fact, Hamilton and Burr alike were away in Albany for much of February, immersed in lucrative commercial lawsuits. The money was cold comfort to Hamilton: The death of George Washington was already proving disastrous to his own political and military career. Washington had been Hamilton's great ally in D.C.—it was he who had engineered Hamilton's promotion to general in the first place, over the angry objections of John Adams. As his most bitter rival in the Federalist Party, President Adams took deep offense at Hamilton's tawdry affairs, as well as to his ill-concealed military ambitions.

"If I should consent to appointment of Hamilton," Adams had complained to Washington, "I should consider it the most irresponsible action of my whole life and the most difficult to justify."

Now without George Washington's protection, the general found even history itself turning against him. Much of Hamilton's previous two years had been spent building up an "additional army," justified by stoking fears of a French invasion of godless radicals. That country's revolution, Hamilton warned, exposed America to a veritable "volcano of atheism, depravity, and absurdity . . . an engine of despotism and slavery." But then France's revolutionary council had capitulated to Napoléon Bonaparte. The new leader had no immediate fight to pick with America; some thought he might actually bring peace to Europe. Hamilton's endless demands for more funding and troops were beginning to look foolish.

"Speculations on a probable war in Europe have almost ceased to occupy the American papers," one Federalist newspaper glumly admitted. About the best threat it could now conjure was a Gallic invasion from the heavens: "The French will not have any cause to regret the loss of their naval power when they find it so amply supplied by their *aerial squadrons*. . . . A whole fleet of balloons is soon to proceed to America upon *commercial* adventures: and, as the voyage will take only eight days, it is evident that sailing cannot enter into competition with *flying*."

Just a few blocks from the newspaper's offices, Colden was un-earthing an altogether more believable tale. It came from Susannah Broad, an elderly Quaker acquaintance of the Ring family—and, it so happened, a neighbor of Ezra Weeks's.

*I remember that night,* she told him. *It was about eight o'clock on a Sunday night, and I heard one of Ezra's gates open. Well, they never used that particular gate—I thought it was someone stealing from Mr. Weeks's lumber yard! But when I looked out, it wasn't anyone carrying out wood at all. . . . It was a horse coming out. Drawing a sleigh.*

Really now?

*Yes, and here was the peculiar thing. It had no bells upon it.*

This was news indeed. The pleasant jingling of sleigh bells was no mere wintertime fancy; it was a basic courtesy of the road, par-ticularly at night, so that others might hear the vehicle's approach. True, some complained of the racket from drunks careening home-ward from taverns in the wee hours—"When you hear sleigh bells jingling along the road, about two o'clock in a winter morning, you hear many a curse from the driver," one contemporary observed—but not to mount bells on a sleigh seemed downright secretive, even dangerous.

*The strangest thing,* Susannah added, *was that it was scarcely gone for long at all. My son and daughter came home from their congregation meeting soon after eight, and I do believe the sleigh had already come back before they turned in for bed.*

What hasty mission had Weeks's sleigh so quietly embarked upon that night?

ALL OF February 1800 passed as the prosecutor painstakingly gathered leads for his assault on Weeks's alibi. By the time Aaron Burr found himself ready to return from Albany in early March to arrange a defense, though, he was stymied by an unexpected problem: even more criminals.

"I sent to take passage for to-morrow," he wrote to his daughter, Theodosia. "And lo! The stage is taken by the sheriff to transport criminals to the state prison. I should not be much gratified with this kind of association on the road."

There had been no lack of crimes to occupy the sheriff or gossiping New Yorkers, and one of them presented a grim reminder of the fate that might await Weeks. At the same time that John Pastano's plea of insanity had been laid out to the assembly and the governor, another case had been brought to them for appeal: the murder conviction of Benjamin Holmes, who stabbed a good Samaritan that intervened as Holmes beat a child with an iron-tipped ox goad rod. The victim left behind a widow and five children of his own; when the whole grisly affair was recounted to the legislature, not only did they not stop Holmes's execution, they also made a point of passing an act demanding it.

In fact, the death of Elma Sands wasn't even the only Manhattan Company crime. At least one enterprising soul upstate was already counterfeiting Manhattan Bank currency. Another one made off with a $350 check drawn upon the Manhattan Bank account of Washington Irving's brother Dr. Peter Irving—something so infuriating to the Broadway pharmacist that he offered the full amount of the check itself in reward for information about the theft. As a close ally of Aaron Burr's, Dr. Irving may have been as troubled by the defrauding of the bank as he was about his own loss.

But for Cadwallader Colden, patiently building up a line of witnesses, his work led him far from the intrigues and transactions of City Hall, Broadway, and the local courts—all the way north, inexorably, into the frozen streams and tracts of Lispenard's Meadow itself.

*Yes,* said Arnetta Van Norden, who lived in the rough terrain about halfway between Broadway and the well. *I heard it that night. A young woman yelling: Lord have mercy on me! Lord help me!*

*That's right,* her husband added. *I heard it, too. I looked out over the field, and . . . I glanced out the window and could see a fellow out by the well. Yes, walking about it. It was dark out, and I could see the stars that night—but I could make out a man's shape out there.*

And yet they did nothing?

*Well,* the husband explained, *we gathered the commotion came from one of the houses in the neighborhood.*

The point was plain enough: It was the reason, perhaps, that Benjamin Holmes's victim had been killed. It was not someone's business to interfere in other people's family affairs. A number of cartmen lived around the meadow—hard physical laborers, like Mr. Van Norden himself, whom it would be unwise to confront in the middle of a beating.

A week before Elma's disappearance, though, one of the other cartmen who lived out in meadow had proven a bit more inquisitive.

*The Sunday before,* Matthew Musty recalled, *I saw a young man out there—working on the well, it seemed like. He said he was a carpenter.*

The young carpenter was with a crew contracted to build the well, the cartman said, and he had thrown off the wooden cover and fastened some poles together in order to sound the dark waters of the now-abandoned hole. The reason he gave when asked was a chillingly simple one. The man was assuring himself, Musty said, of the Manhattan Well's depth.


*TEA, TEN SHILLINGS a pound. Spearmints, nine shillings a pound.*

Many locals had been accustomed to using British currency right alongside American coinage, and in a port city like Manhattan, a grocer had to know the plethora of wildly fluctuating currencies liable to grace his till. There wasn't much William Dustan hadn't seen pass through his neighborhood by now: He had lived and worked in his store off the corner of Broadway and Chambers Street for years, watching these tracts north of City Hall evolve from stinking tanneries and abattoirs to the beginnings of homes that could almost be described as respectable. Even the local Negro

Burial Ground, stretching out for blocks behind his property, had been covered over with a thick layer of dirt and was now platted out for new residences. Dustan's family name was prominent among Manhattan grocers, and William was known to chair meetings of his professional brethren when it met to argue over such matters as the price of bread.

*Soap, ninepence. Turnips, sixpence a bunch. Cabbage, threepence.*

In March, as the morning sun slanted into the grocery shop, Dustan's first customers of the day were arriving and exchanging the usual gossip: word that ice shipped out from Philadelphia had yellow fever in it, a rumor that Bonaparte had hired Thomas Paine and paid him with all the brandy he could drink. And, of course, the election—there was always that to talk about. The local electors hadn't even been picked yet, and one of the previous night's newspapers was already laying into likely presidential candidate Thomas Jefferson: "His household is *French*—his language, his dress, his manners, his associates are *French*—and his library and Philosophy are *French*—Such a number of *French* dishes might be unpalatable to the *American* taste."

*Apples, fourteen shillings a barrel.*

And, inevitably, there was crime to discuss. From Westchester County, there'd come news of a duel between two bickering watchmakers. And Benjamin Holmes was finally scheduled for hanging and dissection—word of that would come on the next incoming coaches, no doubt. But here in Manhattan, new cases were about to come to trial; with the city council session just having concluded the day before, Mayor Varick and Recorder Harison were now ready to sit in on the weightiest cases to demand their attention. Just a couple of days earlier, on March 26, they'd announced that the circuit court was to commence the following Tuesday. But which cases would it hear?

*Sugar candy, five shillings a pound.*

The door to the store swung open, letting in the morning air, still brisk from a crackling electrical thunderstorm during the night—and a customer stalked in, excitable in his movements, and low and quick in voice.

"Good morning, gentlemen," he said hurriedly. The man took no notice of the sacks and barrels of goods around him; he could scarcely contain his news.

"Levi Weeks," he blurted out, "is taken up by the high sheriff."

# PART III

THE TRIAL

# THE PEOPLE vs. LEVI WEEKS

COURT OF OYER & TERMINER, CITY HALL, CITY OF NEW-YORK

MARCH 31ST—APRIL 2ND, 1800

---

His Hon. Mr. Justice John Lansing, Jr.
*Chief Justice of the New-York Supreme Court*

William Coleman, Esq.
*Clerk of the Court*

His Honor Richard Varick, Esq.
Mayor of New-York
*attending*

His Honor Richard Harison, Esq.
Recorder of New-York
*attending*

Levi Weeks
*Defendant*

COUNSEL FOR THE PRISONER
Aaron Burr, Esq.
Alexander Hamilton, Esq.
Brockholst Livingston, Esq.

PROSECUTOR
Cadwallader D. Colden, Esq.
*Asst. Attorney General*

MEMBERS OF THE JURY
Richard Ellis
James Hunt
Robert Lylburn
William G. Miller
John Rathbone
Simon Schermerhorn [Foreman]
George Scriba
Garrit Storm
William Walton
Jasper Ward
Samuel Ward
William Wilson

# II

# The American
# Phenomena

Monday morning dawned bright with promise over the Ring boardinghouse—"a very clear day, but very blustery," one neighborhood resident noted in his journal entry for March 31, 1800. Windows rattled in the panes, and Manhattanites outside gamely clutched for their hats. But for all the freezing nights and scouring winds of the previous week, Spring was surely arriving to the island. Just the night before, one of the boarders—Richard Croucher, the cloth merchant—had aptly marked the new season by marrying one of his customers, the widow Mrs. Stackhaver. The happy occasion still faced certain practicalities; Croucher hadn't moved out just yet to the widow's house on Ann Street, though her teenaged daughter was to come over later to help him pack his belongings. Still, the wedding marked what should have been the first ray of light to pierce the gloomy recesses of 208 Greenwich in many weeks.

But, instead, the sunny morning found the mood in the house curiously dark. Arrayed around the table for breakfast, the boarders were not dressed in their usual work aprons, or shouldering their shipwright and masonry tools. They were dressed respectably, but not to mark the occasion of Croucher's new marriage: Nearly every one of them had been subpoenaed to appear in that day's trial. Instead of a honeymoon, Richard Croucher would be spending his first day of married life in the courthouse.

Then again, the trial of Levi Weeks was where most New Yorkers *wanted* to be that day—"Scarcely any thing else is spoken of," one socialite wrote in her journal. It was a spectacle, as surely as the two-shilling show in the side parlor of the City Hotel. There New Yorkers beheld "The American Phenomena," a single cage containing the improbable menagerie of "A Fine Little Bird, A Beautiful Flying-Squirrel, & A Rattle-Snake"—all living, gawkers were assured, in confounding harmony. Weeks's trial would feature Major General Hamilton, Colonel Burr, and Colonel Livingston—all on the same side, peaceably—a veritable American Phenomenon themselves. How could any New Yorker resist? It would be, as the sideshow's own ad rhapsodized, "one of the most extraordinary occurrences that has been yet exhibited to gratify the curiosity of the Public"—a splendid, awful wonder.

BY THE time the Rings and their boarders reached City Hall, it was almost impossible to get in. Hundreds had crowded outside at the intersection of Wall and Broad Streets—thousands, even—"the concourse of people was so great," one observer wrote, "as was never before witnessed in New York." The only event to compare was the founding of the country itself. City Hall had once served as the place of George Washington's presidential inauguration, and for the first few years of the republic, Congress itself had been held in its grand halls. Weighty matters of the fate of the nation had been decided here, but on the morning of the trial, the mood outside was less deliberative.

"*Crucify him!*" voices yelled out.

The block around the building was usually a more amiable place. It was here that you might hear an anvil ring from Mr. Babb's shop as he wrought iron into his famed specialty, birdcages—"to confine tame birds in a free country," as one local patriot put it. The block had what was long the city's only hosiery shop, though many New Yorkers still remained so poorly dressed that, to earn extra pennies, the proprietor had resorted to offering cheap shaves with castile soap and rainwater. For those needing neither cages nor hosiery, at the corner was an old buttonwood tree, a shady spot traditionally staked out by slaves and servants as their refuge on sunny days.

Today, though, the tree was valued for another purpose: for climbing, in order to see over the crowd.

*"Crucify him!"* they yelled again.

From up the street, in the direction of Grenzeback's grocery and the gloomy Bridewell jail, there came a stirring that parted the crowd.

*Make way, make way for the prisoner.*

Blinking against the sunlight and worn from his long weekend in jail, Levi Weeks was marched through by a phalanx of constables and a citizen volunteer guard. The baying crowd had been well primed by the handbills; New Yorkers knew that Weeks was already as good as convicted by the ghosts and dancing devils seen out by the Manhattan Well. They followed him into City Hall, only to find the way blocked.

"Though that room in which the court was held is very large," wrote one witness, "not one fourth of those who attended could procure admission."

Inside, City Hall was so packed that it was almost impossible even to lead the defendant up to the courtroom's bar. Cadwallader Colden took one table; the defense team of Hamilton, Burr, and Livingston took another with their defendant. Outside the room, filling the hallways and antechambers of City Hall, there waited scores of subpoenaed witnesses. Constables shoved the overflow of spectators out of the room, a task they tackled with relish; they had real power that morning, one reporter mused, and were "disposed to exercise it in its amplest extent."

When those who managed to seize a bench seat sat down and opened the morning's *New-York Commercial Advertiser*, they found a surprise waiting for them. John Furman, who ran a print shop across the street from City Hall, had already staked out his place at the trial. Fresh off a run of hawking door-to-door copies of "A Handsome Edition of George Washington's Will," he had hit upon his next great moneymaker:

THE TRIAL OF LEVI WEEKS, FOR THE MURDER OF
MISS SANDS, NOW PENDING IN THE CIRCUIT COURT,
WILL BE PUBLISHED AS EARLY AS POSSIBLE—BY
JOHN FURMAN, OPPOSITE THE CITY-HALL. IT IS TO
BE PRESUMED THAT IT WILL BE MORE FULL AND
CORRECT THAN ANY WHICH MAY BE MADE, AS IT IS
TAKEN DOWN BY THE CLERK OF THE COURT.

The trial had not yet even begun, but New Yorkers already knew they were about to become a part of history.

FOR THE man who would be recording that history, they needed to look no farther than the center of the courtroom, where at ten o'clock the clerk of the court's voice rose above the crowd.

*Hear ye, hear ye, hear ye!* he called out.

William Coleman's deep timbre carried authority; he towered over most of the crowd, and bore the robust frame of a young man famed for having skated twenty miles up the Connecticut River in a single evening. Spectators in the courtroom were wise to quiet down quickly.

*All manner of persons,* he continued, *that any have business to do at this circuit court and court of oyer and terminer, held in and for the county of New York, let them draw near and give their attendance and they shall be heard.*

Coleman knew these proclamations by heart, for he had once been on the other side of the counsel's table himself. From an unlikely start as an abandoned child at a Boston poorhouse, Coleman had risen as a young lawyer to build one of the finest mansions in Massachusetts—and was then promptly bankrupted by a bad land deal. Fleeing debts to reassemble his life in Manhattan, he'd worked briefly as Aaron Burr's law partner before falling under Hamilton's sway as a Federalist—and it was to Hamilton that the grateful and destitute Coleman owed the coveted patronage job of clerk of the court.

*Sheriff,* he intoned, *return the writs and precepts to you directed, and delivered and returnable here this day, that the court may proceed thereon.*

Behind Coleman, as was the customary for the Court of Oyer and Terminer, the assembled might of Manhattan's political and judicial establishment entered and seated themselves. At the highest chair was the presiding judge, the Right Honorable John Lansing— the chief justice of the New York State Supreme Court, the presiding judge for circuit court cases in this district, and a member of the state assembly's crucial Council of Revision. He was a stout Republican—as one of New York's delegates to the Constitutional Convention, he'd virtually walked out in disgust at its model of a strong central government. And yet he was also a eminently fairminded man. During debates over the Manhattan Company charter in 1799, it was Lansing—not any Federalist—who publicly questioned the curious provisions buried in Burr's bill.

By his side sat Mayor Richard Varick—former speaker of the assembly, former city recorder, and Aaron Burr's predecessor as state attorney general. He was a war veteran with much in common with Brockholst Livingston and Alexander Hamilton: Like Livingston, he'd served as an aide to Hamilton's father-in-law, General Philip Schuyler; and like Hamilton, he'd gone on to serve as General Washington's aide. Nearby sat Varick's second in-command, Richard Harison, the city recorder. He, too, was close to Hamilton—he was the general's former law partner, in fact—and yet by virtue of his office, he was now also a board member of Burr's new water company.

This room, filled with the most distinguished legal eminences in the state, might have seemed a Gordian knot of tangled conflicts of interest: Burr's company owned the murder scene, had employed the defendant, had rejected a bid by a relative of the deceased, had financial relationships with the court recorder and the clerk, and had political alliances and rivalries with his fellow counselors, the mayor, and the judge. In any other time or place, all this might have at least raised an eyebrow. But in Manhattan in 1800, it was just how business was done.

*Hear ye, hear ye, hear ye!* Coleman called out again.

The city's greatest political foes—the very men whose reputation jurors would be weighing at the ballot box in a month's time—now sat before the crowd, united in this case of murder. And now, in the middle of this group of men—these war heroes and skirmishing politicians, these bitter rivals and old comrades in arms—there stood the young carpenter whose life lay in their hands.

*Approach the bar*, the clerk instructed Weeks. The crowd got their first good look at the man: a respectable-enough-looking fellow, the murmur went.

Weeks's presence was a quiet and subdued one—not least because in a capital trial, it was still the custom to not let the accused testify, as their hopeless bias against conviction created a "disqualification of interest." Until 1701, British and American defendants didn't even have the right to counsel or to call witnesses, because holding trials was considered necessary only when there was already overwhelming proof of wrongdoing. That Weeks could retain the talents of Hamilton, Burr, and Livingston, and call witnesses on his own behalf, was the great advance of the eighteenth century. But even now, at the dawn of nineteenth century, defendants remained almost mute during their trial. One of the few times Weeks could speak was during jury selection.

"Simon Schermerhorn!" the clerk called out.

*Here.*

"William Miller!"

*Here.*

One by one, Coleman called out thirty-four members of the jury pool, and then turned to the accused.

"Levi Weeks, prisoner at the bar, hold up your right hand," he commanded. Weeks placed his left hand on the court's Bible and raised his right; in the tense silence there was the scratching of pencils in the gallery as competing local hacks took rapid notes, hoping to beat the clerk himself to writing the story that was about to unfold.

"Hearken to what is said to you," Coleman continued. "These good men who have last been called, and who do now appear, are those who are to pass between the people of the State of New-York, and you, upon your Trial of Life and Death. If, therefore, you will challenge them, your time to challenge is as they come up to the book to be sworn, and before they are sworn, you will be heard."

The clerk steadily called up each potential juror to the stand: *Garrit Storm. Robert Lylburn. George Scriba.*

Weeks immediately cut some of the jurors short as their names were called out: *They are not fit to judge me.* So many New Yorkers had already spoken publicly against him that soon nearly a dozen rejects were sent back. Others excused themselves even as they walked up to the bar.

*I am a Friend,* they explained, and the judge waved them off— for he knew they were not friends of the accused, but rather members of the Society of Friends—and thus forbidden by the tenets of Quakerism from swearing of oaths, let alone accepting a trial that involved capital punishment. Just one Quaker, James Hunt, was willing to bend his theology.

*Place your hand upon the book,* the clerk told Hunt.

"Juror, look upon the Prisoner; Prisoner, look upon the Juror."

The two men locked eyes.

Observing carefully from the defense table, Burr could only be pleased by this choice: Hunt was an old Republican running mate of his, and they'd served in the assembly together. So had the father of juror Garrit Storm. Another juror, Robert Lylburn, was a tobacco and beeswax merchant best known for organizing local Irishmen for the Republicans.

And yet above all, these jurors were reasonable businessmen: Of the twelve men agreed upon, all were merchants, grocers, or provisioners. Not only did the jury box contain John Rathbone—a merchant of everything from shawls to gunpowder, who maintained what was admiringly described as "immense operations" in salt manufacturing—it also contained a former president of the city's chamber of commerce, Boss Walton, known as a lavishly generous and civic-minded "Prince of Merchants." The overwhelmingly mercantile jury was no coincidence. Jurors had to be men between the ages of twenty-one and sixty, and be taxpaying landowners holding property worth at least $250—nearly a year's wages for a common laborer. The jury box was what women and the poor faced, not what they sat in.

And so the jury, like everything else in the room, was a curiously and intimately local affair. Not only did jurors cross paths with the contestants of the trial, they also knew *one another* well: Just a few years earlier, James Hunt and his fellow juror Jasper Ward had even run a grocery store together.

*Swear*, the clerk said to Hunt, "You shall well and truly try, and true deliverance make, between the People of the State of New-York, and Levi Weeks, and a true verdict give according to evidence, so help you God."

Levi looked at the grocer who would help to decide his fate. The day before, the man had been judging apples and weighing plugs of tobacco.

*So help me God*, the juror said.


GENERAL HAMILTON considered his carefully written notes. It was his habit to divide his papers into two columns, the left side with the points of his case, and the right with the legal precedents and citations. *Hale's Plea of the Crown*—yes, that would come into play. For all the new laws and rights that Hamilton's generation had been developing for this new country, he and his fellow lawyers were still deeply dependent on the usages of the colonial era and the old country. A country scarcely a decade old had few legal precedents to draw on, so if there was one place where the king and the crown still received respectful mention in America, it was in its courtrooms.

Hamilton had served the defense many times before, had some small experience with murder cases, and had even served alongside Burr in the past, but this—a murder defense with Burr? It was altogether unique. And yet for all the strangeness of the affair, many eyes in the courtroom were also upon the clerk. For Coleman to keep this patronage job would depend on the Federalists' holding on to City Hall in the next election, of course—Colonel Burr, sitting with his usual unnerving calm, would try to sweep Coleman and the rest out at the first opportunity. But for now, Hamilton's young protégé was confidently holding forth in the center of the courtroom.

"Gentlemen of the Jury," the clerk began. "The prisoner at the bar stands indicted in the words following, to wit."

Coleman peered down at the densely written parchment. The indictment, as was the custom, was a serpentine tangle of flawlessly penned, endlessly redundant clauses.

> *The Jurors and the People of the State of New-York, in and for the city and county of New-York, on their oath present that* LEVI WEEKS, *late of the seventh ward, of the city of New-York, in the county of New-York, labourer, not having the fear of God before his eyes, but being moved and seduced by the instigation of the devil, on the 22nd day of December, in the year of our Lord 1799, with force and arms at the ward foresaid, in and upon one* GULIELMA SANDS, *in the Peace of God, and of the said people then and there being, feloniously, willfully, and of his malice afterthought, did make an assault, and that the said Levi Weeks, then and there feloniously, willfully, and of his malice afterthought, did take the said Gulielma Sands into both the hands of him the said Levi Weeks, and did cast, throw, and push the said Gulielma Sands, into a certain well there situated, wherein there was a great quantity of water . . .*

Coleman took a breath—for the first sentence was not yet even finished.

> *. . . by means of which said casting, throwing, and pushing, of the said Gulielma Sands into the well aforesaid, by the said Levi Weeks, in the form aforesaid, the said Gulielma Sands, in the well*

*aforesaid, with the water aforesaid, was then and there choked, suffocated, and drowned; of which said choking, suffocating, and drowning, the said Gulielma Sands, then and there instantly died.*

A second sentence, at twice the length, went on to say much the same as the first, and in nearly the same words. After carefully navigating through this ornamental maze of verbiage, Coleman turned to the jury and addressed them more plainly—as fellow citizens and neighbors, all puzzling over a mysterious crime.

"Upon this indictment the prisoner at the bar hath been arraigned," he explained gently. "And on his arraignment, hath pleaded not guilty. Your charge is, gentlemen, to enquire whether the prisoner at the bar is guilty or not."

Out in the hallways the scores of witnesses awaited; inside, the young carpenter sat ready for his fate.

"So sit together," Coleman commanded the jury, "and hear your evidence."

## 12

# BY THE HOLLOW STAIR

BEFORE HE BEGAN HIS OPENING ARGUMENTS, THE ASSISTANT AT-torney general pondered the eminences at the defense table. Just a few months back, Colden had personally investigated and success-fully prosecuted Hamilton's libel action against local printer David Frothingham—and it was Brockholst Livingston that he'd prevailed over. Aaron Burr was no stranger to Colden, either: As a lawyer for the prosecutor's own father, Burr helped save Colden land from anti-Loyalist seizures after the war.

Today, though, all three men were arrayed against him.

"The prisoner has thought it necessary for his defense, to employ so many advocates distinguished for their eloquence and abilities— so vastly my superiors in learning, experience and professional rank," the young prosecutor began, as eyes turned toward the de-fense table. "But gentlemen, as a public prosecutor, I think I ought to do no more than offer you in its proper order, all the testimony the case affords, drawn from witnesses. All that they know—the truth, the whole truth, and nothing but the truth."

The wooden floors of the courtroom echoed the footsteps of the prosecutor.

"Levi Weeks, the prisoner at the bar, is indicted for the murder of Gulielma Sands. He is a young man of reputable connections, and for aught we know, till he was charged with this crime, of ir-reproachable character."

For spectators peering at the defendant, that seemed fair

enough—Weeks was a handsome fellow, a hard worker, a man with an honest face.

"His appearance interested us greatly in his favor," one spectator mused. "We waited with anxiety for the testimony." They would not have to wait for long—and, Colden warned, it would be damning, for the carpenter's gentle appearance was deceiving.

"He gained the affections of those who are now to appear against him as witnesses on the trial for his life. The deceased was a young girl, who till her fatal acquaintance with the prisoner, was virtuous and modest—always of a cheerful disposition, and lively manners, though of a delicate constitution. We expect to prove to you that the prisoner won her affections, and that her virtue fell a sacrifice to his assiduity; that after a long period of criminal intercourse between them, he deluded her from the house of her protector under a pretense of marrying her, and carried her away to a well in the suburbs of the city, and . . ."

Colden stopped for a moment—"as if overpowered with his emotions," the court clerk noted—and then gathered himself again.

"No wonder, gentlemen, that my mind shudders at the picture here drawn, and requires a moment to recollect myself," he added weakly. The outrage over the ads placed by Weeks's defenders—the claims that Elma had committed suicide—then revived his indignant anger.

"I will not say what may be your verdict," Colden told the hushed room. "But I will venture to assert that not one of you or any man who hears this cause, shall doubt that the unfortunate young creature who was found dead in the Manhattan Well—was *most barbarously murdered*."

THE FIRST witness called was Elma's cousin, Catharine Ring—the woman in charge of the boardinghouse itself. As a Quaker who refused oath taking, she solemnly affirmed her presence in the court. There was another presence, though, that was more problematic.

*Your honor, that man needs to leave the room.*

The proceedings halted; the defense was demanding that Elias Ring leave the courtroom during his wife's testimony. In the searching looks of the crowd at the witnesses, the unspoken question hung over the moment: Why did Levi distrust Mr. Ring?

"You have a right to it, of course," Judge Lansing replied. Elias was briskly escorted out of the courtroom by the bailiffs.

Composing herself after the room had quieted down again, Mrs. Ring began her tale. She was, she explained, twenty-seven years old—just five years older than Elma—and "I regarded her as a sister.

"In July last, Levi Weeks came to board in our family, soon after which he began to pay attention to Margaret Clark, till about the 28th of the 8th month, when she went in the country." Their former boarder Margaret suddenly found herself under the glare of onlookers' attentions, but Mrs. Ring pressed on. "About two days after her absence, Gulielma Sands asked me—"

*Objection!*

Colden's first witness had been stopped by Weeks's team scarcely two sentences into her testimony; Mrs. Ring, they insisted, was relating hearsay. Colden was ready for it: He pulled out his notes to announce a whole a series of legal precedents for use of a murder victim's speech, from *State Trials* and *Leach's Cases* to *Skinner's Reports*.

*Wrong*, the defense shot back. *Has Mr. Colden actually read those cases?*

Brockholst Livingston, reaching across the table for a copy of Leach's *Cases in Crown Law*, thumbed through to one of the cases Colden cited. It was the trial of one William Woodcock, accused in 1789 of beating his wife to death in a London lane. Her dying accusation against the man had been taken down—but not under oath, not by a jury, and with the wife herself apparently oblivious to just how near death she was.

"His Lordship," Livingston read from the thick quarto volume, "then left it with the jury to consider, whether the deceased was not in fact under the apprehension of death; and said, that if they were under admission that she was, then the declaration were admissible; but that if they were of a contrary opinion, they were not admissible."

Elma Ring was hardly dying back in July 1799; indeed, she was full of life. Far from backing his case, Colden had just cited one that contradicted it. Before the prosecutor could respond, Aaron Burr leaped in: Was the prosecutor aware that another case he'd cited was, in fact, in a *Scottish* court—a different legal system—and not an authority for the United States? Or that in the Woodcock case—

*Very well*, the judge announced. *Please proceed, Mrs. Ring, without resort to hearsay.*

"Levi became very attentive to Elma, to whom I mentioned it, and she did not deny it," she continued, choosing her words carefully. "After my return I paid strict attention to their conduct, and saw an appearance of mutual attachment, but nothing improper. He was frequently in the room when she was sick. One—"

*Objection! . . . What's he doing here?*

The defense pointed into the crowd behind Mrs. Ring. There stood Elias Ring, who had crept back into the courtroom to eavesdrop on his wife's testimony.

*Mind your behavior, sir*, the judge snapped. *Bailiff, you may escort him out again.*

Chastened on behalf of her own husband, Mrs. Ring began her testimony again.

"Not a day passed but convinced me more and more that he was paying attentions to her," she insisted. "I often found them sitting and standing together, and once in particular I found them sitting together on her bed."

It was not quite the decorous behavior expected in a prospective Quaker—"I always thought her disposition rather too gay for a Friend," Mrs. Ring said primly—and on December 22, 1799, she found her niece seeming "much pleased" about something. The boardinghouse mistress recalled the evening carefully for the jury: Elma borrowing clothes and her neighbor's muff to get dressed to go out, and Levi limping back, his knee bandaged, from his early evening visit to his brother's house. Just after Levi returned home, she recalled, "I heard the clock strike eight"—and then, after retiring to her room with Mr. Ring, she heard Levi and Elma leave again within ten minutes.

Yes—she was *certain* that was what she had heard: two sets of footfalls coming down the stairs, and the voices of Levi and Elma whispering in the hall outside her room.

"Mrs. Ring." Prosecutor Colden dramatically unrolled an architect's plan of the 208 Greenwich boardinghouse and exhibited it to the court. "What kind of staircase is it?"

"It is a hollow, closed staircase."

"Would not a person coming down such," he ventured, "make a considerable noise?"

"Any person certainly would."

The jury examined the drawing, seeing just how close in proximity Mrs. Ring's eavesdropping had been.

"How near is your door to the stairs?" Colden asked.

"It opens against them."

"How far is it from the foot of the stairs to the outer door?"

"Not more than four feet."

Upon coming back home at about ten o'clock to find herself and his apprentice waiting up for him, she recounted, Levi seemed "pale and much agitated"—and assumed a quizzical expression when Mrs. Ring remarked that she assumed Elma to be out as well. The next morning had passed with everyone slightly uneasy at Elma's absence—but it wasn't until that Tuesday morning, she testified, that she finally confronted Levi.

"I said, *Stop, Levi, this matter has become so serious, I can stand it no longer.*" And at that moment, she claimed, she'd confronted Levi with the very secret that Elma had revealed on the day she disappeared: "She came down stairs after being with thee, and told me, that night at eight o'clock you were going to be married."

All the suspicion, all the anger of the city, had hinged on this one recollection.

"He turned pale," Mrs. Ring continued, "trembled to a great

degree—and began to cry, clasping his hands together, cried out—*I'm ruined! I'm undone forever, unless she appears to clear me.*"

In the shocked silence, a droll inquiry came from the defense table: Elma said all kinds of things, didn't she? Hadn't Mrs. Ring *also* heard Elma threaten to overdose on laudanum? The very hint of suicide had deeply upset the Rings before—the charge blackened Elma's memory with a grievous sin—and now the raw emotion welled back up again.

"Why Levi! How can thee say so?" she scolded. Being sick so often, Elma easily could have overdosed on opium tincture—"it was always easy for her to get that"—and to have her idle jest over a bottle of medicine perverted like *this* by Hamilton and Burr in the courtroom was infuriating to Mrs. Ring.

"It don't bear the weight of a . . . single . . . *straw* with me," the grieving witness sputtered, and she turned her baleful stare upon the prisoner—on the man who once was to have married into her own family.

"Levi," she spat, "I shudder to think I ever indulged a favorable thought of thee."


*Hope Sands!*—the clerk called.

Levi watched as Mrs. Ring sat back down, and her sister Hope walked up to the witness box. Today was a long way from that hazy summer day when he had visited the museum with Hope and Elma; and now, instead of the pleasant sense of being an upstanding boarder newly introduced to two charming young women, he faced nothing but accusation.

"After she was missing, he denied knowing any thing of her," Hope accused, "though from his looks I was confident he did."

She'd been onto Levi and Elma all along, she insisted. Why, she'd even taken their hint to leave Elma's room once, and heard them quietly locking the door behind her. She'd loudly walked back down the stairs, and then—"I left my shoes at the bottom of them, and went softly up"—she'd put her ear to the door. Hope hadn't quite heard anything, true, but she was sure that they were up to something. And that had made Elma's disappearance most suspicious indeed.

"He soon began to use all possible means to convince me of his innocence," she said disdainfully. "The Sabbath evening after she was missing, he came to me saying, *Hope, if you can say any thing in my favor, do it, for you can do me more good than any friend I have in the world to clear me.* He then pressed me very hard to go to the Alderman's and see him."

This was a revelation to raise some eyebrows: Levi's Seventh Ward alderman, Richard Furman, was sitting in the courtroom as a spectator. Furman and his longtime assistant, the memorably named Mangle Minthorne, were better known for their tireless efforts to get local streets fixed than for being tangled up in murder cases. What Levi had wanted her to give to Furman, Hope claimed, was a signed statement that he'd written himself, claiming that "he paid no more attention to Elma than to any other female in the house"— and that he had never courted or been at all engaged to Elma.

"I refused," Hope told the courtroom. "Levi, if I was to do it, thee knows it would be positive lies."

The reason Hope was certain Levi was lying became apparent as soon as her brother-in-law Elias Ring took the stand. The inventor, spurned for his Manhattan Well proposal, now found himself staring across the courtroom at the very man who founded the company—and at a prisoner who had begun succeeding in the precise business where he himself had failed.

"Levi Weeks was a lodger in my house," he began, "and in the ninth month—"

"What month is that called?" Hamilton interrupted.

"I don't know it by any other name. Thee can tell," he answered stubbornly. As a Quaker, he refused to use pagan names for months or days of the week, and Levi's team was not above making him look foolish for it.

"At this time, when my wife was gone into the country," Elias continued undeterred, "Levi and Elma were constantly together in private. I was alone and very lonesome, and was induced to believe from their conduct that they were shortly to be married."

The boardinghouse, he explained, was nearly empty during the worst days of the yellow fever epidemic—and up in a room that lodger Isaac Hatfield had wisely vacated for a while, he began hearing *someone* creeping around at night.

"One night when Hatfield was out of town, I heard a talking and a noise in his room. In the morning I went up into the room and found the bed tumbled, and Elma's clothes lying on the bed."

"Did you see her in the room?" Hamilton needled.

"No, I saw nothing," the inventor admitted. "But I have no doubt she was there. There was no other person in the house besides Levi and his apprentice, and Elma and myself."

"Did you ever know that the prisoner *and* Elma were in bed together?"

"No."

What had happened in the room, as far as Elias and others were concerned, hardly needed spelling out in the courtroom. But rather than press the point, the defense team seemed curiously distracted into mere trivialities about the home and blacksmith shop run next door by Joseph Watkins.

"What materials is the partition made of between Watkins's house and yours?" Hamilton asked.

"It is a plank partition," the bewildered witness answered. "Lathed and plastered."

"Could you hear the noise of children through it?"

"No," Elias answered warily. "Not as I could recall."

"Is Mr. Watkins a clever man, and a good neighbor?"

"Yes—he is."

For spectators in the benches, shuttling out to grab victuals as the trial continued into the evening, the defense's descent into such trifles was simply too peculiar to explain to the crowds gathered eagerly outside. Hamilton, Burr, and Livingston might have been good and clever men themselves, but with the client's life now at stake—what on earth were they driving at?

THE TALE told by Cadwallader Colden's witnesses was only to become more damning to Levi. As the sky darkened outside, the cloth merchant Richard Croucher took the stand.

"May it please the court and gentlemen of the jury," he said with a smile, his voice low and quick. "I was satisfied, from what *I* saw, there was a warm courtship going on. I have known the prisoner at the bar to be with the deceased, Elma Sands, in private frequently, and at all times of night."

As a newly married man, Croucher's very presence in the witness stand almost seemed to upbraid such wanton conduct.

"I knew him to pass two whole nights in her bedroom," he continued. "I saw the prisoner at the bar come out of her room, and pass the door in his shirt only. Once, too, when they were less cautious than usual, I saw them in a . . . *very intimate* situation."

More than the other witnesses, the cloth merchant seemed familiar with the usages of the courtroom: Along with formally greeting the court and the jury, he'd made a point of referring to "the deceased" and "the prisoner at the bar." But to Levi's team, it was Croucher himself who was the suspicious character in the courtroom.

"Where, sir," Hamilton's voice rang out, "were you on the night of the 22nd of December?"

He'd gone to the coffeehouse and then to a birthday party— at Ann Ashmore's, on the Bowery—and had just missed crossing Lispenard's Meadow that evening. "I wish I had," Croucher sighed. "I might, perhaps, have saved the life of the deceased."

"Do you know where the Manhattan Well is?"

"I do."

"Did you pass by it that evening?"

"I did not."

He couldn't be sure of the route he'd taken—"I believe I might have passed the glue manufactory"—but with the weather bad and the moonlight scarce, he'd had to trek across whatever clear route down the streets and across the fields that he could find—he couldn't remember which, exactly. What he did recall, though, was hearing Levi Weeks pace back and forth in his room all night—at least until four in the morning.

"I thought then that his brother had some great work on hand and that he was drawing plans," he said scornfully. "But since I have accounted for it a *different* way."

The defense team eyed him carefully, their skepticism easily a match now for Croucher's.

"Ever had a quarrel with the prisoner?"

"I bear him no malice."

"But have you never had any words with him?"

"Once I had," Croucher allowed. He'd surprised Elma in a hallway—perhaps by more than just brushing by her—and Levi confronted him.

"I told him he was an impertinent puppy," he sniffed. "I bear him no malice. But I despise every man who does not behave in character."

Annoyed that Elma had taken the side of Levi in the argument, he never talked with her after that exchange.

"She thought," Croucher sneered, "he was an *Adonis*."

# 13

# THE COLOR OF A HORSE IN
# THE NIGHT

ONCE ELMA SANDS WALKED OUT THE FRONT DOOR OF 208 GREEN-
wich Street, it seemed as if she had simply vanished altogether—
except, that is, to the woman who took the stand next. Her name
was Catherine Lyon, and she had been some blocks north on a
stretch of Greenwich Street that cold and snowy night.

"Being in Greenwich Street, at the pump near the door of the
new Furnace, I saw Gulielma Sands a little after eight o'clock," she
testified.

Lyon had been helping up "a lame woman who was laying in
the street"—for, as another witness had recalled, "the going was
very rough that night." The sidewalks were treacherous for anyone
without sure footing, and the handles of the public water pumps
were particularly notorious for catching and tripping the unwary on
the city's poorly lit streets.

"Elma came up to me alone, and asked who it was," she continued, though who had sprawled on the ground was of less import
now than who might have been walking with Elma that night.
"There was a good many people passing, and I could not say if they
was with her or not," Catherine admitted.

She had, though, heard the briefest snatch of conversation.

"I heard someone say, 'Let's go,' and the deceased bid me good
night and went on."

"Did you see the face of Elma?" Hamilton pressed.

"I did not," the witness admitted. "But I knew her form and
shape."

So Colden's witness had not exactly solved the mystery—and it was only to deepen further when he ushered Mrs. Susannah Broad up to the stand. She was, the court clerk noted, "aged and very infirm," but Colden nonetheless interviewed her in his quest to trace Elma's route that night.

"I live opposite Ezra Weeks's lumber-yard," she explained. "On the night when the deceased was lost, I heard a gate open and a sleigh or a carriage coming out of the yard, about eight o'clock."

The gate, she dutifully recounted, was one that she never heard opened—and the vehicle had set out without any sleigh bells, as if on some secret errand.

Levi's team was unimpressed.

"When was this?" Hamilton asked dryly. "What month was it?"

It seemed a ludicrous question to ask—everyone knew the crime had occurred on December 22, 1799; the court had just spent hours recalling the evening.

"I don't know the month," the widow snapped. "I know it was *so*."

"Was it after Christmas?" they pressed. "Or before Christmas?"

"It was after, I believe. In January."

For an agonizing moment, the prosecutor could only watch as Hamilton gently closed the net around his witness.

"You are sure?" the general asked. "It was in January, you say?"

"Yes," she now insisted. "I am *sure* it was in January."

For Mrs. Broad's part, the whole thing seemed rather silly and irksome. War heroes or not, it seemed the men over at Levi's table were almost sporting with her, a frail widow—asking her yet again if she'd *really* ever previously heard Ezra Weeks use that particular gate to his lumberyard.

"No, gentlemen," she snapped at their impertinence. "Do you think I came here to tell a lie?"

It was not Mrs. Broad's first experience of speaking under oath— she had, not so many years before, testified in the estate hearing of a late veteran of the Revolution—but the change that had come over the old woman, perhaps even since the night of the crime itself, was becoming painfully apparent.

"Her memory," one courtroom observer put it delicately, "was not very tenacious on most particulars."

For CADWALLADER Colden, any crime occurring on a Sunday night in the streets of lower Manhattan meant an unexpected source of testimony: Methodists.

Each Sunday evening their church, built just a few blocks east of Broadway, brought the fiery preaching of Dr. Joseph Pilmore. Sent by John Wesley in 1769 as one of two handpicked missionaries to the colonies, the indefatigable Pilmore was known for his marathon "watch-night" services, some of which could stretch to midnight. But on that snowy evening in December, he had parishioners heading home just after eight. One Margaret Freeman, it just so happened, had decided to walk home along Greenwich Street.

"I and my boy were coming home from Meeting," she recalled. "I was holding my boy by the arm."

In the midst of their careful trek up the slippery road, she'd noticed something rather unusual for a quiet Sunday night.

"A one horse sleigh overtook me, as I was walking in the middle of the road," she described. "With two men and a woman in it, all talking and very lively—particularly the woman. I kept out of the way for it to pass."

Like others, though, she could not be absolutely sure of the time.

"When I came in I ran up the stairs, and looking at the watch, I saw it was a quarter past eight," Mrs. Freeman testified, before admitting—"the watch *was* rather slow."

Instead of embarrassing her on the point of the time—which she had already admitted was imperfect—the defense gently approached from another angle.

"Did you ever see Ezra Weeks's sleigh any where?" they asked.

Unlike the previous witnesses, Mrs. Freeman could not be

drawn into looking foolish by claiming anything beyond exactly what she'd seen.

"I don't know as I ever did," she said plainly.

Another fellow parishioner, though, was quite sure that he did indeed know what Ezra's sleigh looked like. A leather worker by trade, Berthrong Anderson was known to be civic-minded and reliable, for he'd served as an election inspector in his ward. Like Mrs. Freeman, he had seen a sleigh of merrymakers charging through the streets that evening.

"I had been to Mr. Pilmore's church the Sunday night before Christmas," he testified. "I went out of the meeting with company, up the Bowery, and down Broadway—on my return, I was overtaken by a one horse sleigh, about half past eight in the evening."

That sleigh sounded curiously like the one spotted perhaps ten or fifteen minutes earlier on Greenwich—it "had two or three men or women in it," Anderson said, though he wasn't quite sure.

"I can't say whether they were men or women," he admitted, before helpfully adding: "The horse seemed to be dark-colored."

Colden was ready for his opportunity.

"Have you not, sir," the prosecutor said triumphantly, "seen *Ezra Weeks* drive such a horse, of the same size and color?"

"I *have* seen him drive one, I think," the leather worker agreed, and two other fellow parishioners dutifully confirmed his testimony: Yes, they had seen the same horse and sleigh as well, and even hailed huzzah to it as it passed—"as is usual on such occasions"—but, they added, the mysterious sleigh had not returned their greeting.

Levi's team could scarcely contain its incredulity at Anderson's testimony.

"Do you pretend to distinguish the color of a horse in the night?" they scoffed.

"Not exactly," the earnest parishioner fumbled. "But I know he was not light colored."

But other witnesses could not be so easily jeered at—for not only had they seen the sleigh, they had also seen where its journey had ended.

Henry Orr was a cartman who lived on Broadway's upper reaches—a man with the tight muscles and calloused hands of his hard work in the delivery trade—and he remembered that snowy December night well.

"On the 22nd of December, after dark," he recalled, "I went from my house near Union Furnace, to a house near Mr. Benson's."

True to his profession, his directions were not by street name but by landmark: Benson was a local colonel in the New-York Regiment, and the Union Furnace was a large iron smithy on Broadway, where fires were kept continually roaring for the manufacture of "jambs, cog wheels, gudgeons, &c." The heat and noise radiating from its doorway made it a vivid presence on a cold December night.

"I stayed there, I should judge, about an hour—and then came down," the cartman continued, recalling his route home in rustic local landmarks once again. "When I got near Lewis's fence, I heard a cry in the direction of the Balloon House."

The house was an infamous local landmark, the site of a doomed attempt a few years earlier by a French aeronaut to launch Manhattan's first aerial ascent. He'd needed to sell three thousand one-dollar tickets for his grand plan, which included an amphitheater and a behemoth balloon sporting French and American flags—but before he could launch, his whole workshop was destroyed by a strong windstorm. What was left behind was perhaps best a quiet spot for getting drunk. That night, though, the area near the Balloon House gained a very different sort of infamy.

"It was," Mr. Orr added, "the voice of a woman—towards the well, in distress. When I got nearer the well I heard another cry, but the second cry was not as loud as the first . . . but rather *smothered*."

He had not, though, gone any farther to investigate.

"When was this?" the defense team asked quietly. "What time in the evening?"

"It was six or seven minutes before," the witness hesitated, "or six or seven minutes *after* nine."

He'd only heard what was happening by the well and hadn't actually seen it—but someone else in the neighborhood had.

Lawrence Van Norden and his wife, Arnetta, who had given the prosecutor such key recollections in his investigation, now took the stand. They patiently recalled how they'd heard cries of *Oh Lord have mercy upon me! What shall I do? Help me!*

"I got out of bed to see what I could," the husband remembered. "I saw a man walking towards the well—and in a little time the cries stopped and I went to bed."

Lispenard's Meadow was not a place where neighbors asked too many questions.

"Did you go to the well the next morning to make any examination?"

"No," Van Norden said bluntly.

But William Lewis, another cartman whose property line ran near the well, had done just that. Examining the ground along a property wall and fence the next morning, he found strange new markings in the snow.

"I discovered the track of a one-horse sleigh, about three hundred feet from the Manhattan Well, up the new road which Colonel Burr had built," he said.

All eyes turned to Burr at the defense table. It was an uncomfortable reminder that the prosecutor could, if he chose, call upon Levi's own attorney to testify. Burr couldn't be compelled to discuss conversations with his client, but it was entirely conceivable that he could be made to pore over the well's maintenance schedule and any visits by company workers to it that week. But for now, at least, the young prosecutor was keeping his attentions on the local cartmen around the meadow.

"The sleigh drove so near the wall, it was a wonder that it had not turned over," Lewis marveled. "The sleigh appeared to have gone up towards the Balloon House—I thought that somebody had missed their way, for there was no road there."

There was something else odd, too—something about the cover on Colonel Burr's new well.

"I observed," he said, "that there was one board off the well."

And around that pried-open well, he added, there were foot-prints.

WHEN THE night-watch bell chimed softly outside the courtroom, it was an occasion for disbelief: *Really? Midnight?*

Criminal trials—even for murder—rarely lasted this long. The courtroom was now lit by candles, the flickering and unsteady light giving an uncanny pallor to the proceedings. Asked to cast their minds back to the darkness of a Manhattan street in December, the witnesses now needed only to gaze upon the darkened windows of the courtroom itself.

*Approach the stand.*

Three young boys came shuffling up in succession, all kept up far past their bedtime. This was like nothing anybody in the court had seen before: Colden was still calling up one witness after another, as if trying to damn Levi Weeks with the sheer weight of his neighbors' testimony against him.

But now—children?

*State your age to the court.*

"Eleven," said one.

"Thirteen," vouched another.

This was most irregular. The court, as a matter of course, did not accept testimony from children under the age of discretion—that is, fourteen years old. This was considered the age of being fully able to discern right from wrong, and to comprehend the gravity of the mortal sin of false witness. Those unable to understand the spiritual import of their oath on the Bible were *incompetent witnesses*—a category one law tome helpfully described as "Idiots, madmen, and children."

The first two boys were promptly dismissed. Colden then brought forward the third, a cartman's son, William Blanck—who didn't even seem to know exactly *how* old he was.

*State your age to the court.*

"About . . ." the boy started. Actually, it was a puzzling question. Some children did not know their own exact ages, or even their own dates of birth. "Thirteen?" he finally guessed.

A groan across the courtroom was warranted by now—it was unfathomably late, and this was who Colden had brought forward? But Judge Lansing gently led the boy through some crucial questions.

*Can you read?*

No, he could not.

*Do you know what an oath is?*

No, the boy hesitated—he didn't.

Colden quickly called forth the boy's father instead.

"Pray, sir," he asked Andrew Blanck. "What is your son's age?"

The father didn't seem sure, either.

"He is . . . thirteen?" he ventured.

Colden, it seemed, was now going to have to rely on the father's testimony instead.

"Go on, sir," the judge harrumphed.

The father remembered his own visit to the well distinctly, not least because he had trod there through the snow on Christmas Day.

"My son brought home a muff which he said he got in the well," he explained. "I went the next day to the well and looked in, but I saw nothing."

He had noticed, though, a disturbance in the snow around the well itself.

"I discovered a sleigh track about eight or ten feet from the well," he recalled, "and I saw men's tracks to the well and about it. One man's track I noticed from the well to the side of the road."

*Someone* had been to the well—but who? And had it even been on that same night?

YOUR HONOR, came the plea from Levi's table, *perhaps an adjournment is called for.*

The trial had now stretched to one thirty in the morning, and it was showing no sign at all of stopping.

*I'm prepared to keep going*, Judge Lansing replied, but a glance at the jury convinced him otherwise: After fifteen tense hours of sitting in judgment of another man's life, they were simply exhausted.

*Very well*, the judge sighed.

If these prosperous citizens thought they were now to head home to their respectable homes and mansions, though, they were much mistaken. As jurors on a capital case where the public was calling for the defendant's blood, they would simply have to be sequestered.

*It is ordered*, the judge announced, *that the jury empanelled have leave to withdraw from the bar of this court, being well and truly kept by two constables duly sworn not to permit any person to speak to them touching any matter relative the trial. The same jury shall come to the bar of this Court at ten o'clock in the forenoon.*

They could leave the jury box—but not the control of the court itself. No grousing by his wealthy jurors could change Judge Lansing's mind. While judges did have some discretion in misdemeanor and felony trials to allow a jury to go home at night, a capital case was a very different matter. Jurors in a contentious life-and-death case like Levi's were, one law text gloomily explained, "as it were, prisoners until they are discharged."

So seriously did courts take the prisoner comparison that bailiffs traditionally denied jurors "food, drink, or fire" until they had reached a decision. Shivering and ravenous men were not, it seemed, inclined to dither endlessly over a case. But in the case of an overnight recess, the court was obliged to provide at least some minimal succor to their twelve unwilling guests. Finding accommodation for twelve men together was not easy, and sheriffs had been known to simply unroll mattresses in courthouses; jurors pleading to go outside for fresh air were told to go walk on the rooftop.

It was going on two in the morning, and every inn would be closed now. The exhausted jury followed the constables down the hallways and filed into what was to be their makeshift quarters for the night: the upstairs of City Hall itself. Blankets were laid out in the Portrait Room, a second-floor reception gallery whose paintings of Revolutionary heroes featured Trumbull's famed portrait of George Washington. Now, though, the room was half sunken in darkness, its glories flickering in the dim light of the candelabras.

The twelve men settled uneasily on the floor, each alone in his thoughts about what he'd seen that day and what was to come in scarcely another eight hours. The tapers in the room were snuffed, and then, curled up against the cold, the jurors slumbered under the impassive painted gaze of General Washington.

# 14

# Asleep, Seemingly

The concourse outside City Hall stretched before Brock-holst Livingston, empty of its crowds in the slumbering night—and yet for him, the place was haunted. As he considered the precedents for their defense, it was hard not to also be reminded of the fate of his client Henry Bedlow.

Bedlow's case had unfolded in this very same courtroom in October 1793. Lanah Sawyer, a seventeen-year-old seamstress, claimed that she had been raped that fever-ridden summer by Bedlow, the rakish scion of a local landholder. The young man had gallantly saved her from local toughs in the street, and introduced himself under a false name—he said he was a lawyer named Smith—and later took her out for ice cream and a midnight stroll around the Battery shoreline. Walking home past a darkened street of brothels, Sawyer claimed that "Smith" had clamped his hand across her mouth, dragged her screaming into the notorious brothel of Mrs. Mary Cary, and brutally raped her. When Lanah tottered home the next morning, her parents and friends soon guessed what disaster had befallen her, and in the courtroom they lined up to roundly condemn the wealthy scoundrel who had soiled her hardworking family's name.

Rape was a capital crime and a perfect charge to enrage the local poor: Bedlow readily admitted the false name and the brothel visit with Lanah. But he'd shown up at court with no fewer than four attorneys who, led by Brockholst Livingston, spent hours assailing the young girl's honor—all to prove that she'd already *known* he was the infamous "Harry" Bedlow, and had willingly fallen for his dangerous charms. She was, Livingston had scoffed, "willing to be deceived"—and the "cloud of witnesses" testifying to the strength of her character was hardly any proof at all.

"Who are these witnesses?" one of Bedlow's team sniffed. "An obscure set of people, perhaps of no character themselves."

When outraged spectators hissed, Livingston remained unrepentant.

"Gentlemen, I stand here in defense of the prisoner," he shot back to the gallery. "I will use every means in my power to detect the falsehoods that have been accumulated to deprive him of life, and neither hisses nor clamors shall make me swerve from what I conceive to be my line of duty."

By the time Livingston's team was done, it took the jury only fifteen minutes to find Harry Bedlow innocent.

Angry mobs rampaged in fury over the verdict, swelling with what one witness described as "Boys, Apprentices, and Negroes, as well as Sailors." They leveled Mary Cary's brothel, demolished the brothel of "Mother" Giles, and then even menaced Livingston's own far more respectable house. By the time the tumult was suppressed, at least one man had been shot dead, and the mayor himself was injured. Nor did Livingston's client escape unscathed: The wronged Lanah quickly sued Bedlow in civil court for seduction, and bankrupted the young man so thoroughly that he landed in debtor's prison.

But it was all a lie.

The accusation, which had been as damning to Harry Bedlow as the charges against Levi were today, evaporated one fine morning five years later. A now-married woman racked with guilt, the former Miss Sawyer confessed what Livingston had suspected all along—namely, that her late stepfather had put her up to making the rape charge. The angry crowds in the streets, she admitted, had been wrong about Henry. They had been wrong about the whole affair all along.

———— ✠ ————

CADWALLADER COLDEN couldn't sleep.

The young prosecutor had just single-handedly led a sixteen-hour-long legal onslaught, and his nerves were jangled. Everyone's were that night: Someone started shrieking *Fire! Fire!*, sending the citizenry piling into the street, only to discover it was a false alarm.

But at least the prosecutor had been free to go wander sleeplessly into the night. The jurors were confined to the Portrait Room with a bailiff keeping watch at the door—and, for them, it might not have been clear if they'd even be *allowed* to leave had the fire proved real. Legal precedent, a bit grudgingly, allowed that prisoners and jurors could flee from a conflagration—but not, perhaps, from a windstorm that might merely knock the building down.

As the sun rose, the jurors rubbed their stubbly faces, stretched painfully under the grand paintings, and looked out past the inaugural balcony into a cold and clear morning. On the street below, crowds reassembled. For anyone near enough to hear, the sentiments of New Yorkers about Levi Weeks remained the same: *Hang him.*

Colden was determined to see that they did.

With the morning sun streaming into the courtroom, the prosecutor called to the stand local grocer James Lent. The man who stood and strode up to the bar was, to anyone observing, immediately recognizable as one of the toughest characters in the room. Lent's namesake father had fought alongside George Washington in the French and Indian War, and was still recalled as "a fierce old fellow, full of fight and full of fun"—and the young Lent had proven himself a chip off the old block by fighting through the entirety of the Revolution. These days, when not contending with troublesome Federalists or tending to his store, the ornery veteran occupied himself with horsebreaking.

And that, he recalled to the courtroom, was just what had brought him out to Lispenard's Meadow on January 2, 1800.

"I, together with Mr. Page, had some business to do in breaking a horse, and we went up to Andrew Blanck's," he explained. "We dined there. Blanck insisted on it. While we were dining, two persons—Mr. Watkins and Mr. Elias Ring—came there to get hooks and poles to sound the Manhattan Well for the body of a young woman who was supposed to be drowned.

"We got the poles and nails," he continued, "and went all together to the well, which we uncovered. Page took the pole first and said he thought he felt her; I took hold then and thought I felt her, too. I took the pole and hooked the nail in her clothes and drew her carefully up to the top of the water: As soon as Mr. Ring saw her calico gown, he said it was she, he knew the gown."

In the dead silence of the courtroom, the crowd paused to envision the horrible sight—the men gathered around the snowy well, the body emerging from the darkness within—but Lent's memory turned to their painstaking care in handling the young victim.

"I put a rope under her and drew her up gently. She slew'd around but there was not a thread of her clothes which touched either side of the well," he explained. "We laid her on a plank, and she appeared in such a situation as if she had been murdered—"

"You are to tell what you *saw*," snapped Hamilton. "Not what conclusion you made. That is for the jury."

Lent, chastened, recalled just what he'd seen: namely, some scratches on her right hand and on her foot, "as if she had been dragged." Except for her shoes, she'd been fully clothed, if disheveled.

"Did you examine her *body*?" the judge asked.

"I did not," Lent said modestly. "The stockings, as far as could be seen without lifting up the petticoat, were whole and good."

"Any bruises upon the face?"

"I do not recollect," Lent hesitated. "There might have been."

"Might you have injured the head with the pole?"

"Not at all," he insisted. Even with all their tenderness, though, the body had been appalling to behold. "Her appearance was horrid enough—her hat and cap off, her hair hanging all over her head, her comb yet hanging in her hair—"

"Was she not a natural corpse?"

An old veteran like Lent knew all too well what both natural and violent deaths looked like—and yet this one was puzzling indeed.

"She looked as if she was asleep, seemingly," he mused.

Amid all this, though, what struck Lent most was the extraordinary exclamation he'd heard when, accompanying a police officer, he'd tracked down Levi Weeks.

"He dropped his head," he recalled, "and said, 'Is it the Manhattan Well she was found in?'"

At this, the jurors leaned in carefully.

"Was there any mention made," a juror interrupted, "of the Manhattan Well, in the presence of the prisoner, *before* he asked the question?"

One of the most damning and infamous public accusations against the young carpenter now hung in the courtroom, awaiting the horsebreaker's reply.

"I did not hear any," Lent said.

HAVING MADE some palpable hits on the defendant already, Colden was ready for his coup de grâce: the doctors. His first medical witness, Richard Skinner, possessed just the sort of theatrical flair that might impress a crowd; as the sort of fellow who would attire himself with a gold watch from Paris, a walking stick, and a scarlet cloak, he immediately stood out.

Skinner, though, proved curiously demure regarding his qualifications.

"Dr. Skinner," the prosecutor began, "are you not a surgeon in this city, and did you not see the body of Elma Sands after it was taken out of the well? Pray, sir, inform the court and jury."

"I follow a branch of surgery," he replied, "but I do not pretend to be a professed surgeon."

This was news to many in the crowd. For years Skinner had been advertising himself in local papers as a surgeon, boasting that he was "the only operator in America that sets artificial eyes"; he would also, in a pinch, install artificial ears, noses, and legs. But the only actual training that Skinner would aver before a judge was rather different.

"I am a dentist," he explained.

Skinner had always been ambitious, though. As an unknown new arrival from London, he immediately tried hitting up Benjamin Franklin for a twenty-dollar loan, and proceeded to make a name for himself by picking a fight with George Washington's dentist. And his sidelines in glass eyes and peg legs notwithstanding, Skinner had, in fact, built a respectable dental practice in the city, selling gold teeth at four dollars apiece, hawking his own patented dental tincture for a half guinea per bottle, and yanking out teeth at four shillings apiece in his Partition Street office—or, for his more well-to-do customers, for seven shillings on a house call.

His heart, though, had always belonged to the finer arts of the scalpel and the saw.

"I *have* made the subject of surgery generally my study," he added; and it was such medical curiosity that had brought him to the Ring boardinghouse in January. "I saw the corpse of the deceased twice."

The first time he viewed Elma was in the dim, hushed interior of the Rings' house, where she had been laid out; the next time was in broad daylight, when her coffin was thrown shockingly open to the multitudes on Greenwich Street.

"I had but a superficial view, though, as it lay in the coffin, exposed to the view of thousands," Skinner said with some regret. "I examined such parts as were *come-at-able*, such as her head, neck, and breast. I discovered several bruises and scratches—particularly a bruise upon the forehead and chin, and upon the left breast or near it."

Judge Lansing knew enough of medical testimony that he quickly halted the witness.

"How long was this after she was taken out of the water?" the judge inquired.

"I do not know," Skinner admitted.

This was an awkward admission, and the prosecutor quickly moved his witness back to firmer ground.

"Will you describe those marks more particularly?" Colden asked.

"I think that the mark upon the neck had the appearance of a compression, but not by a rope or handkerchief. The appearance on the breast was about as large as the circumference of a dollar. It was a small bruise, but it was more difficult to examine than the other," the dentist said, pausing delicately to explain. "There were a number of women present."

As Levi watched, the prosecutor moved in for his most damning question.

"Was the compression which you spoke of round her neck," he asked expectantly, "such as might have made by the hand?"

"My impression then was—and now is—that it was."

"Were the spots in a chain round the neck?"

"There were several spots pretty much in a row round the neck," Skinner agreed.

Considering that he did not know how long the body had been out of the well, Skinner seemed eager to agree with Colden's sly imputations—and for an experienced criminal lawyer such as Brockholst Livingston, such assertions beggared belief. The prosecutor had chosen not to call to the stand the two doctors at the inquest, who had seen the body shortly after its recovery, and had instead called up this—this *dentist*.

Skinner quickly found himself caught in a cross fire of questions from the defense and the prosecution.

"Do you say, *sir*, you are *certain* that the spots were in a ring round the neck?"

"I cannot say they were in an exact circle," Skinner faltered. "Not particularly. I think they were regular . . . but cannot exactly say."

"May such spots not have happened from a different mode than that of strangulation?"

The dentist, who just moments before had been happy to impute the spots to a strangler's hands, now claimed not to have made any such discernment at all.

"I am incapable of judging how they might have happened," he insisted.

For Colden, it was clear that the wiles of the defense team were undermining another one of his witnesses, and he quickly stepped in to rescue him. It was critical that the jury's attention be kept on the matter at hand: that Levi Weeks had strangled this poor woman.

"Suppose, Doctor," he interrupted, "a person *had* been strangled by the hand. Would it not leave such an appearance upon the body?"

"I think it would," Skinner eagerly agreed.

*No further questions for this witness,* Colden announced triumphantly.

For onlookers, the introduction of Skinner as a witness raised an obvious question: Where were Doctors Prince and McIntosh, who had handled the autopsy at the coroner's inquest? Given the remarkably crude state of affairs in autopsies for criminal cases, perhaps Colden simply hadn't trusted the two to provide any useful evidence on the stand. But his next witness—Dr. James Snedeker, a young doctor with a practice on Barley Street—certainly did *sound* like an expert.

"There were many discolorations on the teguments of the skin," Dr. Snedeker announced to the prosecutor. "There was a dislocation of the clavicle from the sternum."

There was a confused silence.

"Be so good, sir, as to speak in less technical language, so that the jury may understand you."

"The left collar bone was broke," the doctor sighed.

Like so many New Yorkers, he'd looked at Elma's body after it had been out of the well for two or three days—and like Skinner, he had noticed the telltale marks along Elma's neck, as well as the bruise on her breast. "I saw a mark upon her breast as large as a dollar, black and blue," Snedeker explained.

But the most persuasive evidence would come from Cadwallader Colden's crowning witness: Dr. David Hosack, the chair of Columbia's nascent pharmacology department. A powerful public speaker, Hosack had only narrowly avoided a law career himself to become one of the most brilliant young doctors in the country. What was more, Hosack could hardly be considered partial to the prosecutor: Not only was he a friend of Aaron Burr's, he was also Alexander Hamilton's friend and family physician. Indeed, one time after saving the general's beloved young son from scarlet fever and collapsing into a guest room with exhaustion, he'd awoken to find Hamilton kneeling by his bedside—the great man overcome with emotion and thanking God for the medical talents of "this ministering angel."

But Hamilton and Burr could only watch in dismay from the defense table as their friend laid out the grim evidence against their client.

"Upon looking at the neck I observed three or four dark colored spots," Dr. Hosack said from the stand. "Not in an exact line as if by a cord, but rather the effect of violent pressure. The largest spots, those near the wind-pipe, were about an inch and a half."

Like Skinner and Snedeker, he had noticed scratches on Elma's hands, as well as the disturbing hue of her skin.

"Could such appearances as you saw have been produced by suffocation merely?" asked Colden.

"I ascribed the unusual redness of the countenance to the sudden extinction of life, and the exposure to air. For in many cases of sudden death—by opium, lightning, poison, or a blow on the head—the florid appearance of the countenance have that appearance."

"Are you not, sir, *decidedly* of the opinion that the livid spots you have described, were the effect of violence?" Colden emphasized for the benefit of the jury. To Columbia's most esteemed physician, there was no doubt in the matter.

"I am," the doctor replied plainly.

That still left open the question of self-violence, though; and the ads placed in support of Levi in the days after Elma's discovery had, to the fury of the Ring family, raised that very notion. But if that was the last leg that Levi's defense had to stand on, Colden was now ready to kick it out from under them.

"Could any person, in your opinion," the prosecutor asked Dr. Hosack, "have committed such an act of violence on their own person as to have produced such effects?"

Dr. Hosack regarded the exhausted and yet keenly interested crowd in the courtroom before him, and the steady gaze of the accused Levi Weeks. Hosack had saved the lives of his friends, but today he could not save the life of their client. Their theory of suicide simply did not make sense.

"I do not think it could be done," he answered.


THERE WAS little question that the strapping young Levi Weeks had the ability to overcome Elma Sands. But the crime had occurred out in the middle of a meadow and not in the lumberyard of Ezra Weeks or the boardinghouse of Elias Ring. Would the carpenter have had the *time* to get there to commit the deed?

It was a question that Colden had prepared carefully for: Just as he had taken the unusual step of drawing up an architectural plan of the layout of the Ring household, the prosecutor had also taken the nearly unheard-of initiative of hiring a man to ride a horse from Ezra's house and out to the well. Even with the bad roads, the trip had taken just fifteen minutes in one direction, and sixteen minutes coming back—and that was without ever breaking out of a trot and into a canter. It was a stunning form of evidence. While on rare occasions courtrooms had heard of rooms or distances in a backyard being measured, measuring the entire route of a crime was altogether more ambitious. And with hours having passed between Levi's appearances at the boardinghouse, Colden's point was clear: There was plenty of time for him to have committed the deed.

But had anybody actually seen Levi do it?

Much of the evidence *seemed* to point to the prisoner's guilt, but there was no eyewitness and no exact murder scene. Dramatically taking up an influential legal text, John Morgan's *Essays Upon the Law of Evidence*, the prosecutor thumbed to page 208 and read it aloud to the jury.

"Circumstantial evidence is all that can be expected, and indeed all that is necessary to substantiate such a charge," he recited.

In a carefully hidden murder, Colden reminded the jury, circumstantial evidence was not only warranted but vital—because the victim herself could not give any testimony.

"The prejudice entertained against receiving circumstantial evidence is carried to a pitch wholly unreasonable," he read from Morgan. "In such a case as this it must be received, because the nature of the inquiry, for the most part, does not admit of any other; and, consequently, it is the best evidence that can possibly be given."

Far from being a weakness, he claimed, the circumstantial nature of his evidence was *more* damning to Levi Weeks than any eyewitness account.

"A concurrence of circumstances—properly authenticated, otherwise they weigh nothing—forms a stronger ground of belief than positive and direct testimony generally afford, especially when unconfirmed by circumstances," the prosecutor continued reading aloud. "The reason of this is obvious: A positive allegation may be founded in mistake, or, what is too common, in the perjury of a witness."

The prosecution was concluded, and the jurors would now almost certainly see the defense present a series of powerful alibis by powerful friends. And that, the assistant attorney general said, was just what Morgan and others were warning them of. Colden carefully enunciated a crucial line from Morgan before snapping the text and his case shut.

*"Circumstances,"* he read, *"cannot lie."*

# 15

# THE DEVIL'S ADVOCATE

Aaron Burr was not impressed by the case against his client.

"Gentlemen of the jury," he began, as he arose and solemnly paced the packed courtroom. "I know the unexampled industry that has been exerted to destroy the reputation of the accused, and to *immolate him* at the shrine of persecution without the solemnity of a candid and impartial trial."

Everyone there knew Burr was no stranger to attacks on reputation himself—attacks, in fact, that sometimes came from his fellow counsel Alexander Hamilton. But after the raking fire of General Hamilton's cross-examination of prosecution witnesses, it was now Colonel Burr's duty to begin the defense's counterattack. Their strategies could not be more different: Unlike the passionate and eloquent Hamilton, Burr was known for speaking slowly and precisely in the courtroom, each word considered and emphatic, each sentence like a line of silk in a spider's patient, ensnaring web.

"Extraordinary means have been adopted to enflame the public against the prisoner," Burr continued. "Why has the body been exposed for days in the streets in a manner most indecent and shocking? Such dreadful scenes speak powerfully to the passions: They petrify our mind with horror—congeal the blood within our veins."

Burr's defense table was scattered with his careful notes and volumes of *Pleas of the Crown*—the very emblems of enlightenment and reasoned thought over bloody terror that stood in mute contrast to the multitudes outside who had rushed to judge the prisoner guilty.

"Notwithstanding testimony of an intimacy between the prisoner and the deceased, we shall show you that there was *nothing* like a real courtship," Burr emphasized. And the tales of nighttime sleigh rides, of marks upon Elma's body, of guilty signs by the prisoner afterward? These, he assured jurors, would all fall apart under close scrutiny. The very slowness and care of Burr's speech seemed to mark him apart from the prosecutor, with his wild barrage of accusations. "The story, you will see," the colonel remarked scornfully, "is broken, disconnected, and *utterly impossible.*"

And that was just the problem: Through an almost malicious sloppiness in prosecution, a good name could already be damaged. Everyone there knew too well how justice could catch the innocent and unwary in its gears.

"Even in this city a case had occurred, not many years ago—a young man had been charged with the crime of rape," Burr mused in grim recollection of the Harry Bedlow case. "It is yet fresh in the minds of everybody. The public mind was there highly incensed, and after the unfortunate man had been acquitted by a verdict of the jury, so irritated and enflamed were the people, that they threatened to pull down the house of the prisoner's counsel."

The attention of the crowd turned to Brockholst Livingston at the defense table; they knew about his narrow escape, as well as his client's destitution after the civil trial that followed. The gravity of this example had just the effect Burr had hoped for—"it was one of the most eloquent speeches we have ever heard" one onlooker remarked—for Livingston was a war hero who had nearly lost everything he owned to the public's distrust of an impartial trial.

"*Now* it comes out that the accusation was certainly false and malicious." Colonel Burr paused to let the mournful realization sink in. "What remorse of conscience must a juror feel for having *convicted* a man who afterwards appeared to be innocent?" And this, he emphasized, was the heavy duty that fell upon those given mere circumstantial evidence of a man's guilt.

Aaron Burr's final, most dramatic assertion was not directed at the prosecutor or the jury at all—but rather to someone else in the case—someone, perhaps, watching at that very moment from the courtroom gallery.

"We shall show you," he added, "that if suspicions may be attached anywhere, *there are those on whom they be fastened with more appearance of truth.*"

Burr wasn't just saying that their client was innocent—he was also saying they knew who might be guilty.


THEY BEGAN with the humblest of witnesses: an apprentice.

*State your name to the court.*

"Demas Mead."

Alexander Hamilton had sat quietly through Aaron Burr's stately opening argument—and it had been an effective one. But then Hamilton, as the brisk cross-examiner, took the stage again.

"Do you live with Ezra Weeks, and did you the 22nd of December last?" the general asked the apprentice. "Relate all that you know."

"I live with Mr. Ezra Weeks, as an apprentice, and take care of his horse and sleigh," Mead answered. "I lived with him December last. I remember perfectly well taking care of the horse that night, and I either left the key—after locking the gate as usual—on the mantelpiece, or I put it in my pocket. I can't say certainly which."

One of the jurors, perhaps remembering the elderly neighbor's hapless confusion over when she'd seen those gates open, tried the same gambit on the lad.

"Was it a week day," the juror asked, "or on a Sunday?"

"On Sunday," Mead answered flatly. "I lock the gate every night—I locked it that night a little after dark, and before 8 o'clock."

"Did you miss the key in the morning?"

"I did not."

"Has the harness bells?" Hamilton asked.

"It has eight, tied in four places," the boy recalled.

"How many minutes would it consume to take the bells off and put them on?"

"Five or six."

The prosecutor was still thinking about the key on the mantelpiece, though, and he called out a question from his table.

"If you had laid the key upon the mantelpiece," Colden ventured, "and some person had taken it off and put it there again after keeping it for half an hour, might it not have been done without your knowledge?"

"I don't know—it might," the apprentice hesitated. "But I don't think it could, for I was only once out of the kitchen to fetch an armful of wood."

Crucially, the apprentice recalled hearing someone come in at about eight thirty; glancing into the room just before nine o'clock, he saw that it was Levi. When Ezra Weeks was called to the stand, his own recollection of the evening matched his apprentice's account: Levi had left to go to his boardinghouse around eight, just as the Ring family claimed, and he had then come back alone in about half an hour. That also matched the Rings' testimony, except that he was not with Elma. Nor did it give Levi time to also get over to Lispenard's Meadow. Aside from the physical impossibility of it, Levi had simply been too busy that evening.

"Levi came in to enquire about the business of the next day," the contractor explained. "He had charge of the shop, understanding the business as well as myself. I took dimensions of work on a memorandum, and gave it to my brother in writing. His business was to give directions to the journeymen for execution."

Ezra paused to draw out a slip of paper.

"Here is the eight doors on my memorandum, of different dimensions for Mr. James Cummings's house, which he took down that evening on a piece of paper as I called them off," he explained, handing the paper over to the court.

Hamilton knew that still left one of the most damning allegations unaddressed: that Levi had immediately asked about the Manhattan Well when the body was found. And who but the killer would have known that?

"Did your brother inform you that the muff and handkerchief were found prior to the arrest?" the general asked Ezra.

"Levi told me that Mrs. Forrest had told him that the muff and handkerchief were found in a well near Bayard's Lane. *I* told him that I supposed it must be the Manhattan Well."

At this, the prosecutor pounced.

"How came *you* to mention the Manhattan Well?" Colden interrupted.

For Ezra Weeks, it was a moment almost comic in its absurdity. Before him were two defense attorneys that he was building homes for; sitting by the judge was a city recorder who had helped approve his municipal contracts. How the city's most successful contractor could identify the well by Bayard's Lane was simplicity itself.

"I had furnished the wood materials for that well," he said.

OF COURSE, one might expect an accused murderer's brother to be good for an alibi—and for an apprentice to not contradict his employer. But testimony from Mrs. Forrest quickly confirmed where Levi had heard about the muff being found, and with both Ezra and his apprentice placing Levi in the house from 8:30 to 10 P.M., the prosecution still lacked any witnesses who actually saw Levi anywhere else during that time. At best, they had witnesses who saw *somebody* struggling by the well around 9 P.M.—just when Levi was apparently taking down door measurements in his brother's house.

Colden's lack of direct witnesses to the murder meant that the prosecution's case against Levi Weeks relied on a string of suppositions—that *if* one thing happened, *then* the next observation was likely part of a murder plot. "In cases depending on a chain of circumstances," Burr reasoned, "all the fabric must hang together or the whole must tumble down."

But although they'd countered Colden's case with an alternate scenario of how Levi had spent his evening, there was still a final link in the prosecution's chain: the assumption that a murder *had* taken place. Since that was what the coroner's report had claimed, it seemed like a safe assumption to make.

Or was it?

*We call Dr. Benjamin Prince to the stand.*

The society physician walked up and took the oath. Unlike the "dentist-surgeon" that the prosecutor had called upon, Hamilton's defense witness had an unquestioned role in the case.

*Tell us, sir, what you saw on January third.*

"I was called upon by a constable to attend the Coroner's Jury on the body of Elma Sands," the doctor explained. "When I came in I saw the body lying on the table before the Jury. I proceeded to examine it. I saw some scratches, and a small bruise on the knee. The body was then dissected."

This was news to the jury, for they had not been told that Elma's body had been manhandled and cut into for dissection *before* the prosecution's doctors had seen it.

"*I* saw no spots about the neck," Dr. Prince said pointedly. "No marks of violence. I saw no appearance but what might be accounted for by supposing she drowned herself."

"If there *had* been any very remarkable spots," Hamilton asked, "would you not have seen them?"

"I should," the doctor replied dryly. "I examined particularly—I was called for that purpose."

Why, then, had the coroner's report claimed murder as the cause of death? The mystery only deepened when the next witness stepped up: the other doctor at the inquest, Dr. William McIntosh.

*Tell us, sir, what you saw that evening.*

"I was called together with Dr. Prince to attend a Coroner's inquest on the body of Elma Sands," the almshouse physician recalled. "I was desired particularly, by the jury, to examine and see if she was pregnant. There were no marks of violence—and we discovered, to the satisfaction of the jury, that she was not pregnant. It was suggested by some of the jury that her neck was broke: I examined and found it was not. Neither was the collar bone dislocated."

That directly contradicted the testimony of the prosecution's witness, Dr. Snedeker—but that doctor had seen Elma body's three days later, after it had passed through innumerable hands, not least of which had been those of Prince and McIntosh at the dissecting table.

"The scarf skin of the face was scratched with gravel," McIntosh continued, meaning that Elma had minor abrasions that might have come from the side of the well itself, as *scarf skin* was a term used for the outermost layer of skin, the epidermis. "Near the instep there was a small spot like a blood blister. It seemed as if the knee had been injured by falling upon coarse gravel. There was a small spot on the breast, but there were no marks of violence upon the belly."

The marks on her body were of the type that jury members themselves might have—and for McIntosh, who saw the results of both stumbles and fighting among his almshouse charges, the determination had been simple.

"I think there were not marks of violence sufficient to occasion her death," he said.

But what of the row of spots seen around her neck: Surely that was proof of a strangling, was it not?

"I have been in the custom of seeing numbers of drowned people who have been brought to the Alms-House," McIntosh responded. "And I have often seen livid spots of the skin, much as I saw in this instance."

The courtroom was now so unsettled by this revelation that the prosecutor immediately began his cross-examination.

"Would that produce a row of spots round the *neck*?" Colden asked incredulously.

"Why, if the body was gangrened . . ." The doctor left the point unfinished. Elma's body had, after all, already been dead for twelve days when it was brought to the inquest. "It would be no matter. It might or it might not."

Judge Lansing, still troubled by the reports of scratches on El-ma's knuckles, quickly interrupted.

"If the hand had been hurt by a blow, would you have seen and noticed it?"

"Undoubtedly."

"Was there any water in the body?"

"A small quantity." Dr. McIntosh shrugged it off. "But very little is sufficient to drown. There might have been a quart."

"Would a spoonful drown?" a juror asked.

"Yes—unless it could be thrown up by the effect of a cough."

"Suppose," the juror added, "she had been killed first, and *then* thrown in the well? Would the body have any water in it?"

"It *might*," the doctor admitted.

The inquest doctors, while not entirely discounting this possibility of murder, had favored drowning as a cause of death—and the lack of many bruises and scratches meant either a stealthy killer *or* suicide. But the coroner's determination hadn't mentioned the latter possibility, because *he had ignored the consulting doctors.*

This was one reason Elma's inquest may have taken so long. Not only were the coroner and his jury liable to be men with little training in forensics, they had also faced the very real possibility of riots—just like in the Harry Bedlow case. With rumors spreading about Elma's death, and Levi already arrested as a suspect, they had decided to note only *one* possible cause of death—the one that had been the less convincing explanation to the doctors themselves. And in agreeing with the darkest suspicions of New Yorkers, the coroner had left out the most important detail of all: doubt.


THERE HAD been some doctors on the case worth ignoring, perhaps—just not the ones the coroner thought.

For one doctor, what was now happening looked all too familiar. Dr. Nicholas Romayne was one of the city's leading physicians. Formerly a trustee of Columbia, he'd gone on to run his own private medical school. Like many of the best American doctors, he had completed his training in Britain, where the medical profession had once been shaken by a disturbing murder case.

If Harry Bedlow was the precedent that haunted lawyers, then Theodosius Boughton was the name that Levi's case called to mind for physicians. A baronet and a young wastrel, he had died in convulsions on his genteel estate in Warwickshire in 1780; suspicions immediately fell on his brother-in-law, who stood to inherit a fortune. But in the trial that followed, it emerged that the victim's body wasn't exhumed and examined until two weeks after his death; the three local doctors who testified had found it too putrid to dissect, and after a brief visual inspection *supposed* that the brother-in-law had poisoned him with cyanide. The suggestion had come not from a coroner or from a consulting physician, but from the victim's excitable mother—a woman who failed to note that her son was a hypochondriac, or that he made a hobby of mixing his own rat poisons. With little other tangible evidence, and to the horror of medical professors around the country, the victim's brother-in-law went to the gallows on inept and vague suppositions.

As far as Dr. Romayne was concerned, Colden was nearly reenacting the appalling scandal: Once again, unqualified physicians were prepared to send a man to the scaffold based on brief, almost worthless visual inspections. As a young doctor, Romayne had seen the Theodosius Boughton case roil his profession after the more cautious testimony of Dr. John Hunter, widely regarded as Britain's greatest surgeon, was passed over by the judge and jury in favor of the emphatic but less informed responses of the three other doctors in the case. Now Dr. Romayne was in the same position that Hunter had been in. Called to the stand by Hamilton, he was withering in his judgment of Colden's doctors.

"An *experienced* person of good judgment might *perhaps* discover, upon inspection, whether the bruises made upon the body were done before or after death," he warned. "A body which had been taken out of the water would assume a different appearance from what it had at first—and every day the *appearance* of injury done would acquire more visibility as it advanced in putrefaction."

His words were a lancet, and they were particularly aimed at the one man in the room who should have known better: Dr. David Hosack.

The ambitious young Dr. Hosack had once been among Romayne's most promising students. For Hosack to join a dentist and a local hack in guessing the causes of death, on the basis of a brief viewing in the street two weeks later—it was unconscionable. The one medical jurisprudence text to emerge after the Boughton case, in fact, had warned of just this danger: that drowning and strangulation "are chiefly discovered by the facts, rather than by any peculiar marks they make on the body."

Shamed by his old teacher, Hosack was called back up to the stand. The defense lawyers proceeded gingerly—he was still Hamilton's friend and personal physician, after all, and the man who had saved the life of the general's son.

"Is there any way," Hamilton asked gently, "in which the testimony we have heard may be reconciled?"

"I think it may in either of two ways," replied the chagrined doctor. "At first there may have been very little change of color in the injured part, but after some time it undergoes a very considerable alteration."

The other possibility, he admitted, was that the injuries came after death—from the inquest doctors themselves.

"It occurs to me"—he paused—"that as it was supposed that the neck and collarbone were broken, when she was first taken out of the well, and as I did not see her until the day of interment—it is possible that the frequent turning and bending of the head, and the frequent examination of the neck to ascertain the injury done to the collarbone, may have produced the appearance on the neck I before mentioned. Especially as the body had been dead for several days, and the vessels had become tender. Very little violence might have produced an effusion of blood under the skin."

So the injuries could have been caused by murder . . . or they might not have been.

As powerful as Levi's alibi and Hosack's recantation were, they didn't answer everything. The prosecution's doctors and witnesses might have been slipshod, but they weren't responsible for Levi's arrest. He was jailed *before* the inquest, after all. Why, the defense team mused, had his name come up so quickly as a suspect? Where had the whisperings in the crowd come from, or the mysterious printed broadsides about ghosts haunting his boardinghouse room?

*Someone* had tried to pin Elma's death on Levi Weeks. But who?

PART IV

THE VERDICT

# 16

# LOOK UPON THE PRISONER

AARON BURR HAD BEEN MAINTAINING HIS USUAL OPAQUE AND UN-
nerving silence. Hamilton himself had been frustrated by his rival's
sly lawyering in the past—"at the bar he is more remarkable for
ingenuity and dexterity than for good judgment or good logic," he
complained. But one of Burr's old law partners observed that setting traps was simply what gave the colonel joy: "He delighted in
surprising his opponents, and in laying, as it were, ambuscades for
them."

The ambush Burr had planned for the Weeks trial would be one
of the most remarkable of his long legal career—and this time, he'd
mapped it out alongside General Hamilton.

*We call upon Joseph Watkins as our witness.*

The blacksmith took the witness stand, his work-scarred hands
and powerful physical presence a striking contrast to the lawyers
and doctors around him. Watkins had been hammering nails and
tongs for New Yorkers for years, and as the immediate neighbor to
the Ring boardinghouse, he'd been the first to join Elias in recovering Elma's body. He knew the family and its boarders well—better,
in fact, than anyone imagined.

"Do you remember," General Hamilton asked carefully, "any
thing in the conduct of *Mr. Ring* that led you to suspicions of improper conduct between him and Elma?"

Things were not what they seemed in the reputable Ring
boardinghouse—and hadn't been for months before the
disappearance.

"About the middle of September," the blacksmith said, casting his mind back to the evacuations from yellow fever, "Mrs. Ring being in the country, I imagined one night that I heard a shaking of a bed and considerable noise there—in the second story, where Elma's bed stood. I heard a man's voice and a woman's. I am very positive the voice was *not* Levi's."

For the jury, there was a shock of recognition—the inexplicable questions the defense had kept asking the Rings about the shared wall the between the houses now made sense.

"Could you hear through the partition?" an astonished juror asked.

"Pretty distinctly," Watkins said. And what he heard, as one observer put it delicately, was a "rustling of beds, such as might be occasioned by a man and wife," by Mr. Elias Ring and Elma. "It continued some time and it must have been very loud to have awakened me," the blacksmith continued. "I heard a man's voice, pretty loud and lively, and joking; the voice was loud and unguarded."

What was more, he could tell whose voice it was—because Ring had a distinctly high-pitched voice, while Levi had a low and quiet way of speaking.

"I said to my wife," he added, "*it is Ring's voice.*"

Three months before Elma disappeared, as the boardinghouse proprietor, the young carpenter, and the beautiful niece tried to survive the fever season in the sweltering Ring house on Greenwich Street, the blacksmith could already see it would come to a terrible end.

"I told my wife, *That girl will be ruined next.*"

The courtroom was shocked—and doubly so when an affidavit from Watkins's ailing wife was read, attesting that she, too, had heard the noise. As Cadwallader Colden stepped in to grimly cross-examine the witness, it only got worse for him.

"When was this?" he demanded.

"A little after the middle of September."

"How often have you heard this . . . noise of the bed?"

"From eight to fourteen times, in the time of the sickness."

"Did you ever hear this noise after Mrs. Ring came from the country?" Hamilton interrupted.

"I never did."

What he *did* hear later, though, was almost as remarkable. After Elma disappeared, in the days that Mrs. Ring now claimed to be agonizing over Elma's alleged betrothal to Levi, she hadn't made any mention of it at all to her neighbors. In fact, Mrs. Ring had gone out of her way to praise Levi.

"I heard her say," Mr. Watkins recalled, "the Thursday after she was missing, that he was very kind and friendly to all the family, particularly when sick—but not more so to this girl than to the rest—he was more like one of the family than a boarder."

Others had the same puzzling recollection. Watkins's young daughter, Betsy, had heard similar sentiments from Mrs. Ring. Yet others—including one of Levi's own coworkers—had heard by that fourth day of Elma's disappearance that Levi was suspected. If the Rings weren't the ones feeding these whispers, then someone else had encouraged them to change their story. A person, perhaps, with a motive to implicate Levi—someone who knew that the Rings faced ruin if the husband's adultery with the missing girl became public.

"Did you ever speak of this noise which you and your wife heard in the night to anybody else?" Watkins was asked.

Why, yes, the blacksmith recalled—there *was* one other person he had told.

"Croucher," he said.

THE GRAYING cloth merchant, who was sitting among the crowd in the courtroom, now seemed to shrink back into the darkness of the falling night.

"When did you first mention to Croucher what you heard in the chamber?"

"At the Coroner's jury," Watkins said. Quietly armed with the knowledge of Elias Ring's adultery—the kind of knowledge that could blackmail the Rings into changing their stories—Croucher proceeded to heap guilt on Levi for Elma's murder. "The day she was laid out in the street, I saw him very busy in attempting to make people believe that the prisoner was guilty."

Hugh McDougall, a Broadway glazier and sign painter, took the stand with a similar recollection of Croucher.

"I have been acquainted with this *Mr. Croucher* for some time, but I never liked his looks," he sniffed. "He used to bring apparel, such as shawls, to dispose of, but I noticed that he always managed to come *just* at dinner time. I told my wife that I did not like the man—and in the future, if he wanted anything of me, that *I* would call on him."

Soon, though, McDougall found even more reason to dislike him. Croucher had already been spreading accusations from the moment Elma's body was discovered.

"The day when the body was found," the sign painter recalled, "he was extremely busy among the crowd to spread improper insinuations and prejudices against the prisoner—who was *then* taken." That explained why Levi was arrested so quickly after Elma was raised from the well. What was more, Croucher had claimed that the seemingly upright carpenter was a thief. "Among other things, he told a story about his losing a pocket book. This conduct I thought unfair, and I told him so plainly. *Oh*, says he, *there's the story of the pocket book . . .*"

But Croucher couldn't let the story go. In fact, McDougall mused, the fellow had visited him again just the previous week, interrupting him in his garden for no other reason than to claim that there was new proof of Levi's guilt.

"I told him I thought it was *wrong*," McDougall snapped, "and highly improper that he should persecute Weeks in such a manner when he had a difference with him. For my own part, I wanted some further evidence before I should condemn the man."

Croucher, though, did not need further evidence. David Forrest, a boardinghouse neighbor who ran a Greenwich Street grocery, took the stand and recalled how Croucher burst into his shop just before the trial, filled with malicious glee.

"On Friday last, Croucher came running to the store and said, 'What do you think of this innocent young man now? There is material evidence against him, and he is taken by the High Sheriff, sir, and carried to jail—he will be carried from here, sir, to the court and be tried—and from there he will carried back to jail, and from thence to court again, sir—and from thence to the place of execution, and there be hanged by the neck until he is dead.'"

There was no such new evidence, in fact. And the curious thing, Forrest said, was that Croucher didn't even come into the store to buy anything—didn't have any purpose at all, in fact, but attacking Levi Weeks.

For another grocer who also testified, that customer sounded curiously familiar. That same Friday, an utter stranger had also burst into *his* store and, without buying anything, had launched into the same attack on Levi Weeks.

Alexander Hamilton snatched up a candle from the table and thrust it though the gathering gloom, up close to the face of a startled member of the courtroom crowd.

*Is this the man?*

The grocer peered from the stand, and at the candlelight flickering over the countenance of Richard David Croucher.

*Yes*, he said. *That's him.*

LEVI'S FELLOW boarder was now the very picture of wounded innocence.

"Did you ever publish the handbills about apparitions? Murder?" General Hamilton demanded.

"No," Croucher vowed. "I never did."

For the prosecutor, it was clear that the attacks by the defense had to be stymied. With the case now stretching past midnight for a second night in a row, Cadwallader Colden looked exhausted, but he asked the judge for leave to call in an additional prosecution witness—his one last chance to implicate Levi Weeks.

*The people call Matthew Musty to the stand.*

The cartman, now up appallingly late in a courthouse instead of asleep in his home by Lispenard's Meadow, took his oath.

*Tell us what you saw out by the Manhattan Well*, Colden urged.

"I saw a young man, the week before the girl was missing, with a pole in his hand—"

"Do you know Levi Weeks?" Hamilton interrupted. "Should you know the person you speak of if you saw him?"

"I don't know," the cartman admitted.

Exasperated, the prosecutor grabbed up a candle. If Hamilton could resort to such tactics, then so could he.

"Take the candle," he said, placing the taper into the witness's hand, "and look round and see if you can pick him out."

Given that the prisoner was at the bar, it was not quite a triumph of deductive skill. Musty dutifully held up the candle by Levi Weeks's face.

*That's Levi*, he said.

"Will you undertake to swear," Hamilton interrupted again, "*that* is the man you saw at the well?"

"I cannot . . ." he hesitated.

"Well, sir," Colden snapped, "tell what you saw."

Musty dutifully recounted his tale of the depth of the well being tested by a man—"he had on a blue coatee, red jacket, blue breeches and white stockings," the witness helpfully recalled. There was just one problem: Levi didn't own any clothing like that.

"If the court please," the prosecutor slumped back down, "we give up this point."

Hamilton, though, was not about to stop.

*We call Ann Ashmore to the stand.*

As the widow whose house Croucher gave as his alibi for the night of Elma's disappearance, her testimony was crucial. Though no longer in mourning—she had lost her husband to yellow fever back in the outbreak of '98—she had been left to care for her young son.

"On the 22nd of December," she began virtuously, "being my little boy's birthday, I invited some of my friends to come and sup with me, among the rest Mr. Croucher. Between 4 and 5 in the evening he came, and remained there till 4 or 5 minutes after 11."

"Could he have been absent twenty minutes during the time?"

"No," Ashmore insisted.

Several others from the party quickly offered the same recollection. But they were not witnesses of great public reputation—and when Hamilton laid out the simplest of pitfalls yet again for them, they went tumbling in.

*Mrs. Ashmore's birthday party—what day was that on, exactly?*

On a Sunday, came the response. Yes—a Sunday—which was Christmas Day, said another. No, the party was after Christmas, said a third.

*No further witnesses*, said Hamilton.


AARON BURR sized up the room: It was obvious that the jury was exhausted. The midnight bell had softly chimed from the almshouse more than two hours before, marking the arrival of Wednesday, April 2, 1800. The trial was now about to run into an unheard-of third day—not because of the defense, but because of the prosecutor's sprawling, almost uncontrollable succession of witnesses. But Cadwallader Colden had been guilty of much more than trying the jury's patience.

The prosecutor had misled them.

In explaining to the jury the importance and acceptability of circumstantial evidence, Colden had used an impressive quote from John Morgan's *Essays*: "Circumstantial evidence is all that can be expected, and indeed all that is necessary to substantiate such a charge"—the beginning of a passage that seemed to give legal precedent for using an intricate chain of suppositions in a capital trial.

But that was not what Morgan's essay meant at all. Colden had, in fact, left out the rest of the paragraph *preceding* his quote:

> Positive and direct proof of fraud is not to be expected.... The nature of the thing itself, which is generally carried out in a secret and clandestine manner, does not admit of any but circumstantial evidence; and therefore, if no proof of actual fraud were allowed in such cases, much mischief and villainy would ensue, and pass with impunity. *Circumstantial evidence is all that can be expected, and indeed all that is necessary to substantiate such a charge.*

"Such a charge" in the original was not a capital murder charge, but maritime insurance fraud—specifically, a case involving the fraudulent policy on a £110 cargo of oats. It was this standard of evidence, incredibly, that Colden had fobbed off onto the jury as a justification for sending Levi Weeks to the scaffold.

Catching the prosecutor on this point would have been child's play for Burr, but whether the jury would understand Colden's malfeasance was another question altogether. What they surely could understand, however, was the evidence that Hamilton had placed before them—and they also understood that Levi was a man whose moral character bore testimonials by local worthies.

*I now have a passage that I wish to read to you,* Burr announced, as he drew out a copy of Matthew Hale's *Pleas of the Crown.*

"In some cases, presumptive evidences go far to prove a person guilty, tho' there be no express proof of the fact to be committed by him, but then it must be warily pressed," Burr read to the candlelit chamber, "for it is better that five guilty persons should escape unpunished, than one innocent man should die."

To this, the prosecutor scarcely had an answer—in fact, he had little answer to anything at all by this point, because in the process of exhausting the judge and jury, he had also managed to exhaust himself. It was now 2:30 A.M., and after battling the three more experienced defense lawyers, Colden was "sinking under the fatigues he had suffered in the course of this lengthy trial," as one observer put it.

From where he stood, even closer to both the prosecutor and the defense team, court clerk William Coleman was even blunter about the state of the prosecutor. "Really," he mused, "he had not the strength to proceed that night."

*Your honor,* Colden began, *I have not slept in forty-four hours.* If the defense were allowed the first summation, he complained, then he "was obliged to at five or six in the morning to enter a reply." He just couldn't do it: The trial would need to adjourn and then enter a third day. Perhaps the jury could be sequestered in City Hall's Portrait Room for another night, and everyone return to the courtroom in the morning?

The sentiments of the crowd did not bode well for this notion. The jurors were among the city's most prominent and powerful merchants; several were older gentlemen, and at least one was quietly teetering on the edge of insolvency. Another night spent sleeping on a courthouse floor, away from their homes and businesses, was simply an intolerable prospect.

*Two nights passed in this manner might make some of them sick, and prevent a determination,* Judge Lansing admonished the prosecutor.

"The examinations of the paintings must doubtless be very edifying and amusing to the jury on the former night," one man in the crowd agreed drolly afterward, adding that they'd scarcely appreciate "a repetition of the pleasure."

Sensing his opportunity, Hamilton pounced.

*Your honor,* he interrupted, *if it please you, we relinquish our closing argument. The merits of our case are such that they require no summation.*

Almost before Colden knew what had happened, his sprawling spectacle of a murder trial was over. The verdict, Judge Lansing brusquely informed him, was now to be decided by the jury—immediately.

For the state's chief justice and the mayor of Manhattan, and for the prominent men that stood on either side of this case, there was nothing left but to trust in their fellow citizens. Judge Lansing turned to the exhausted jury: The matter of the prisoner's guilt or innocence had now arrived.

*The question involves considerations of great moment*, he warned them, *regardless of the consequences attached to your determination.* There could be riots yet again—and if they hadn't recalled that from the riots last summer at Mrs. Murphy's brothel on their own, then Aaron Burr's opening argument had refreshed their memories of that danger. Still, the judge remained unequivocal.

*You must find the prisoner guilty if in your conscience you believe him so from the evidence—and to acquit him if you find him innocent*, he added. *The obligation incurred when you became jurors limits you to the evidence produced by the trial.*

Some of that evidence, Judge Lansing reminded them, did not exactly flatter the prosecution's case. *If* the testimony of the defense witnesses was true, then Levi's movements that fatal evening were accounted for, save for one gap that left Levi about *ten minutes* to run one mile from Ezra's house to the Manhattan Well and back, and to commit the murder—all without becoming the least bit discomposed. *If* the testimony of the prosecution witnesses was true, none of them had actually sighted Elma or Levi together outside of the boardinghouse. In fact, aside from the allegation by Mrs. Ring about the two being engaged, the only link between the prisoner and that night's events was what one old and confused widow had seen out of her window.

*Regarding the widow Susannah Broad*, the judge reminded them, *if the account that the sleigh was taken out of the lumberyard of the prisoner's brother on or about the time Gulielma Sands disappeared does not satisfy you, then it must be evident that the accounts of the other witnesses respecting a sleigh, or cries of distress heard near the Manhattan Well, have no application to the prisoner.*

It just depended on whose word they believed. To the judge, the matter was simple: While in the previous decade the notion of "beyond a *reasonable* doubt" had started to gain currency as a legal concept, men of Judge Lansing's generation had been trained to believe that jurors were in danger of mortal sin if they convicted on insufficient evidence in a capital case. And so, the judge added, as for himself, the mayor, and the recorder—*we are unanimously of the opinion that the proof is insufficient to warrant a verdict against the prisoner.*

Whether that unanimity would be shared with other New Yorkers was a different matter. The crowds that might gather outside—as well as the accounts of the pamphlets, the hauntings, and the body in the street—could not be far from the merchants' minds. With a state primary coming up in a few weeks' time, half of Manhattan was already convinced that the other half was about to lead the nation to ruin. If they couldn't trust their government to prosecute a man nearly everyone was *certain* was guilty of murder, whom could they trust?

By the time the jurors left the room, it was crawling toward 3 A.M. A chill had settled into the air, and the spectators and legal teams had scarcely sunk back down into their chairs with exhaustion, huddling together for warmth in the dimly lit room, when the door to the courtroom swung open again.

Some said afterward that it had taken ten minutes; others said it was four or five; another still was quite sure that it was "less than two." But what everyone remembered, after the longest murder trial in the city's history, was how little time it had taken the jury to reach their verdict.

William Coleman stood up and gravely called a final roll of the jury's members: "Jasper Ward," the court clerk's voice rang out. "Garrit Storm. John Rathbone . . ." It was Simon Schermerhorn, though—the most humbly employed of the group, and bearing one of the oldest names from the city's Dutch past—that the jurors had chosen as their foreman. He raised his right hand, dutifully following the instruction of the clerk.

*Look upon the prisoner, you gentlemen of the jury,* Coleman commanded. *How say you? Is he guilty or not guilty?*

The young carpenter stood at the bar, knowing as he gazed back at the jury that it had all come down to this moment. All Hamilton and Burr could do now was watch—and hope.

"Not guilty," the foreman said, and the courtroom erupted into shouts and applause as the judge gaveled loudly for order.

Levi Weeks walked out into the night air of Manhattan unshackled—a free man.

# 17

# THE CATCHPENNY
# CONTRIVANCE

*NOT GUILTY?*

After all the vitriol expended upon Levi Weeks—the darkly in-
sinuating handbills, the scores of witnesses summoned from around
Lispenard's Meadow, the ill-wishers outside the courthouse that one
chronicler numbered in the "many hundreds, perhaps thousands"—
it seemed inconceivable before the trial that the fellow could be anything but guilty. The city's Court of Oyer and Terminer did not
have a reputation for leniency, after all: In one of the cases after
Levi's an unfortunate miscreant drew four years of hard labor for
stealing a black mourning cloth from a local church.

But for those watching closely, Levi's verdict was not entirely a
surprise. "Although some circumstances point to him as the perpe-
trator of the horrid deed," one local judge had written privately after
his arrest, "there has not yet been sufficient proof to convict him of
the fact." And as far as the reporters attending the trial were concerned, nothing in Colden's case for the prosecution changed that
damning assessment.

"Mr. Burr opened the defense with perspicuity and force, as he
disentangled every circumstance of perplexity; tore away the suspicions that had obstinately hung upon the public mind. . . . If the deceased was murdered, this at least was not the man," the *New-York
Daily Advertiser* weighed in. The fact that Hamilton had forgone
closing arguments also impressed the paper: "By the evidence of the
facts alone is this young man's innocence completely established.
Not a single doubt remains on the mind of any person who was

present at the trial. . . . Every one had come more or less impressed with the idea that he was GUILTY . . . [but] were, as soon as the verdict NOT GUILTY was given, just bursting into involuntary and exulting acclamations."

Within hours of the acquittal, a new pamphlet was on sale:

---

A

## Brief Narrative

of the

# TRIAL

for the

## *Bloody and Mysterious*

# MURDER

of the

## *Unfortunate Young Woman,*

in the

# FAMOUS MANHATTAN WELL.

---

It was an admirably theatrical title, and that suited its publisher just fine. David Longworth was known for publishing plays and possessed a impresario's pragmatism in offering any fare that would sell. He also hawked a city directory, sentimental prints of the late General Washington being lofted heavenward, and now this hastily assembled account "Taken in Short Hand by a Gentleman of the Bar." In his race to trump the competition, Longworth set the type even as his "Gentleman" wrote it and handed him the sheets.

The sixteen-page trial summary completely left out Mr. Ring's affair and Richard Croucher's machinations. Few witnesses were even identified by name. Still, it was the first, and it found quick sale among crowds eager for an account of the trial. Longworth was unabashed in his motives: "The narrative I published was too hastily written to be anything but a 'catchpenny,' " he cheerfully admitted.

The "Gentleman of the Bar" he hired confessed as much himself: "The careless and inelegant style in which these are recited, we account for on three principles," the writer said unapologetically. "First is, the excessive fatigue we have undergone in attending this trial, which has deprived us of two nights rest, and rendered us unfit for any occupation. The second is, the extreme haste. . . . The third is, our complete indifference to whether our readers are pleased with our style or not."

One reader was certainly not pleased: William Coleman. The publisher's ads that John Furman had bought throughout the trial— promising that "he had procured the clerk of the circuit court to take down in short hand the particulars of the evidence"—had instead only stoked demand for this flimsy knockoff by "a Gentleman of the Bar," released before Coleman could even get his own started. Infuriated, the court clerk marched down to Noah Webster's office to place an ad in the next morning's issue of the *New-York Commercial Advertiser*.

"The miserable shift of trying to put off this catch-penny contrivance under the insinuation of a falsehood, render it fit and proper to say implicitly that this is not the report promised to citizens by Mr. FURMAN," he sputtered. Anyone wanting the genuine article, he added, would have to wait at least another four days.

David Longworth was gleefully unrepentant: Catching wind of Coleman's ad, he immediately paid for a notice to run underneath it, mocking the very accuracy and dogged stenography that Coleman laid claim to. *His* pamphlet, Longworth promised, could "gratify the public curiosity . . . without entering into unnecessary detail of the tedious and unimportant part of the testimony." The publisher jeered at Coleman's self-importance: "By what privilege does this man insult me for printing an account of a trial, of which the whole world has a right to publish narratives? By what privilege but that of unending, insolent and vindictive *prejudice*?"

Coleman's temper had gotten the better of his commercial judgment. By revealing the earliest possible publication date of his account, he'd put rival printers on notice that they still had four more days to leap in with their versions of the Levi Weeks trial. And so it was that the next morning, Coleman awoke to find *another* pamphlet.

His catchpenny rival was right: The trial did belong to the public, and the latest member to seize this opportunity was James Hardie. As a brilliant young Scottish scholar, Hardie came to New York after the war with the hopes of becoming a professor at Columbia—a dream that slowly dissolved in a sea of drink. For years he'd boozily turned to anything at all to support himself. One year he was a tutor, teaching "Greek, Latin and English languages grammatically, writing, arithmetic, bookkeeping, geography and navigation"; the next he was running a Literary and Intelligence Office that professed to offer everything from drawing up indenture documents to a servant employment board to a real estate service. This particular year, he was a court reporter . . . of a sort.

"Not being acquainted with the art of stenography, I am incapable of giving verbatim what was said upon this solemn and awful occasion," Hardie explained, before adding that his haste was all in the service of seeing justice done to Levi Weeks. Yet *An Impartial Account*, as he titled it, was indeed a serious work. Twice as long as Longworth's "catchpenny," it featured every major witness from the trial, identified all the members of the court and jury, and delved into the sordid revelations of Ring's adultery and Croucher's slanders. Hardie's account was such an improvement on Longworth's that when four days had passed without any sign of the court clerk's long-promised book, few were likely surprised. The rest of the week passed with no sign of anything new in the window of Furman's shop; surely Coleman had simply given up and dropped the idea.


In fact, the court clerk had been writing like a man possessed. And when curious New Yorkers arrived in John Furman's shop on

Monday, April 14, 1800, what they found on offer for thirty-seven and a half cents almost defied description, even as the title gamely tried to cover it: *A Report of the Trial of Levi Weeks: On an Indictment for the Murder of Gulielma Sands, on Monday the Thirty-First Day of March, and Tuesday the First Day of April, 1800. Taken in Short Hand by a Clerk of the Court.* Transcribed and set entirely by hand in just under two weeks, the ninety-nine-page book was easily the longest murder trial account ever published in New York, not to mention the most painstakingly created.

"When it was promised at an earlier day, it was not foreseen what degree of labor or painful attention would be required to render it correct," Coleman explained. Rather than the customary summary of testimony with a few scattered quotes, Coleman had one-upped his competitors by including *everything.* The testimony, the cross-examiners' questions, the scoffing interjections, the collaring of Mr. Ring from the courtroom and the candle held up to identify Richard Croucher—it was all there, in direct quotation.

It was the first such transcript ever published in the new republic—the first fully documented murder trial in U.S. history. Without meaning to, his rivals had goaded William Coleman into pioneering a new genre. But there had been competing catchpennies for past murder trials as well; why had this trial created something new?

One clue lay in the publication date: 1800. In past centuries, before the adversarial system of trials allowed defendants to have lawyers, a murder trial was effectively a ceremony of laying out a person's guilt and punishment. The form of literature followed the trial's function: crudely inked confessions and dying words on the scaffold, and execution sermons that hectored readers not to act like the woeful, condemned sinners. This remained a thriving genre, and readers could still amuse themselves with such gratifyingly moral and exhaustive titles as *The Reprobate's Reward; or, A Looking-Glass for Disobedient Children, Being a Full and True Account of the Barbarous and Bloody Murder of One Elizabeth Wood, Living in the City of Cork, by Her Son, as She Was Riding, upon the 28th Day of July, to Kingsdale*

*Market. How He Cut Her Throat from Ear to Ear; as Also How the
Murder Was Found Out by the Apparition of Her Ghost; the Manner
of His Being Taken; His Dying Words at the Place of Execution: With a
True Story of Verses Written with His Own Hand in Cork Jail, Being a
Warning to All Disobedient Children to Repent, and Obey Their Parents.*

The adversarial trial system created an argument—a space for
uncertainty in the unfolding of the story—and a narrative tension
to take the place of old-fashioned sermonizing. It was a subtler form
of storytelling, and one not unfamiliar to readers of the burgeoning new genre of novels. The era's desire for vivid narrative also encompassed the use of quoted dialogue, which found its own curious
reflection in another important clue within Coleman's title: *Taken in
Short Hand.*

Court transcription was still a new art. Though stenographic
systems had been around for two centuries, it was only within the
past generation that they had found widespread use. The method
of abstract geometric shapes that Coleman favored—known as Byrom's New Universal Shorthand—had initially been developed by
a brilliantly deceitful courtier as a method of writing in code. Now
it served to reveal rather than conceal, as courtrooms and legisla-
tures began adopting stenography. Full transcripts were published
of Harry Bedlow's rape trial in 1793, and readers had become accustomed to seeing complete parliamentary and congressional speeches
in newspapers.

The nearest precursor to Coleman's achievement—a 1798 transcript of the Pennsylvania trial of four murderous conspirators
against one Francis Shitz—also showed a level of detail that likely
relied on shorthand. But unlike Coleman, that account's author
hadn't thought to include the questions asked of witnesses, only
their answers. In creating his account of the Levi Weeks trial, Coleman understood the electrifying effect of including both sides of
such transcribed speech to create actual dialogue.

With stenographers ready to take down dialogue, and an adversarial trial system to fuel the drama of the trial, all that was
needed for the first true-crime mystery was, in fact, an unsolved

murder—and the Elma Sands case had been the final key element needed to create an explosive new form of literature.

NOT EVERYONE was happy with Coleman's literary invention. Rival pamphleteer James Hardie pointed out in an open letter that Coleman's book was riddled with misspelled names for the witnesses—a jab at the clerk's pride that hurt all the more for being entirely true. Hardie's harshest criticism, though, cut to the heart of the case itself: "Let me ask, what strict regard to the truth could be expected from a reporter who, though clerk of the court, has shewn himself to be actuated by prejudice against Levi Weeks, as to have repeatedly said that if he had been on the jury, he would have starved before he acquitted him!"

Hardie was not alone in this suspicion. Coleman's rumored antagonism toward Levi so worried Ezra Weeks that the builder had quietly tried to bribe the author into making America's first complete trial transcript a little *less* complete, offering $500 to sweeten it or $1,500 to suppress it entirely.

"Mr. Weeks," Coleman rebuffed him. "You are not worth money enough, neither is the City of New York, to buy me."

Ezra Weeks was so impressed—an incorruptible writer in Manhattan!—that he and Coleman became fast friends. In fact, Ezra found he had little to fear from the clerk's studiously noncommittal rendition of the facts. Coleman invited Ezra to read the manuscript before it went to press—and in a response to his critics, Coleman revealed that he'd consulted "Mr. Ezra Weeks, and the prisoner's counsel, to whom the proof-sheet was *particularly submitted.*" Waiting for Ezra Weeks and Alexander Hamilton to read the transcript was part of what had delayed his release date, he explained. The revelation was a startling one, not least because it confirmed what everyone likely suspected: that Ezra was the real client behind Levi's powerful defense team.

AMID THE dueling trial narratives, locals had plenty else to distract themselves after the trial. A huge crowd watched the launch of a new frigate, the USS *President*, and loudly celebrated with newly penned songs such as "Huzza for the President." For those less patriotic in their entertainments, the local theater was offering *Ground & Lofty Tumbling, Posture and Equilibriums*, in which a Signor Joseph Doctor would "go through a HOOP, with a PYRAMID of thirteen Glasses of Wine on his Forehead."

The lawyers, too, remained busy. Within days, Livingston and Hamilton were on one side of an insurance suit, with Burr on the other—while in another lawsuit, it was Livingston and Burr versus Hamilton. Their work was a lucrative courtroom waltz, though the stunning victory for Levi Weeks had not profited them. Instead, Burr took out another $1,500 loan, and Hamilton received a politely humiliating note from a cashier at the Bank of New York—the bank that Hamilton himself had founded—reminding him that his "account, by the former ones being charged, is now overdrawn $5300." Yet Hamilton in particular was wise not to bill Weeks; he already owed so much to Ezra that he could be thankful simply for keeping out of debtor's prison.

More vexing to Hamilton was another mighty contest that led inexorably back to Lispenard's Meadow, and to the sly banking scheme that Aaron Burr had slipped into the municipal water supply. With Thomas Jefferson the likely Republican presidential nominee, Burr was positioned to become vice president—and his new bank's influence would pay off in Republican electoral votes for the country's most crucial swing district.

"It is universally acknowledged," admitted a Federalist writer signing himself *Marcellus*, "both by Federalists and Jacobins, that the election of the President on either side, depends on the city of New-York—that is, if the Federal ticket for the state legislature is carried, a Federal President will be chosen; if the Jacobin ticket succeeds, Mr. Jefferson will be President." Savvy New Yorkers could spot the pen name of the president's ambitious son, John Quincy

Adams, in Marcellus's editorials—and they could also spot the increasingly dire rhetoric of the Federalist Party: "Mr. Jefferson, and of course the Jacobins at large, wish to destroy the Constitution of the United States."

Federalists, though, apparently wished to destroy *themselves.* By the time they caucused in the Tontine City Hotel on April 15, 1800, they were weakened by the party's unpopular Alien and Sedition Acts, and by incessant bickering between General Hamilton and President Adams. Their resulting local slate landed with a thud: The list, one Republican aide smirked, consisted of "two grocers, a ship chandler, a baker, a potter, a bookseller, a mason, and a shoemaker." The most prominent man willing to run was Cadwallader Colden; his fame, alas, was now for bungling the Elma Sands case.

When advance word of the slate was delivered to Burr, he calmly slipped Hamilton's list of hapless loyalists into his pocket.

"Now I have him all hollow," the colonel said coolly.

Two days later he hit Hamilton with the most assuredly solid slate in New York political history: The Republican candidates included former four-term governor George Clinton and a raft of war heroes ranging from Major General Horatio Gates to none other than Brockholst Livingston. After campaigning as a party of law and order, Federalists now found themselves facing a wall of bona fide soldiers and prominent politicians.

"What means these gigantic figures?" one Federalist editorial complained weakly. "Why this parade of Governors, Generals, and Senators for the lowest civil office?"

Hamilton knew all too well why. The Republican faithful that he'd denigrated as mere anarchists had been whipped by Burr into a disciplined force—and the colonel's Richmond Hill mansion had become an election war room, roiling with constant planning and sifting of voter information from each ward. "Committees were in session day and night during the whole time at his house," one local merchant marveled. "Refreshments were always on the table, and mattresses were set up for temporary repose in the rooms. Reports were hourly received from sub-committees—and in short, no means left unemployed."

Burr had virtually invented modern electioneering—canvassing across the city, he fought Federalists house to house through the Sixth and Seventh Wards, which encompassed both the Ring boardinghouse and Lispenard's Meadow. Even when the import of an election was nationwide, the impracticality of a traveling campaign in the far-flung nation meant that this savvy local groundwork was crucial. Yet Hamiltonians were bewildered that reputable men such as Aaron Burr and Brockholst Livingston would lower themselves to such vote scrounging. "Many people wonder that the ex-Senator and would-be Vice President can stoop so low as to visit every low tavern that may happen to be crowded with his dear fellow citizens," puzzled one Federalist newspaper.

But among those men in the taverns were grateful Bank of Manhattan customers—men whose votes could now reward their great benefactor.

"The leaders of the aristocratic faction bewailed the establishment of the Bank of the Manhattan Company, as an institution whose well-timed liberality secured to the merchants a free exercise of their political principles," one Burr editorialist explained. Not only had the bank allowed merchants to vote Republican without fear of reprisal from a monopolistic Bank of New York, it had also allowed the "middling classes" to start acquiring enough property to qualify as voters. "Merchants, mechanics, cartmen, men of all grades," the editorial claimed, "are interested in preserving this important source of independence and prosperity."

The project that began in the hidden waters of Lispenard's Meadow was ending happily for Burr. It was ending quite well, in fact, for a great many people—but not for the unfortunate young woman whose name was now so inextricably and mysteriously tangled up with its history. And for her mourners, a mystery remained to be solved.

# 18

# EVERY MARK OF

# A VILLAIN

WHO KILLED ELMA SANDS?

The answer hinted at by the defense team in the trial—"herself"—never did seem satisfactory, and the case was still universally referred to as a murder. After all, Elma had left no note, nor made any comment in the day or week leading up to her death that could be construed as a sign of distress. Her occasionally melancholy disposition might not be considered a notable quality in an unmarried woman of twenty; nor even was her remark, made months earlier, that if she had a bottle of opiate she'd drink it. Probably most members of the courtroom, if they searched their own lives in the months preceding the trial, could imagine a gloomy day or half-joking comment of their own that could be held up as equally specious evidence of suicidal intent.

And for Elma Sands to kill herself in a well required that she not only kill herself, but that she do it *in a well*. New York's records are rich with self-annihilation by pistol, by hanging, by poison, and by river. Suicide by water system, though, would constitute an altogether novel approach. *Murder* would not: In fact, not long before Levi's trial, a young woman upstate was charged with fatally precipitating a neighbor's baby into a well.

There was another problem with suicide in the Manhattan Well: If Elma Sands had wanted to drown herself, all she needed to do was walk a few blocks from her boardinghouse and jump off a pier. This was why, fearing a possible suicide, Elias Ring quite sensibly ordered the river dragged at this spot: "We swept near

Rhinelander's Battery," he had explained to the court, "because I thought it was the handiest place." And while the depth of the failed Manhattan Well was uncertain—for all Elma knew, she might have found herself in four feet of muddy water—the efficacy of plunging into the icy Hudson River on a December night was beyond doubt.

Nor was the medical evidence in the trial much help. Though the defense team had convincingly thrown doubt on the shoddy evidence offered by the prosecutor, their own testimony by inquest doctors Prince and McIntosh could hardly be considered trustworthy. The state of medical jurisprudence remained primitive, and the body they examined had already been dead for nearly two weeks; moreover, the crime scene was not secure during that time. The inquest did ascertain that Elma was not discernibly pregnant, a crucial fact in ruling out possible murder or suicide motives. She had not been stabbed or shot. But beyond that, little entirely reliable information could be hoped for.

Curiously, the most suggestive evidence may have come from the humblest of witnesses: the cartman and his wife who lived on the outskirts of Lispenard's Meadow. Lawrence Van Norden testified to hearing a woman's loud cries for help out by the well, and that "in a little time the cries stopped." Their having stopped in a short time, rather than dying out, suggests the possibility of Elma's strangulation, at least to the point of unconsciousness before she was dropped into the well.

The inquest doctors testified that Elma's lungs indicated possible drowning, which suggests a likely explanation for all the evidence: that Elma Sands was strangled to the point of unconsciousness but not death. Believing her dead, her assailant then dropped her body into the Manhattan Well, where, just as the inquest doctors claimed, *she drowned without a struggle.*

But who would have done such a thing?

In fact, there *was* a person of suspect character living at 208 Greenwich Street—but it wasn't Levi Weeks. The quiet boardinghouse had hosted someone with both the means and the motive to kill Gulielma Sands—someone who, unknown to Hamilton and

Burr or the prosecutor, was hiding a criminal past, and who had been known to be dangerously unhinged. Someone whose record, for more than two hundred years, has evaded detection in one of our country's oldest unsolved murder cases—until now.

It is hidden deep within the *Proceedings of the Old Bailey* for September 20, 1797, recorded on a blustery Wednesday at London's fearsome criminal court. Below the case of a woman sentenced to whipping for having pawned a stolen calico petticoat in Kentish Town, and a young mute caught stealing silver buttons in a pub, another case appears. This one, from a shoemaker's shop by St. Paul's, involved a well-dressed fellow absconding with a pair of boots worth twelve shillings. The shop's apprentice chased him for blocks into King's Head Court.

"I saw the boots in his hands, and hollered, *stop thief*!" he testified.

Dressed in a blue coat and with powdered hair, the thief was almost too genteel to be caught; one bystander in the street admitted: "Seeing him so much a gentleman, I let him pass." When he was finally collared, the suspect proved to be no ordinary thief at all, but a respectable shopkeeper from Leominster.

"I am a musician at the Theatre Royal," one neighbor testified. "I have known the gentleman at the bar twenty years."

"Is he a man of decent situation in life?" the court asked.

"Very respectable indeed."

"He has a wife, daughters grown up?"

"Yes," the musician replied, before adding, "I think, from some circumstances in the last four or five years, he has not been collected in his mind."

He recounted how the accused would suddenly fling his store's money till upon customers' heads, and how the man had cruelly abused his wife and daughters until they received a court order of protection against him. Another neighbor testified that "he is at times deranged," and recalled that "he has threatened to buy a pair of pistols, insisting that I should fire at him, or he would fire at me, for no reason upon earth."

Atop the court docket is the name of this homicidal lunatic:

## RICHARD DAVID CRUTCHER, *OTHERWISE* CROUCHER.

His neighbors knew him by a different name, though.

"I was coming down Holborn, and met the waggoner," another witness testified. "I asked him if he knew Mr. Croucher, and he said—*what, Mad Croucher!*"

Croucher never denied stealing the boots, and indeed the court was scarcely interested in that question; the man was clearly insane. As such, Croucher was found not guilty. Yet instead of occupying a cell in the Bedlam asylum, he had managed to flee and secure a passage to Manhattan.

Nobody in the Rings' boardinghouse—or in the courtroom at Levi Weeks's trial—had any idea of the true nature of their new boarder. But had the jurors or lawyers known the Bowery a bit better, they'd have seen right through Croucher's alibi for the night of Elma's disappearance. He'd been at a birthday party at the house of Ann Ashmore, he said. But who was Ashmore? Why, she ran a brandy-making firm in her house: *Croucher's alibi was a party in a distillery.* It was no wonder that the attendees couldn't even remember what month they'd seen him there.

Croucher's old neighbors in London could have warned of what was liable to happen next. "I have seen him very often in liquor, and look as wild as he possibly could," one testified. "In fact, he was not bearable when he had any liquor."

If Croucher or anyone else had told Elma about the party that evening—and, though he held back from using it in the trial, Burr claimed that Elma was known to sneak out at night sometimes—then an encounter between her and Croucher could have been disastrous. Burr and Hamilton already had their suspicions about Croucher, and after the trial one newspaper pointedly warned "those who have been instrumental and active in misleading public sentiment, and stirring up public indignation . . . Suspicion at length may fall on them." But the task of Levi Weeks's defense team had been to free their client, not to convict someone else. And so it was that Croucher was free after the trial to prepare to set up house with his new American bride—and her thirteen-year-old daughter.

Soon enough, New Yorkers would learn just how dangerous Croucher truly was.

*COME HELP me scrub my old room clean, so that I may move here,* Croucher told his new stepdaughter on the evening of Wednesday, April 23, 1800. Just three weeks had passed since the stunning Weeks verdict, but it was time for the cloth merchant to move on from his old life at the boardinghouse. A forty-year-old man such as Croucher could hardly hope for much assistance in packing from a slight, slender girl like Margaret Miller; still, it was not her place to object to a cleaning job. Her mother had already been upbraiding her for sauciness, though others hardly discerned much impertinence in the meek young girl. She dutifully followed her new stepfather out into Ann Street, and the two made their way toward Croucher's old lodgings on Greenwich Street.

FALSE SHAME! cried the ads for that evening's theatrical production, while over at the street corner in Rhinelander's brew house, the Federalist and Republican faithful argued over the following week's election. Peter Schermerhorn had just that day announced his withdrawal from the local Federalist slate; it was obvious that Hamilton's party was now a sinking ship. Those tired of arguing politics had the competing accounts of the Weeks trial to discuss; Coleman's had been out for scarcely a week.

*I was there—at the trial,* Croucher boasted to the girl. *Shall I tell you how the young woman died?*

Margaret had been learning her lessons at school, where pious and edifying readings were the usual fare, and hadn't looked at any of the books about Levi Weeks. It was hardly proper reading for a child. And at that time of evening, with the sun already down, there was little reading to be had anyway. The two stopped in front of the darkened boardinghouse at 208 Greenwich Street, and Croucher ushered her in through the crooked front door, through which, just a few months earlier, Elma Sands had last departed.

*We shall pack and clean in the morning,* he explained, and they walked past Mr. and Mrs. Ring's bedroom by the foot of the stairs, and then up the creaking steps. *Tonight, you'll sleep in the servant girl's room—it's on the third floor.*

Margaret walked up obediently, and into the darkened hallway that locals had idly imagined to be haunted. There was scarcely any light at all up here, it seemed. Margaret walked into a room and heard the click of the lock on the door behind her.

Hands seized her in the dark, pulling her clothes off.

*If you scream,* Croucher's voice hissed, *I will kill you.*


TWO MONTHS later, Margaret Miller peered anxiously from the same witness stand where so many others had testified against Levi Weeks back in the spring. Before her stood the very man who had questioned her predecessors: Cadwallader Colden. At the defense table there was another familiar face: Brockholst Livingston. But next to him sat a new prisoner: Richard David Croucher.

*How old are you?* the prosecutor asked Margaret.

"Thirteen," she said.

Her faced flushed with embarrassment, and she began crying, the tears coursing uncontrollably down her cheeks. She scarcely looked her age to begin with, and now the grave gentlemen of the court found themselves flustered by an altogether unaccustomed sight in the City Hall courtroom: a terrified, weeping girl.

*I know that it is difficult,* the judge comforted her. *But you must tell us what happened next.*

"He took me and undressed me and put me on the bed," she said haltingly, regaining some composure. "Then he undressed himself, and came to bed . . ."

She burst into tears again. To face her stepfather across the courtroom while testifying had simply become too much; Croucher, one spectator remarked, bore "every mark on his face of a crafty, unprincipled villain." He seemed not at all discomposed that he was being tried for rape.

"He used force," the girl continued. "He did what he would, and hurt me very much, so that I could hardly get home the next morning. After he had done, he fell asleep, and I got up and sat on some wood till I could see to find the door."

In the weeks that followed, Croucher had abused her terribly, calling the girl a whore in front of her mother. "He whipped me, and turned me out of doors," the girl testified, and finally broke down altogether into sobs.

Striding before the jury, defending lawyer Brockholst Livingston seemed as confident as ever: He was now a state assemblyman-elect, thanks to a Republican sweep of the elections back in the spring. And Colden, sitting grimly across the courtroom—well, he had lost. This rape charge against Croucher, Livingston genially announced, was just like the Henry Bedlow rape trial all over again . . . which Livingston had also won.

"If any thing of an improper nature has passed between them, *I* am inclined to believe it has been with her consent," he mused thoughtfully. "It is said, her youth renders it impossible she should have been a lewd girl. Who that is acquainted with the dissolute morals of our city does not know that females are to be found living in a state of open prostitution at the early ages of 12 and 13 years?"

Perhaps, he added helpfully, the real culprit behind her wantonness was "our ill-judged mode of educating the sexes together in our public schools."

This time, Colden was ready for him in his closing argument. Consent was legally impossible in a girl her age, he pointed out; and what was more, Croucher had plainly threatened her with Elma's fate.

"She *knew* that a young woman had been cruelly murdered," he reminded the jury. "She learned the particulars of that trial from *this* prisoner. The threats of the prisoner to murder her if *she* was not silent, must have had a greater influence than they would have at any other time."

It took the jury just five minutes to find Croucher guilty.

A MONSTER, read headlines announcing his sentence of life with hard labor, and the word spread quickly to other cities as well. "Every one must rejoice that the community is freed from a demon so artful and unfeeling," the *Philadelphia Gazette* announced. And while Croucher's threats to his stepdaughter stopped just short of a confession of Elma's murder, they were enough for the *Gazette* and other newspapers to revive distrust of a witness "who was absent at a suspicious place that very evening, and pursued the suspected young man with the utmost malignity." The brilliant and unlikely pairing of Hamilton and Burr in the defense of Levi Weeks had, it seemed, almost certainly saved the life of an innocent man after all.

Saving their own lives, however, was a different matter.

*[ Four Years Later ]*

# 19

# DUEL AT DAWN

FOR THE MAN WHO HAD TRIUMPHED IN THE 1800 ELECTION, THE next would prove far less kind.

"AARON BURR . . . is using every wicked art to promote his own election," the *New-York American Citizen* warned in April 1804. "Degraded as he is, beyond contempt in the opinion of all good men. Vain dotard! Does he aspire to public honor? Let this hint suffice—Let it shew what I could relate—I know the rottenness of their character, and could *torture the marrow of their very bones.*"

A hint was all that was needed, for the rumor was already afoot: The newspaper's editor claimed that he had had assembled a list of "upwards of twenty women of ill-fame with whom [Burr] has been connected." For good measure, the editor then ran a letter claiming that the colonel was actually a British secret agent.

And this was in a *Republican* newspaper.

Engineering his party's victory in 1800 had been curiously unrewarding to Aaron Burr. He'd spent four years as an unwelcome vice president, spurned by President Jefferson through internal feuding; once it was clear that Jefferson would prefer New York's Governor Clinton on his 1804 reelection ticket, Burr returned to run for Clinton's vacated post. There was just one problem: The judge from the Levi Weeks case, John Lansing, was already tipped for the Republican candidacy. Ambitious as ever, Burr dodged a looming loss with a simple solution: He'd run to the middle and seize both Republican and Federalist voters. The opposing party's disarray, he realized, had left many of their voters his for the taking.

Hamilton, not surprisingly, was appalled.

"I had rather seen Lansing governor & the [Federalist] party broken to pieces," he wrote in despair.

General Hamilton traveled around the state, lobbying to keep Burr from capturing the Federalist Party—*his* party. Hamilton had already hired William Coleman, the chronicler of the Weeks trial, to head his newly founded *Evening Post*; it now joined Republican papers in attacking this monstrous Republican-Democratic-Federalist candidate. This time Hamilton's tactics worked. Burr lost the resulting election by a crushing margin, and retreated in humiliation to his mansion—dodging friends, his own family, and—above all—his creditors.

He was a ruined man, and he wanted revenge.

"I send for your perusal a letter," Burr began in a terse note to Hamilton dated June 18, 1804. It contained an account of a Federalist dinner where Hamilton had heaped scorn on Burr; in it, one Dr. Cooper claimed he could quote "still more despicable" opinions from Hamilton. "You must perceive, Sir," Burr wrote, "the necessity of a prompt and unqualified acknowledgement or denial."

The account of the slander was undated and gave no direct quotes. How could Hamilton acknowledge or deny anything so vague? And, Hamilton added in a reply—"Tis evident that the phrase, 'still more despicable,' admits of infinite shades, from very light to very dark."

"The question is not . . . grammatical accuracy," Burr shot back.

For two weeks the pair reprised their roles as a trial team: Burr as the wily exploiter of formalities and Hamilton as the rigorous cross-examiner. Burr demanded respect, and Hamilton demanded evidence. But what Burr really wanted was a fight—a duel—one that would return him to political power. Hamilton, ever the lawyer, asked to finish his current cases first: "I should not think it right in the midst of a Circuit Court to withdraw my services from those who have confided important interests to me."

When the two finally met on a New Jersey shore in the early

morning of Wednesday, July 11, 1804, it was with all the attention that two legal minds could bear upon the task. They'd crossed the river to a state that had not outlawed dueling; they were taken over by bargemen who were not to look up, so as to witness nothing; they were refereed by judges who would look away at the appropriate moment of firing, and would then depart with their duelist under cover of an umbrella, so that nobody could witness the entire fight.

But this much is known: Hamilton shot into the trees. Burr, leveling his pistol at his foe, did not.

Hamilton crumpled to the ground almost instantly. Burr's assistant saw the colonel step forward, a seeming expression of apology flickering momentarily across his face, but he then turned away and departed without a word, in keeping with the code duello. Dr. David Hosack—a key witness in the Weeks trial, and still the physician to both men—was the first to aid the fallen General Hamilton. The veteran soldier already knew just how badly he'd been hit.

"This is a mortal wound, Doctor," he gasped.


VICE PRESIDENT Burr now found himself at the middle of the most shocking homicide case in America since—well, since the last one that he'd also been at the center of. New York was in mourning, and no matter how much he insisted that Hamilton had brought it on himself, many believed that it was Burr's fault.

"The streets were lined with people," reported William Coleman of Hamilton's funeral that Monday. "Doors and windows were filled, principally with weeping females, and even the house tops were covered with spectators."

Nobody had seen anything like it since George Washington had died—doctors and lawyers and judges were all out on Broadway, marching gravely and attired in black; so were local politicians, veterans, merchants, diplomats, the students and faculty of Columbia—everybody, in short, except for Aaron Burr. It was a mark of just how much a part of the city's fabric he and General Hamilton were that, in ordinary times, the two men might have reasonably chosen from at least five different places to march in a city funeral procession: with the veterans, with the bar association members, with the bankers, with the civic associations, or among the pallbearers.

Now Hamilton had been torn from the city he'd helped rebuild, and the populace was in shock. They boiled with such anger at Burr that, as Gouverneur Morris gave the eulogy in Trinity Church, he feared setting off a riot—"their Indignation amounts almost to a frenzy already," he warned.

Where had it all gone so wrong for the vice president?

To Burr, the cause of his troubles remained none other than General Hamilton himself. "The last hours of Genl H (I might include the day preceding the interview) appear to have been devoted to Malevolence and hypocrisy," he wrote bitterly a few days after the funeral. In particular, the general had devoted the day before the duel to composing a lengthy farewell note. Carefully enumerated in the same neat hand as his court briefs, it explained that he disapproved of duels, and planned to "throw away my first fire" all along.

"I have thoughts even of reserving my second fire—and thus giving a double opportunity to Col. Burr to pause and reflect," he piously added.

Burr was flabbergasted: Hamilton had been in far more duels than he had, and it was Hamilton who had attacked Burr's reputation in the first place. For Hamilton to posthumously present himself as the victim beggared belief. Nor did Hamilton's throwing away his shot have the sanction of proper dueling. Yet General Hamilton had perfectly designed his letter, by sincere intent or calculated design, for the possibility of a loss—and to loft himself into sainthood. He now looked like a martyr, while Burr appeared to be a cold-blooded killer.

Outrage poured forth from newspapers and pamphlets, not least from William Coleman, who published the exchange of letters between Burr and Hamilton, decrying "the shocking catastrophe which deprived America of its most useful citizen." Dueling was certainly a subject Coleman knew well: Earlier that year, *he'd* killed

New York's harbormaster in the middle of a snowstorm, and then trudged back to the *Post* and "got the paper out in good style, though half an hour late." But now that dueling had claimed Hamilton as a victim, the editor was utterly grief-stricken—and like so many others, he found his opinion of dueling had been upended.

"Dueling," he approvingly quoted one newspaper, "is now looked upon with something like the detestation it deserves."

Instead of securing Burr's political future, his victory on the dueling field had turned the country against him. With a murder charge being mulled, the vice president fled the state, abandoning his mansion and all his possessions to his creditors. For days he kept off main roads and used a false name; what money he had in his pocket had been borrowed at the last moment.

At one time Aaron Burr had battled to defend New York's most notorious accused murderer. Now the notorious killer he'd have to defend was himself.

DECADES LATER, a popular tale arose about the Levi Weeks murder trial: that as his triumphant defense team left City Hall, they were accosted by Mrs. Ring. Shaking her fist, the boardinghouse mistress yelled at Hamilton, "If thee dies a natural death, I shall think there is no justice in heaven!"

The tale is balderdash, but it derives its mythical potency from a simple fact: Many people in the Weeks case *did* come to a bad end. Hamilton's bereaved family was, for a time, left nearly destitute by his chaotic personal finances. Burr, after serving the brief and awkward remainder of his term as vice president, became a stateless and bankrupt shadow of a man. It would be years before he dared to return to New York.

But if anything sealed the popular notion of the Quakeress's Curse, it was the strange fate reserved for the trial judge, John Lansing. Though he retired to take a respectable position as a university regent, his most lasting fame would come from the day he left a hotel room to post a letter, and then . . . vanished. Decades later, political kingmaker Thurlow Weed claimed he'd heard a confession about Lansing, but that he kept silent to avoid embarrassing the respectable descendants of the judge's assassin. If so, then Weed took the secret to the grave. Judge Lansing's disappearance remains unsolved to this day.

Some of the key witnesses in the Levi Weeks trial probably wished *they* could also disappear. Elias Ring, cursed with a infamous boardinghouse now associated with a murder and a rape, lost his home within a year of the trial. The upstart inventor who had once proposed an entire water system to Aaron Burr was now reduced to humbler quarters and work as a mechanic. Ring's name shows up in debtor and bankrupt notices for decades afterward, and the Friends finally ejected him in 1816 "for the continued intemperate use of intoxicating spirits." Set adrift, he moved his family to Mobile, Alabama, where he was swiftly mown down by yellow fever. His widow, Catharine, and sister-in-law Hope soon moved back to rural New York, far from the baleful reach of cities.

Their fellow accuser in the boardinghouse, Richard Croucher, proved more fortunate—at first. Though convicted of rape, he had been wise in his choice of Brockholst Livingston as his defense counsel. Less than three years into his life sentence, Croucher was granted a pardon from Governor Clinton, on the condition that he leave the country at once. It was the same conditional pardon that Livingston had secured for a previous client, the crazed Portuguese murderer John Pastano. Since Croucher had employed an insanity defense before in Britain, it was clearly a fine strategy for his lawyer to have pursued again.

And then—just as he had in London—Croucher escaped justice.

Instead of honoring his pardon agreement to emigrate, Croucher fled to Virginia. There, mingling among Richmond merchants, within months he had insinuated himself into the city's respectable society—and promptly robbed them. Soon Virginia bounty notices sought a "villain": "R. D. CROUCHER, about six feet high, very thin, sallow complexion, with grey hair, genteelly dressed but ill-looking large eyes and long nose."

After his arrest in Norfolk, it was said that Croucher returned to England. There, apparently, his luck ran out at last—and, one of Hamilton's sons later recalled, "he was executed for a heinous crime."

NOT EVERYONE succumbed to ill fortune. William Coleman, the court clerk and the great chronicler of the Levi Weeks trial, had been a brilliant choice by Hamilton to lead his new newspaper, the *New-York Evening Post*—Coleman would become, as one competitor put it, "the generalissimo of Federal editors"—and the *Post* has proven far more long-lived than the major general himself. In the decades that followed, Coleman championed such reforms as better municipal sanitation: He was the sworn enemy of pigs running free in the streets. His special editorial umbrage, though, was reserved for New Yorkers who bought lottery tickets. "The stranger that walks through this street," he wrote of Broadway, "might almost imagine that the city was one great lottery shop, and that one half of the citizens, at least, got their living by affording the opportunity of gambling to the rest."

Coleman's unlikely new friend from the trial, Ezra Weeks, also continued to prosper. He became one of the city's great hoteliers and developers, and his respectability was such that he served without incident on an 1806 jury where the defense counsel was none other than Cadwallader Colden. The hotelier was so clearly trustworthy that Colden did not use a peremptory dismissal on the man—even though it was Ezra who, just a few years earlier, had been key in destroying his case against Levi Weeks.

For despite the doomed Elma Sands case, and the hapless Federalist candidacy that followed, Cadwallader Colden's fate had hardly been sealed. He returned to private practice, even serving as a defense counsel to a man charged with aiding Alexander Hamilton at the duel—and he lost that case, too. But over time his reputation grew, and he steadily rose in the Federalist ranks to become mayor of New York in 1818. In his later years he was a tireless advocate for his best friend, the steamboat inventor Robert Fulton—and when not fulminating over canals and steam engines, Colden helped found the state's first formally chartered scientific society.

New York's elite could hardly keep from crossing paths, particularly in a grand intellectual enterprise such as a new scientific society. And, in fact, there were two other curiously familiar names among the founding officers of the Literary and Philosophical Society of New-York: Brockholst Livingston and David Hosack.

Having quietly worked on the Weeks case in the shadow of Hamilton and Burr, Livingston proved to have the most durable career by far. In time he rose to the state supreme court and, in 1807, earned an appointment by Thomas Jefferson to the U.S. Supreme Court, where he served as a justice until his death in 1823.

The career of Dr. David Hosack, the physician to Hamilton and Burr and one of the most prominent witnesses of the Weeks trial, was no less distinguished. Along with helping to found Bellevue Hospital and leading vaccination drives across the city, he joined Livingston as one of the eleven founding members of the New-York Historical Society. Their first meeting was in the Portrait Room of City Hall—and there, where years earlier the sequestered Weeks jurors had spent a restless night, the men who had witnessed history now began the great task of preserving it.


HISTORY, THOUGH, was something that Levi Weeks wished only to escape.

Even with the vindications of his trial and Croucher's conviction, the young carpenter never could settle easily into his adopted city. After a couple of years of living in his brother's home, he gave up and moved back to Deerfield, Massachusetts, to the inauspiciously named neighborhood of Bloody Brook. Here, at least, he lived among people who trusted him, though he had to leave his old carpentry trade to work in selling liquor and dry goods.

But like many a city dweller since, he found returning to his parents' home was not an easy burden to bear.

"Son," his pious father lamented, "I wish I knew whether *any* topics on religion are agreeable to you."

Levi was no longer cut out for sleepy rural western Massachusetts; he was restless. And, perhaps understandably with his history, he found himself still a bachelor as he approached his thirtieth birthday. For someone chafing against his home and his past, there was just one place to go. In 1805, he ended his dry goods partnership, packed his belongings, and struck out for the western frontier.

The Appalachians and the lands out to the Mississippi were still wild, barely settled lands. For a while he tarried in Cincinnati, and from there moved on to Kentucky, whose residents he did not care for—"they were brought up among slaves," he explained to a friend, "and their manners especially of the lower class is very disgusting." Soon he left yet again, pushing farther westward, all the while recording his travels in a diary that he had brought along.

Even this was not fated to last; as he forded a tributary of the Mississippi with his horse, Levi and his belongings went toppling into the water. He barely escaped with his life—and his diary vanished into the muddy waters. Disappearing into the hinterlands of the West, he truly was becoming a man without a past.

"Ultimately," his hometown chronicler in Massachusetts recorded in 1838, "he became a vagabond."

But that's not quite what happened.

# 20

# A Complicated Evil

For a man looking to start over again, it was hard to find anyplace farther away from Manhattan—in distance or in temperament—than the river city of Natchez, then the capital of the Mississippi Territory. It had been only a decade since the last Spanish garrison had left and ceded the port to the United States. Even as its citizens grew wealthy on a burgeoning flatboat traffic of cotton and sugar, the place still had the wild feel of a frontier outpost.

"Its vicinity is very uneven," Levi marveled in a letter to a friend back east. "You are constantly ascending and descending as you pass through in any direction. . . . The houses are extremely irregular and for the most part temporary things."

It was, in short, perfect for an aspiring architect looking to make his mark. Toppling with his supplies into the river had been nearly a disaster for Levi, but it had also been a kind of baptism: He'd lost his past, but kept the skills he'd honed back in New York as Ezra's trusted foreman. In a new city that had plenty of cash but few architects, he brought a trained eye for fashionable Georgian and Federalist neoclassical design—and he'd arrived at just the right time.

"The brick house I am now building is just without the city line, and is designed for the most magnificent building in the territory," he reported. "This is the first house in the territory on which was ever attempted any orders of architecture. The site is one of those peculiar situations which combines all the delights of romance—the pleasures of rurality and the approach of sublimity."

His client was a fellow Massachusetts native, Lyman Harding, a wealthy attorney whose presence in Natchez was invaluable to Levi. As it happened, Lyman was an old and trusted army friend of Aaron Burr's. He'd even served as Burr's defense counsel after some frontier adventurism saw Burr unsuccessfully tried in 1807 for treason after trying to foment a Mexican revolution. And like Levi, Harding had made his fortune after arriving penniless in Natchez; the two men, in short, were admirably matched.

Colonel Burr had saved Levi's life. Now his comrade would help him start a new one.

Harding's trust in Weeks was amply repaid. His new architect created all the comforts of a classic home for his client, with grand Ionic columns along the front of the house, topped by Corinthian entablature; inside, Weeks fashioned a dramatic black walnut helix staircase that spiraled up from the front entranceway toward the sleeping quarters. The mansion, dubbed Auburn, became the inspiration for other grand mansions in the region—and for Weeks, commissions for Natchez's new city hall and college building would follow.

Levi flourished in his new land: He married at long last, and in short order fathered four children. His buildings—and his many descendants—live on to this day.

"Colonel Burr has been here," Ezra wrote from New York to Levi Weeks in 1812, "and is at his old profession of the law."

It had taken nearly a decade for the former vice president to even dare setting foot again in Manhattan; the man behind one of the first recorded murder trials in the United States had by then gone through many personal trials himself. After narrowly escaping a murder charge in the East, and then a charge of treason in the West, he'd drifted through Europe until he eventually found himself nearly penniless in Paris.

Just a few years earlier Burr had risen to the vice presidency and had been the proud owner of one of Manhattan's grandest mansions; now he found himself living in a ten-by-ten rented room, desperately dodging petty debts to Parisian shopkeepers. He was in debt to the shoemaker who had patched his boots; he spent months evading an optician who wanted payment for a pair of spectacles.

"Had one sous left," Burr wrote in a typical journal entry for December 1810, "and took one pound cheese on credit."

His poverty, he knew, was positively dangerous. After he accidentally bumped a pane of glass with his umbrella one morning, Burr had the frightening premonition that he'd have been unable to pay had he broken it—and that "I must, infallibly, have been taken before a *commissaire de police.*"

His modest quarters, Burr drolly noted, did possess one virtue: "I can sit in my chair and reach every and anything that I possess." His low point came when, after pawning nearly everything, he finally landed work translating a book into French—only to discover that it was a volume containing "abuse and libels" about himself. He took the job all the same.

Burr did not find New York much more welcoming when he returned; one judge, recognizing the prodigal politician in the street, ran up to him and shouted: "You are a scoundrel, sir! A scoundrel!" Burr doggedly resumed practicing law nonetheless. He had to—for the aging vice president and hero of the Revolution found his requests for a military pension denied by a Congress that had still not forgiven him.

Burr would haunt New York's courts for the rest of his long life; one Manhattanite recalled a genteel old man, "very thin and straight, dressed in black, and his hair so profusely powdered that a superfluous portion adhered to his coat collar." He took on cases that other great lawyers would not tangle with, becoming one of America's first specialists in family law—for if some respectable men still scorned the infamous Aaron Burr, women desperately seeking help in divorce cases did not. And after he died at the age of eighty in 1836, it was a curious realization among his friends that they'd almost never heard him speak again of Alexander Hamilton.

But there was one tragedy that the old man had sometimes mused over: the death of Miss Elma Sands.

THE MANHATTAN Well mystery lived on in the public's mind as well. Within weeks of Croucher's rape trial in 1800, Charles Brockden Brown—a brilliant Gothic novelist and friend of William Coleman's—published a short story based on the case, "The Trials of Arden." In it, a tragic maiden is found strangled in a riverbank grotto, and her titular paramour is instantly suspected by a vengeful populace.

"A recent instance has occurred, in which this state of mind was felt by almost every person within the precincts of the city," Brown reminded his readers, before reflecting upon the destroyed reputation of the accused. "Of all men his lot was most disastrous, the most intolerable! Such a complicated evil! A mystery so impenetrable, so fatal to fame, peace and life of one who merited a better fate!"

To drive home the timeliness of his story, the same magazine that ran Brown's story also included reviews of both Coleman's trial transcript *and* the newly published transcript of Croucher's trial. Just as in the Weeks trial, Brown's central character of Arden is found innocent—to the fury of the crowds outside, who then riot and attack Arden and then even the jury itself. It is only later that Mayo, a Croucher-like figure, proves to be the true culprit—"Europe had been for a long time the theatre of his crimes," Brown hinted presciently, "but at length he withdrew to America, as to a new scene."

The Weeks case also attracted the pen of Philip Freneau, an old Princeton classmate of Burr's who had become America's preeminent epic poet. His poem "The Reward of Innocence"—which included a long introductory footnote on "Gulielma Sands—the unfortunate event alluded to in these lines"—went on to muse upon the Manhattan Well itself:

*Detested pit, may other times agree*
*With swelling mounds of earth to cover thee,*

*And hide the place, in whose obscure retreat*
*Some miscreant made his base design complete.*

Freneau soon got his wish: a few years later the city filled in and platted out Lispenard's Meadow, and the crime scene vanished beneath the orderly, soaring brick blocks of an unstoppably expanding city. The blocks once occupied by Ezra Weeks and Aaron Burr were bought by John Jacob Astor, and the waterworks that they'd created was itself passing into history. The Manhattan Company was turning into a full-fledged bank, just as Aaron Burr intended, with its old identity faintly evident in the middle name of a modern descendant: Chase Manhattan Bank.

But for decades the memory of the crime still lingered, not least among the Ring family. When the anonymous 1870 novel *Guilty, or Not Guilty: The True Story of the Manhattan Well* appeared in bookstores, its rather ordinary artistry concealed an extraordinary connection to the case: The author was Keturah Connah, the granddaughter of Mrs. Ring. The novel was virtually factual, she insisted, as it was "our story, or rather, *history*, for we chronicle most faithfully things that have been."

Connah took liberties nonetheless, not least by originating the popular story of Mrs. Ring's curse on Alexander Hamilton. Not surprisingly, her grandfather's adultery with Elma gets no mention; nor does the implication that Elma was a little fond of laudanum. Conveniently, in her account Levi is implicated in a melodramatic deathbed confession by an accomplice.

If parts of *Guilty, or Not Guilty* are fanciful, there is still something strikingly suggestive about the book. Unlike the court accounts and the newspapers of 1800, it describes the boardinghouse residents. Connah's preface reveals that her great-aunt—Elma's cousin Hope Sands, a witness in the trial—was *still alive* in 1870. Out of print for more than a century and hidden in obscurity, Connah's novel may be the closest we will ever get to an eyewitness description of the Rings, the Sands, and Levi Weeks.

In it, Mrs. Ring is fair and blue-eyed, with "an abundance of light auburn hair plainly arranged" under a lace cap. Hope Sands has short, dark hair, and a mischievous expression from "small, piercing, black eyes that sparkled with intelligence and fun." Levi's charms are even admitted, albeit a bit grudgingly.

"He was tall, and well formed—what the world would call good looking," Connah writes. "His hair was dark and long, worn, in the fashion of the day, tied in a cue. A casual observer would have said his eyes were black, the lashes were so long and dark, but a second glance showed them to be blue."

Her most striking description, though, is reserved for Elma herself. In Connah's account, we have a girl from upstate New York who arrives in the city to find herself behind others in her learning; her classmates dub her "the little mountain maid." Yet she proves a quick study, and despite her illness—"she had been always a delicate child, unable to perform her share of household duties"—she retains a passionate fondness for listening to the piano.

"The eyes were dark—dark as midnight—and soft, and sad," she writes of the doomed young woman, whose ringlets were "black, and the soft, glossy curls fell around the young face like a sable curtain."

However true or fictive such recollections were, Connah could give readers one absolutely solid empirical fact: Her family still remembered, decades after it had vanished beneath the vaulting tenements of the city, where the old well was located.

"Were you to ask me now to give you the exact location of this well," Connah wrote, "I should tell you to go to the corner of Spring and Greene Streets, and, being there, you might feel assured that you were in the immediate neighborhood, possibly upon the very spot where the waters of the Manhattan Well rose seventy years ago."

When it was published in 1870, though, this page of her novel contained a footnote—the only time, in fact, during the story itself that the author used one—because there had been a startling development.

"Since the above was written," she noted in amazement, "the exact location of the well has been discovered."

THE WELL is still there. It has *been* there all along—it becomes lost for a lifetime, found again, then lost for another lifetime still.

Its first rediscovery came just as Connah was finishing her novel. Under the headline "Old New-York," the *New York Times* for April 18, 1869, reported: "The old well, known as the Manhattan Well, down which was thrown the corpse of GULIELMA SANDS, murdered, as is believed, by her lover, LEVI WEEKS, some seventy years ago, and the locality of which had been forgotten, has been rediscovered."

The occupant of 129 Spring Street had been digging out a flower garden when they uncovered the infamous relic. "It is of large diameter," the reporter added, "and was covered over with large flat stones." And the location—behind a building on the corner of Spring and Greene Streets—was just where Connah's family had said it was.

New Yorkers had been going about their business in the spot for years without any inkling of its history. For a time the address had been that of a pawnbroker; after that, it had been a mail order depot for "O. Spotswood's Antidote for Tobacco," which promised relief from "the extreme nausea and disgust inflicted on many ladies by their male relatives and friends who persist in Chewing Tobacco." In its latest incarnation, the building was a German beer hall frequented by political radicals; it was there, carelessly walking over the maiden's infamous murder scene, that a Communist meeting elected Victorian firebrand Victoria Woodhull as a central council member.

Every few decades, a newspaper would recall the tragedy and visit the spot again; if they were in the mood for storytelling, like one *Brooklyn Daily Eagle* reporter, they'd also claim that "on the anniversary of her murder the Quaker girl rises from her tomb and goes wailing through the house." In 1889, another reporter was amused to note that the current occupant shared Levi's old profession, if not any concern over the supernatural: "a sturdy German carpenter works above the well where she was murdered and never thinks about it."

In 1957, the *Times'* top local reporter—Meyer Berger, a Pulitzer Prize winner—got the notion to go back again. He took a cab to "an untidy factory alley" one October evening and found a melancholy scene: "Winds stir sooty papers in it and high walls hem it in. In twilight it has a sinister, brooding air." With a dramatic flourish, he snatched up one of the discarded papers, fashioned it into a torch, and wandered down into the dark alley while the waiting cabbie asked what he was doing. "Just checking on a murder," Berger explained, "a girl was killed here."

And then it was forgotten again.

In 2010, the owner of the Manhattan Bistro set about excavating his basement at the corner of Spring and Greene to make more space for his wine bottles and other supplies. He unexpectedly struck an expanse of brick in the dirt—a wall where there wasn't supposed to be one. Only it wasn't a wall—the brick structure curved, back and back, and then around—it was a *well*.

He had, for the first time since 1799, uncovered the very depths of the murder scene. The well now stands as a crumbling brick column, casting its shadow over the widened restaurant basement— and the owners and employees like to trade stories about mysterious flying glasses, ghostly dropped bottles, and restaurant lights suddenly dimming.

But then, from the very day that Elma Sands's body was discovered, her murder has evoked an impulse to tell stories—even among those at the center of the case. In the years after the trial, it was said that Levi's defense counsel became fond of recalling how he'd dramatically held up a candle to the face of Richard David Croucher in the courtroom, revealing him to a shopkeeper as the man who had been spreading falsehoods about Levi. But in the retellings, his unmasking of Croucher became more damning, and the story kept getting grander:

"He used to say that he once saved a man from being hanged by a certain arrangement of candles in a court-room. As the trial proceeded, suspicions arose against the principal witness. . . . He set forth the facts which bore against the man, and then seizing two candelabras from the table, he held them up toward the witness, and exclaimed, *'Behold the murderer, gentlemen!'* "

The tale had a curious twist. When Hamilton's son recounted it, it was the late *major-general* who had held up the candelabras—but when Burr's biographer told the story, it was the *colonel* who had revealed the murderer.

Some rivalries, it seems, never will be settled.

# [ ACKNOWLEDGMENTS ]

THIS BOOK SIMPLY COULD NOT HAVE HAPPENED WITHOUT THE IN-spiration of my sons, Bramwell and Morgan, or without the love of my wife, Jennifer, who is the first reader of everything that I write.

Marc Thomas, as always, valiantly held down the fort while I was off poking around in musty ledgers. My many thanks also go to my agent, Michelle Tessler, and my editors, Rick Horgan and Nate Roberson—and a tip of the powdered wig to John Glusman for get-ting this project rolling.

I remain indebted to many librarians, particularly those at Port-land State University, the New-York Historical Society, the New York Public Library, the Library of Congress, and the University of Oregon. A special thanks as well to Sally Stanley of the Friends of the Sands Ring Homestead, and to Ted O'Reilly of the NYHS, who drew my attention to their wonderful 1798–1803 diary of Joshua Brookes.

Finally, I'd like to thank my predecessors in this subject. Be-cause much of this book derives from primary sources, later com-mentators on the case don't show up too often. But it was the work of Julius Goebel, Jr., Mildred McGehee, and Estelle Fox Kleiger that kept the memory of the case and its participants alive in the past fifty years, and their earlier studies were helpful in pointing me toward some of those original sources.

# [ Notes ]

While the competing trial accounts of David Longworth, James Hardie, and William Coleman were crucial for this book's exploration of the death of Elma Sands, my portrayal of life in New York frequently draws upon the newspapers of the era. They are abbreviated in the notes as follows:

*New-York American Citizen (NYAC)*
*New-York Commercial Advertiser (NYCA)*
*New-York Daily Advertiser (NYDA)*
*Greenleaf's [New-York Journal; New Daily Advertiser] (GNDA)*
*New-York Mercantile Advertiser (NYMA)*
*New-York Evening Post (NYEP)*
*New-York Gazette (NYG)*
*New-York Spectator (NYS)*
*New-York Weekly Museum (NYWM)*

## 1. The Great Sickness

7 **Giant lobster claws:** "Journal of Joshua Brookes," 555.

7 **Gilbert Stuart's grand oil portrait:** *NYDA*, 22 February 1798.

7 **two shillings to view:** *American Minerva* (New York, N.Y.), 26 July 1796.

7 **Baker's splendid Electrical Machines:** *Diary; or, Loudon's Register* (New York, N.Y.), 8 May 1797.

7 **"a TRANSPARENT MONUMENT":** Ibid., 31 October 1793.

8 **Greenwich Street:** *NYCA*, 23 July 1799.

8 **a menagerie:** *Diary; or, Loudon's Register* (New York, N.Y.), 8 May 1797.

8 **wax figures:** *American Minerva* (New York, N.Y.), 26 February 1796.

8 ***Musical Concert Clock is for sale:*** *NYCA*, 23 July 1799.

8 **signs hung along the streets:** Morhouse, "Boy's Reminiscences," 344.

9 **William Maxwell's, Distiller:** *NYDA*, 14 January 1795.

9 **next shop over for some godless tract:** *NYMA*, 19 March 1803.

9  gunsmith Joseph Finch: *NYEP*, 10 December 1803.

9  tinsmith Tom Eagles: *Public Advertiser*, 20 April 1808.

9  involving the *boiling* of coffee: Ukers, *All About Coffee*, 699.

9  Ben Franklin claimed you could spot visiting New Yorkers: Monaghan and Lowenthal, *This Was New York*, 30.

9  with elevated first stories and stoops: Blackmar, *Manhattan for Rent*, 47.

9  "two lean men to walk abreast": Stone, *History of New York City*, 187.

10  "totally stripped of trees": Koeppel, *Water for Gotham*, 50.

10  shining brass pumps installed along the thoroughfare: Ibid., 34.

10  nearly caused local wells to run dry: Ibid., 50.

10  "The water is very bad to drink": Quoted in ibid., 55.

10  more free-spirited cousin Elma: William Coleman, *Report of the Trial of Levi Weeks*, 33.

11  tried for three nights to pull down a local brothel: *NYG*, 18 July 1799.

11  "We understand (for we resort to no such place)": Ibid.

11  thousand rioters . . . called out a regiment of mounted troops: *NYWM*, 20 July 1799.

11  "The plea is, the necessity of *correcting* abuses": *NYG*, 19 July 1799.

12  "BRANDY Exchanged for PORK": *NYDA*, 10 July 1799.

12  "a Negro MAN, named Henry": *NYS*, 3 July 1799.

12  "A letter received in town yesterday": Ibid., 6 July 1799.

12  along the Atlantic seaboard for nearly a century: Janvier, *In Old New York*, 143.

13  "Those periods, in general, have been most distinguished": Webster, *Brief History of Epidemic and Pestilential Diseases* 2:15.

13  "vessels from one of the sickly ports": Hardie, *Account of the Yellow Fever*, 8.

13  blamed on a load of rotten coffee: Powell, *Bring Out Your Dead*, 17.

13  "exhalations from the ground": Hardie, *Account of the Yellow Fever*, 8.

13  Hosack later estimated that fully one-twelfth of Manhattan's: Koeppel, *Water for Gotham*, 121.

13  "an almost innumerable number": Arnebeck, "Yellow Fever in New York City."

13  "in all the streets where buildings": Ibid.

14  "The late rains in the city": Powell, *Bring Out Your Dead*, 23.

14  "Idle tales . . . A false report": *NYS*, 13 July 1799.

14  Philadelphia had misled other cities: Arnebeck, "Yellow Fever in New York City."

15 In the dock at that moment: *NYMA*, 13 July 1799.

15 Philadelphia's board of health: *NYCA*, 17 July 1799.

15 Bleecker, would be one of the first to find out: Bleecker, Diary, 26 July 1799.

15 "they void and vomit blood": Powell, *Bring Out Your Dead*, 13.

15 the fever's stigmata: Ibid., 27.

15 "by no means alarming": *NYMA*, 18 July 1799.

15 now in Providence: *GNDA*, 24 July 1799.

15 in Newburyport: *NYG*, 29 July 1799.

16 in Philadelphia: *NYDA*, 30 July 1799.

16 was dead from yellow fever: Bleecker, Diary, 23 August 1799.

## 2. A BOARDINGHOUSE BY CANDLELIGHT

17 By September 11, 1799: Laight, Diaries, September 1799 entries.

17 "Rumor of Yellow Fever": Ibid., 3 July 1799.

17 "Dog days begin": Ibid., 29 July 1799.

17 "A shower in the night": Ibid., 10 August 1799.

17 "Oh, oh!": Ibid., 11 September 1799.

17 "near 1/3 of the inhabitants": Ibid., 27 August 1799.

17 "Autumn Residences" of those "removed for the sickly season": *NYG*, 14 September 1799.

17 "As soon as this dreadful scourge": Janvier, *In Old New York*, 140.

18 firing off muskets and cannons: Powell, *Bring Out Your Dead*, 51.

18 kill a little girl: Bleecker, Diary, 24 September 1799.

18 Lee's True and Genuine Bilious Pills: *NYMA*, 30 July 1799.

18 Four Herb Pills: *NYWM*, 10 July 1799, 4.

18 New York Anti-Bilious Pills: *NYCA*, 16 September 1799.

18 Laight had closely allied: Bank of the Manhattan Company, *Act of Incorporation of the Manhattan Company*, 7.

19 landlady hadn't stayed around: Hardie, *Impartial Account of the Trial*, 11.

19 flour mill he'd tried: *GNDA*, 19 February 1794.

19 a mechanic and an inventor: *Aurora General Advertiser* (Philadelphia), 23 February 1798.

19 running a general store: *Longworth's American Almanack* (1798), n.p.

19 running a millinery: Kleiger, *Trial of Levi Weeks*, 2.

20 apprentice, William Anderson: William Coleman, *Report of the Trial of Levi Weeks*, 46.

20 recently immigrated English merchant: Ibid., 43.

20 **Dapper and beginning to gray:** *Alexandria (Va.) Expositor*, 22 July 1803.

20 **as he approached the age of forty:** *Philadelphia Gazette*, 10 July 1800.

20 **his tall and thin form:** *Alexandria (Va.) Expositor*, 22 July 1803.

20 **another boarder, named Margaret Clark:** William Coleman, *Report of the Trial of Levi Weeks*, 19.

20 **a *roomer* but not a *boarder*:** Ibid., 43.

20 **Humbert's bread and Aunt Roach's pies:** Morhouse, "Boy's Reminiscences," 337.

20 **stall placarded JEW'S MEAT:** Ibid., 336.

21 **Girls went barefoot:** "Journal of Joshua Brookes," 579.

21 **"Our streets are filled with straggling fellows":** *NYDA*, 19 September 1799.

21 **found his Pearl Street shop broken into:** Ibid., 17 September 1799.

21 **Flood and Tracey grocery shop was raided:** *NYG*, 19 September 1799.

21 **thieves robbing him of fifty vests:** *NYMA*, 3 October 1799.

21 **208 Greenwich:** Kleiger, *Trial of Levi Weeks*, 1. Although court transcripts note that the boardinghouse was on Greenwich, Kleiger appears to be the first to specify the address, noting that there is a listing for Elias Ring at 208 Greenwich in the 1798 *Longworth's American Almanack*. I note that the presumably adjoining address 209 Greenwich is also given by Ring in his waterwheel ads from 1799.

   The address would place them at or near the corner of Greenwich and Barclay Streets; that this was also the location of the boardinghouse, and not just Ring's business, can be confirmed from the testimony of Margaret Miller in the trial transcript of Richard David Croucher (5). She testifies that the Ring boardinghouse was "almost by Rhinelander's brew house." Advertisements by Rhinelander from this period (for example, *Albany Gazette*, 23 January 1800) specify it as "at the corner of Barclay and Greenwich Streets."

22 **Elias Ring wrote to his wife:** Hardie, *Impartial Account of the Trial* 11.

22 **"Cassie, our neighbor":** Laight, Diaries, 27 September 1799.

22 **laborer . . . and a cart driver:** *NYDA*, 4 October 1799.

22 **tenant died at a boardinghouse:** *NYCA*, 7 October 1799.

22 **"In this pestilential period":** *GNDA*, 1 August 1799.

22 **Hosack confidently presented a sweating cure:** Sherk, "David Hosack, M.D., and Rutgers," 20.

22 **"draw off the noxious electrical fluid":** Young, *Toadstool Millionaires*, 25.

22 **"Having obtained from various experiments":** *NYCA*, 30 July 1799.

23 **"To pour buckets of cold water":** Ibid., 18 October 1799.

23 "First frost": Laight, Diaries, 18 October 1799.

23 "General movement back": Ibid., 26 October 1799.

23 An abandoned flock of sheep: *NYDA*, 23 October 1799.

23 two cannons were simply dropped: *NYG*, 26 October 1799.

23 PEACHES, PLUMBS, GREEN GAGES: *NYCA*, 9 October 1799.

23 English and geography: Ibid., 21 October 1799.

23 gouging dying families: Koeppel, *Water for Gotham*, 63.

23 speculators were now buying up local supplies of wood: *NYMA*, 2 October 1799.

24 "I should not be afraid to drink it full": William Coleman, *Report of the Trial of Levi Weeks*, 32.

24 their peculiar love of Halloween . . . in the graveyard: "Journal of Joshua Brookes," 31 October 1801.

## 3. THE YOUNG QUAKER

25 "But a few days ago our city": *NYMA*, 6 November 1799.

25 "I therefore humbly hint": Ibid.

26 Tea-Water Men: Koeppel, *Water for Gotham*, 32.

26 "They pretend their water is pure": Ibid., 64.

26 a plan to pipe Manhattan: Ibid., 39.

26 "Had I been brought up a hatter": Ibid., 36.

26 calls for a solution had grown louder: Ibid., 59.

26 "The health of a city": Ibid., 65.

27 received five proposal bids: *Report of the Manhattan Company*, 9.

27 operating a mill upstate: *GNDA*, 19 February 1794.

27 run an ad in Philadelphia and New York newspapers: e.g., *Aurora General Advertiser* (Philadelphia), 23 February 1798; and *GNDA*, 6 December 1799.

28 "The Collect has been unjustly stigmatized": *Report of the Manhattan Company*, 29.

28 the pleasingly round sum: Ibid., 36.

28 same rounds were the milk merchants: Morhouse, "Boy's Reminiscences," 343.

28 stank of Long Island meadow garlic: Monaghan and Lowenthal, *This Was New York*, 22.

28 off-putting about his sales manner: William Coleman, *Report of the Trial of Levi Weeks*, 82.

28 *accompany me to my brother's*: Ibid., 38.

29 on the corner of Greenwich and Harrison: *Longworth's American Almanack* (1799), 389.

29  "Why don't you ask me?": William Coleman, *Report of the Trial of Levi Weeks*, 38.

29  Levi still took pains to attend to her: Ibid., 21.

29  "turtle feast": Janvier, *In Old New York*, 219.

30  "when one man offered to present": Dietz, *1913*, 120.

30  Minetta Brook . . . fine trout to be had from it: Mines, *Tour Around New York*, 22.

30  Ezra Weeks had the contract: William Coleman, *Report of the Trial of Levi Weeks*, 87.

30  white and yellow pine logs needed: *NYMA*, 18 May 1799.

30  "People are paying the enormous fee": *NYDA*, 23 November 1799.

31  *Do you want to go to the Charity Sermon?*: William Coleman, *Report of the Trial of Levi Weeks*, 24.

31  sermon by the Bishop Prevoost . . . on December 8, 1799: *NYDA*, 9 December 1799.

31  They stopped off first at Ezra's: William Coleman, *Report of the Trial of Levi Weeks*, 34.

31  THE YOUNG QUAKER . . . THE AGREEABLE SURPRISE: *NYMA*, 30 November 1799.

31  bone-chilling lack of heat and its rather makeshift orchestra: Monaghan and Lowenthal, *This Was New York*, 125.

32  he'd asked her to come, too: William Coleman, *Report of the Trial of Levi Weeks*, 34.

32  carpenter had fallen off a scaffold: *NYCA*, 16 November 1799.

32  live wolves . . . had broken out: *NYG*, 19 November 1799.

32  Thanksgiving, in gratitude to God: Ibid., 29 November 1799.

32  $138 had been collected: *NYDA*, 9 December 1799.

32  the first snow of the year: Bleecker, Diary, December 1, 4, and 5, 1799.

32  pelting of the house at Garden and Broad: "The Olden Time," 424.

32  sleigh rides northward . . . the Kissing Bridge: Janvier, *In Old New York*, 252.

32  on moonlit nights like this, the city saved: Monaghan and Lowenthal, *This Was New York*, 246–47.

33  three and a half feet underground, of piped water: *Independent Gazetteer* (Worcester, Mass.), 7 October 1800.

33  "NOTWITHSTANDING THE INTERVENTION OF A MALIGNANT FEVER": *NYMA*, 13 November 1799.

33  "the wish of every citizen": *NYG*, 20 November 1799.

33  "of a quality excellent": *NYMA*, 13 November 1799.

33  service was to be expanded another twofold: *Independent Gazetteer* (Worcester, Mass.), 7 October 1800.

34 **a primitive pump supplied by one Nicholas Roosevelt:** Ibid.

34 **he'd sold Roosevelt thousands of acres:** Lamb, *History of the City of New York*, 3:382.

34 **$1,500-a-year position of water superintendent:** *NYMA*, 13 June 1799.

34 **business partner from years earlier:** *NYDA*, 26 July 1793.

34 **brother-in-law of the board's president:** Koeppel, *Water for Gotham*, 69.

34 **ad . . . had quietly been withdrawn:** I do not find any further publication of the ad after the 6 December 1799 issue of *Greenleaf's New-York Journal*.

## 4. The Black Veil

35 **sodden city:** Bleecker, Diary, 19 December 1799.

35 *"This is a day of mourning to us":* *NYDA*, 19 December 1799.

35 **"He made his exit last night":** *NYCA*, 20 December 1799.

36 **Shaw had a busy wine shop:** *NYG*, 27 May 1799.

36 **"It is a pity General Washington had not died":** Bleecker, Diary, 27 December 1799; and Abraham Bancker to Abraham B. Bancker, 12 January 1800, Bancker Papers.

36 **British flag over the Merchants':** *Columbia Museum and Savannah Advisor*, 11 April 1797.

36 **"WASHINGTON was our pride":** *NYDA*, 19 December 1799.

37 **A NEGRO MAN TO BE SOLD CHEAP:** *NYG*, 24 December 1799.

37 **"It's a damned lie!":** Abraham Bancker to Abraham B. Bancker, 12 January 1800, Bancker Papers.

37 **"What means this melancholy sound of Bells":** *NYCA*, 24 December 1799.

38 **he trooped over to his brother's:** Hardie, *Impartial Account of the Trial*, 12.

38 **Ezra Weeks himself hadn't:** William Coleman, *Report of the Trial of Levi Weeks*, 86.

38 **growing business on Broadway:** *NYDA*, 21 May 1799.

38 **a new two-story home:** *NYEP*, 16 December 1803.

38 **an order for eight doors:** William Coleman, *Report of the Trial of Levi Weeks*, 86.

38 **a gash in his knee:** Ibid., 21.

38 **"Levi, you won't be able to go out":** Ibid., 22.

38 **followed him upstairs and plastered his knee:** Ibid.

38 **boardinghouse beds:** Watson, *Annals and Occurrences of New York City and State*, 260.

38 **he and Elma were back downstairs:** William Coleman, *Report of the Trial of Levi Weeks*, 22.

38 **The theater had even canceled:** *NYCA*, 21 December 1799.

39 **"Which looks best?":** William Coleman, *Report of the Trial of Levi Weeks*, 22.

39 **calico gown and a white dimity petticoat:** Ibid., 56–57.

39 **"Where's Elma?":** Ibid., 22.

39 **their cockeyed door:** Ibid., 24.

39 **Elias settled into the commons room:** Ibid., 22.

39 **"The clock has just struck eight":** Ibid., 23.

40 **Mrs. Ring . . . put her ear to the door:** Ibid., 24.

40 **Levi's apprentice . . . was locked out:** Ibid., 26. The remainder of this evening's scene is drawn from this passage of Coleman's trial transcript.

41 **a cold and cloudy sky:** Bleecker, Diary, 23 December 1799.

41 **expect bread, cheese, preserved apples:** Maude, *Visit to the Falls of Niagara in 1800*, 29.

41 **warm beer remained the drink:** Koeppel, *Water for Gotham*, 34.

41 **"Is Elma got home?":** William Coleman, *Report of the Trial of Levi Weeks*, 27.

41 **Clement, up by Lispenard's Meadow:** *Longworth's American Almanack* (1799), 189.

42 **"I guess she has gone to be married":** William Coleman, *Report of the Trial of Levi Weeks*, 29.

42 **Gideon Washburn got caught in sin with his horse:** *NYG*, 25 September 1799.

42 **guides such as *Aristotle's Master-Piece*:** Bullough, "Early American Sex Manual," 240.

42 **attributed on the title page to "The Company of Flying Stationers":** *Aristotle's Master-Piece*, title page.

42 **"the action of the clytoris in women":** Ibid., 58.

42 **"brifk and vigorous . . . glafs of rofy wine":** Ibid., 62.

42 **"Married or not":** William Coleman, *Report of the Trial of Levi Weeks*, 29. The remainder of this section is drawn from this passage in Coleman's trial transcript.

43 **"Twelve Silver tea SPOONS":** *NYDA*, 24 December 1799.

43 **Female Humane Society:** Ibid., 11 December 1799.

43 **Breakfast passed uneasily:** William Coleman, *Report of the Trial of Levi Weeks*, 29.

43 **"Mrs. Ring, don't grieve so":** Ibid., 30.

44 **German settlers down in Pennsylvania made much:** "Christmas in America," 171.

44 "passionless immoveable countenance": Stone, *History of New York City*, 205.

44 "A green Christmas makes a fat Church-yard": *NYDA*, 29 December 1800.

44 tradition of slogging out into the swamps: Watson, *Annals and Occurrences of New York City and State*, 123.

44 shooting on the wing, and had started a new fashion: Ibid., 211.

45 city had tried . . . to end these hunts: "Journal of Joshua Brookes," January 1799.

45 she wore a . . . muff: Bleecker, Diary, 4 January 1800.

## 5. THE MYSTERY IN THE MEADOW

46 strolls up Greenwich Street: Hardie, *Impartial Account of the Trial*, 28.

46 warden of the port: *Minutes of the Common Council of the City of New York*, 3:676.

46 *Have you heard of a muff turning up anywhere?*: William Coleman, *Report of the Trial of Levi Weeks*, 75.

46 coming into port from New Orleans and . . . St. Thomas: *NYDA*, 7 January 1800.

46 "It's an *odd* question": William Coleman, *Report of the Trial of Levi Weeks*, 75.

46 Ring's high-pitched voice: Ibid., 74.

46 "A young woman": Ibid., 75.

47 workers by Norton's Wharf found a despairing man: *NYCA*, 19 September 1799.

47 gentleman who had recently stood in Bowery Lane and applied a pair of pistols: Ibid., 18 October 1799.

47 "The nearest dock": William Coleman, *Report of the Trial of Levi Weeks*, 89.

47 down their cross street of Barclay: *NYG*, 26 May 1801.

47 "Rhinelander's Battery": William Coleman, *Report of the Trial of Levi Weeks*, 89.

47 trained as a cooper: *Collections of the New-York Historical Society for the Year 1885*, 222. He is listed as a cooper under "Freeman, 1769."

47 appointed office of Culler of staves and hoops: Law, *New York Directory*, 52.

47 ready to man the local fire pumps: New York Common Council, *Manual of the Corporation of the City of New York*, 797.

48 many sailors scarcely knew a single stroke: "Fatal Accidents: How Far Preventable," 109.

**48 Ice was forming in the river:** Laight, Diaries, 9 January 1800.

**48 the decrepit old fortifications:** *Balance and Columbian Depository*, 5 February 1805, 47. The article notes that the state legislature authorized tearing down Rhinelander's Battery for winter firewood for the city's poor.

**48 a "creeper," a line dragging a claw:** Burney, *New Universal Dictionary of the Marine*, 111.

**48 a long tube with a glass bulb . . . recovery men were hired by smugglers:** "Seal Stalking in the Orkneys," 585.

**48 "Levi . . . give me thy firm opinion":** William Coleman, *Report of the Trial of Levi Weeks*, 31–32.

**49 sixteen rifles, marking the dawn of New Year's Eve:** Washington, *Washington's Political Legacies*, 169.

**49 businesses were closing . . . and carriages had been barred:** *NYG*, 30 December 1799.

**49 "Hope" . . . "Will you accompany me":** William Coleman, *Report of the Trial of Levi Weeks*, 37.

**49 As ten o'clock approached:** *NYWM*, 4 January 1800. This is a particularly long and detailed account of the processions; except where indicated, the details in the remainder of this section are taken from this source.

**49 woodcut diagrams of the positions of Washington's pallbearers:** *NYCA*, 26 December 1799.

**50 "this great national calamity":** Washington, *Washington's Political Legacies*, 168.

**50 "our late brother mechanic":** *Meyer Berger's New York*, 154.

**51 girls dressed in white robes . . . dropping laurel leaves:** "The Olden Time," 433.

**52 *"Bring the laurels"*:** *Sacred Music*.

**52 "Its appearance was really splendid":** Abraham Bancker to Abraham B. Bancker, 12 January 1800, Bancker Papers.

**52 confectioner's shop on Pine Street:** Stone, *History of New York City*, 207. Along with his account of Singeron, Stone has some fascinating vignettes of refugees from the French Revolution—most notably of a hairdresser dubbed Adonis. Like the rest of New York's enclave of fine Parisian dressmakers and dancing masters, he'd fled the country along with his noble clientele during the Revolution. Adonis made house calls, but he had one curious trait: He never wore a hat. He'd resolved to never wear one again until France's king was back on the throne, so he always carried his hat like a purse, with his shears and combs poking out of it (ibid., 221).

**52 plum cake, rich with candied oranges:** Hudson and Donat, *New Practice of Cookery*, 226.

53  frosting unaccountably patterned into Cupids: Stone, *History of New York City*, 209.

53  "Some think it is the first year": Bleecker, Diary, 1 January 1800.

53  Greenwood had advertised himself as "Dentist to the Late President": *NYMA*, 9 December 1799.

53  a portrait of Washington (guaranteed to "afford peculiar satisfaction"): *NYCA*, 28 December 1799.

53  Washington's *urn* ("executed by the original designer"): Ibid., 2 January 1800.

53  debut of "the Washington Minuet": *NYWM*, 11 January 1800.

53  in Mayor Varick's house . . . "they broke the first cookie": Thorburn, *Fifty Years' Reminiscences of New-York*, 208.

53  laid out the riches of the city: "Journal of Joshua Brookes," 556.

53  oysters: Fawcett, "New Year's Day in Old New-York," 137.

53  pickled in white wine: Hudson and Donat, *New Practice of Cookery*, 39.

53  cold jellied lamb, plates of macaroons: Fawcett, "New Year's Day in Old New-York," 137.

53  "Before the moon sunk behind the blue hills": Thorburn, *Fifty Years' Reminiscences of New-York*, 208.

54  Mrs. Blanck heard the curiously offhanded piece of news . . . reached among her winter clothing: Bleecker, Diary, 4 January 1800.

54  Ring and his neighbor Joseph Watkins marched up: William Coleman, *Report of the Trial of Levi Weeks*, 56.

54  Blanck's house on the Bowery: *Longworth's American Almanack* (1800), 138.

54  lunch with James Lent and a fellow named Page: Coleman, *Report of the Trial of Levi Weeks*, 56.

54  a horse . . . had been stolen nearby: *NYS*, 18 September 1799.

54  an ownerless steer had just turned up: *NYDA*, 6 January 1800.

54  *The well*: William Coleman, *Report of the Trial of Levi Weeks*, 53.

54  about midway between Broadway and Bowery: Morhouse, "Boy's Reminiscences," 339.

54  hadn't been found suitable for the pipeline: *GNDA*, 6 January 1800. Most subsequent accounts seem to have assumed that it was a working well for the Manhattan Company, but its disuse is also noted in Stone, *History of New York City*, 342f.

54  William had found the muff . . . and had brought it home: Bleecker, Diary, 4 January 1800.

55  "I went to the well the next day": William Coleman, *Report of the Trial of Levi Weeks*, 53.

55  water . . . nearly six feet in depth: Ibid., 91.

55 swept it gently through the water, then suddenly stopped: Ibid., 56.
55 Lent tried it as well . . . there was a mass deep in the water: Ibid.
55 ironmonger banged irons into the wooden poles: Ibid.
55 too heavy . . . a flash of calico cloth: Ibid.
55 hemp were hurriedly procured: Ibid.
55 now joined in—Lawrence Myer: Hardie, *Impartial Account of the Trial*, 19.
55 a fellow teamster: *Longworth's American Almanack* (1799), 305.
55 rigged into a makeshift net: William Coleman, *Report of the Trial of Levi Weeks*, 56.

## 6. Some Person or Persons as Yet Unknown

59 *Levi Weeks is to blame*: William Coleman, *Report of the Trial of Levi Weeks*, 82.
59 Policing largely existed to guard property: Oliver, "Modern History of Probable Cause," 3.
59 Leatherheads: Costello, *Our Police Protectors*, 72.
59 tipping the boxes over: Ibid., 73.
59 generally had only two constables apiece: Ibid.
59 Constables were not to investigate: Oliver, "Modern History of Probable Cause," 9.
60 "Is *this* the young man?": William Coleman, *Report of the Trial of Levi Weeks*, 58.
60 "It is very hard to accuse—": Ibid., and *GNDA*, 6 January 1800.
60 front of the gathering crowd: William Coleman, *Report of the Trial of Levi Weeks*, 59.
60 "like a person walking against the wind": Ibid., 57.
61 "I think I know the gown": Ibid., 59.
61 auctioneer Jimmy Smith: *NYDA*, 31 December 1799. The advertisement includes details for the auctions scheduled for Thursday, January 2, 1800.
61 building of gray stone . . . by Theophilus Hardenbrook: *Fifteenth Annual Report, 1910*, 394.
61 neglected to provide an open yard . . . they'd even been given a bell: Stone, *History of New York City*, 191. After Bridewell was demolished, this bell was moved to a firehouse on Beaver Street, where—after ringing out a final warning—it was destroyed in the great city fire of 1845.
62 central tower: Dwight, *Travels in New-England and New-York*, 455.
62 the jail keeper, Alexander Lamb: *Longworth's American Almanack* (1800), 252.

62 **flanked on either side:** Dwight, *Travels in New-England and New-York*, 455.

62 **Bib and Gilbert:** *NYDA*, 10 December 1799.

62 **petty larceny . . . less than $12.50 in goods:** Dwight, *Travels in New-England and New-York*, 455.

62 **newly captured runaway slaves and apprentices:** *NYMA*, 8 February 1800.

62 **son of an upstanding Massachusetts family:** Diamond, *Episode in American Journalism*, 34.

63 **a "disgrace to humanity":** Tiedemann and Fingerhut, *Other New York*, 75.

63 **issued . . . *The Rights of Animals*:** Pelletreau, *History of Long Island*, 2:512.

63 **Burr shrewdly recruited him:** Diamond, *Episode in American Journalism*, 51.

63 **and it paid a mere eight dollars a week:** Ibid., 52.

63 **"An effort was recently made to suppress the AURORA":** Quoted in ibid., 53.

63 **Federalists *had* tried to shut down the *Aurora*:** Blumberg, *Repressive Jurisprudence in the Early American Republic*, 115.

63 **"a vile sans-culotte":** Diamond, *Episode in American Journalism*, 77.

63 **"I have long been the object of the most malignant calumnies":** Wharton, *State Trials*, 650.

64 **Greenleaf, claimed to have no authority:** Diamond, *Episode in American Journalism*, 54.

64 **"This is not a question that concerned the liberties":** *NYG*, 5 December 1799.

64 **confined for so long that nobody even knew why . . . "Paul from New Jersey":** Eddy, *Report of a Committee of the Humane Society*, 12–13. This report, issued in 1810, notes that "Paul from New Jersey" had been in Bridewell for at least a decade at that point, as a jail keeper hired ten years earlier found that even back then nobody knew why "Paul" was there.

64 **An inmate's supper . . . about five or six cents:** Stoutenburgh, *Report of the Inspectors of the State-Prison*, 4.

65 **"a mean, insipid, and musty drink":** Moulton, Sampson, and Fernald, *Centennial History of Harrison, Maine*, 457.

65 **Stagg was spotted near a polling station:** *NYCA*, 3 May 1799.

65 **"French Bullies":** Ibid.

65 **he'd been heroically pulling it *out* of the prisoner's hands:** *NYS*, 15 May 1799.

65 **Michaels did not last:** He is not listed with Alexander Lamb in the 1800 *Longworth's American Almanack.*

65 **Michaels crowed that the fellow was a deserter:** *NYS*, 15 May 1799.

66 **Prince . . . saw his colleague:** Hardie, *Impartial Account of the Trial*, 29.

66 **Charles Dickinson, the local coroner:** *NYDA*, 4 November 1799.

66 **meant a "representative of the crown":** Rapalje and Lawrence, *Dictionary of American and English Law*, 1:297.

66 **such unhelpful causes of death as "horseshoe head":** Paris and Fonblanque, *Medical Jurisprudence*, 1:145.

66 **a leader among Aaron Burr's faction:** Myers, *History of Tammany Hall*, 41.

66 **Born to a pauper family in the Bridewell almshouse:** Nolosco, *Physician Heal Thyself*, 170.

66 **they paid for his medical education:** Mohl, *Poverty in New York*, 97.

66 **a tamed deer had sprung free from its pen:** *NYCA*, 23 November 1799.

67 **a coroner's jury sat waiting for them:** William Coleman, *Report of the Trial of Levi Weeks*, 77.

67 *Is her neck broken?*: Ibid.

67 **rumors had been circulating:** *GNDA*, 6 January 1800, 3.

67 *Is she with child?*: William Coleman, *Report of the Trial of Levi Weeks*, 77.

67 **first two books in English on the subject:** Davis, "George Edward Male M.D.," 117.

67 **"It is murder in fact":** Bartley, *Treatise on Forensic Medicine*, 2.

67 **tansy wafting over the room as the corpses were opened up:** For example, Wharton and Stillé, *Treatise on Medical Jurisprudence*, 526.

68 **believing that a rape could not produce a child:** Farr, *Elements of Medical Jurisprudence*, 46.

68 **pointedly disagreed with this notion:** Paris and Fonblanque, *Medical Jurisprudence*, 1:437.

68 **signs of virginity that their texts relied upon:** Ibid., 1:417.

68 **"A report prevailed injurious to her honor":** *GNDA*, 16 January 1800.

68 **"A verdict of WILFUL MURDER":** *NYCA*, 6 January 1800.

## 7. The Glooms of Conscious Night

69 HORRID MURDER!: *Independent Gazetteer* (Worcester, Mass.), 26 January 1800.

69 **"She was that evening to be privately married":** *Claypoole's American Daily Advertiser* (Philadelphia), 8 January 1800.

70 **"The city"** . . . **"is much agitated":** Abraham Bancker to Abraham B. Bancker, 12 January 1800.

70 *"Could beauty, virtue, innocence, and love":* Freneau, "The Reward of Innocence" in *Collection of Poems, on American Affairs, and a Variety of Other Subjects,* 1:113.

70 **gazed at the cold and ashen features:** Hardie, *Impartial Account of the Trial,* 19.

70 **offices at 47 Wall Street:** *Longworth's American Almanack* (1800), 191.

70 **building had served as a coffee merchant:** *NYDA,* 9 May 1796.

70 **a shop selling hogsheads of rum and porter:** *NYG,* 26 November 1799.

71 **Bleecker** . . . **opening a stockbroker office:** *NYDA,* 10 February 1800.

71 **local Tammany Society** . . . **"Is there implanted in the human breast":** "Records of Tammany Go to Public Library," *New York Times,* 25 September 1927.

71 **set up a few years earlier:** *Diary; or, Loudon's Register* (New York, N.Y.), 3 March 1797.

71 **young Cadwallader got the nod:** *Albany Gazette,* 19 January 1798.

71 **counterfeit ten-dollar notes:** *NYMA,* 12 July 1799.

71 **five-dollar bills altered to look like twenties:** *NYCA,* 25 November 1799.

71 **shoplifting duo had been hitting fabric merchants:** Ibid., 2 November 1799.

72 **incorrigible pair known as Rap and Baker:** *NYG,* 14 November 1799.

72 **Jacob Weiser** . . . **"a monster in human form":** *NYDA,* 20 September 1799.

72 **"the damn'd villain guilty of the theft":** *NYCA,* 1 November 1799.

72 **advertise a reward for over $1,200 worth of stock certificates:** *NYG,* 1 November 1799.

72 **immense crowd that filled the court and the street:** Ibid., 25 November 1799. The *Gazette* had by far the most extensive account of John Pastano's crime and trial to run in any newspaper of the time. The rest of this passage on Pastano is drawn from that article, except where otherwise noted.

73 **considered a great patriot:** Simonhoff, *Jewish Notables in America,* 53.

73 **The jury deliberated for just minutes:** *NYMA,* 20 November 1799.

73 **that coming Tuesday, in fact—sentenced** . . . **to hanging and dissection:** Ibid., 2 December 1799.

73 **conflagration that Greenwich Street narrowly avoided:** *NYCA,* 6 January 1800.

74  **breasts ... showed dark bruises:** *Claypoole's American Daily Advertiser* (Philadelphia), 8 January 1800.

74  **"Her fingers appear to have been scratched":** William Coleman, *Report of the Trial of Levi Weeks*, 59.

74  **an equally enraged Richard Croucher:** Ibid., 82.

74  *If I should meet Levi Weeks in the dark:* Ibid.

74  **pistols had replaced rapiers:** Sabine, *Notes on Duels and Duelling*, 30.

74  **The very first duel in America:** Ibid., 164.

74  **journalists, politicians, and military officers:** The entries in Sabine's compendium of known duels are especially rich in these professions.

74  **newspaper letter that year proposing a "dueling club":** *NYDA*, 6 June 1800.

75  **"two French nobles could not agree":** Sabine, *Notes on Duels and Duelling*, 35.

75  **an army colonel and a navy captain dueled:** Ibid., 247.

75  **"seconds"—to** *also* **take offense:** Ibid., 34.

75  **a pair of French immigrants ... met in the storied dueling ground:** *NYMA*, 17 August 1799.

75  **dueled with pistols not once but twice in a single week:** *NYCA*, 9 and 13 September 1799. This particularly argumentative fellow was William Chambers, who is listed on page 160 of the 1800 *Longworth's American Almanack* as being a ship chandler.

75  **Aaron Burr himself had dueled with John Barker Church:** *Political Correspondence and Public Papers of Aaron Burr*, 1:410.

75  **bullets in both legs during a duel in Paulus Hook:** *NYCA*, 13 November 1799.

75  **Any Quaker coffin was a plain one:** Clarkson, *Portraiture of Quakerism*, 25. The other details regarding Quaker funerals are also largely drawn from Clarkson's account.

76  **show off silver coins as buttons:** Watson, *Historic Tales of Olden Time*, 151.

76  **sooner walk into street posts than wear spectacles:** Ibid., 154.

76  **"Mr. Weeks will no doubt speedily meet the reward of his demerits":** *Independent Gazetteer* (Worcester, Mass.), 26 January 1800.

76  **James Snedeker was a surgeon and physician:** *Longworth's American Almanack* (1800), 334. The few modern accounts of the Levi Weeks case spell his name as "Snedecher," presumably because this was the spelling used in Coleman's trial transcript. However, both the Hardie transcript and the 1800 *Longworth's American Almanack* render it as "Snedeker"; moreover, while I find no examples from that time of the name Snedecher in local newspapers, there are occurrences of "Snedeker."

76 **practice still newly established in town:** Snedeker, while listed in the 1800 *Longworth's American Almanack*, does not appear in earlier editions. In his trial testimony (William Coleman, *Report of the Trial of Levi Weeks*, 59) he notes that he is just twenty-eight years old.

77 **carefully turned her head and examined her neck and chest:** William Coleman, *Report of the Trial of Levi Weeks*, 59–60.

77 **"blows on her brow, chin, and breast":** *Claypoole's American Daily Advertiser* (Philadelphia), 8 January 1800.

77 **"a sudden extinction of life":** William Coleman, *Report of the Trial of Levi Weeks*, 60–61.

77 **The Friends Burial Ground:** This location and the afternoon of burial are noted in *NYWM*, 11 January 1800.

77 **To see a funeral:** Clarkson, *Portraiture of Quakerism*, 25.

78 **unmarked with any headstone:** Ibid., 28–29.

78 **"being moved . . . and seduced by the instigation of the Devil":** William Coleman, *Report of the Trial of Levi Weeks*, 10.

## 8. WHATEVER IS BOLDLY ASSERTED

79 **"The public are desired to suspend their opinion":** *NYDA*, 9 January 1800.

79 **pamphlets were even circulating accounts of ghosts:** Hardie, *Impartial Account of the Trial*, v.

79 **"Handbills were generally distributed throughout the city":** Ibid.

80 **a New Jersey coroner's claim:** *NYWM*, 11 January 1800.

80 **a live "Beautiful African LION":** *NYDA*, 29 January 1800.

80 **THE NEWTONIAN SYSTEM OF ASTRONOMY REFUTED:** *NYCA*, 15 January 1800.

80 **gentlemen had built a perpetual motion engine:** *NYMA*, 6 February 1800.

80 **spot the masterful hand of Aaron Burr:** Isenberg, *Fallen Founder*, 192–93. While the editorial is not specifically identifiable as Burr's handiwork, a number of writers and biographers (including Isenberg) have noted Burr as a likely source for this newspaper notice.

80 **plumbing for the Manhattan Well:** Kleiger, *Trial of Levi Weeks*, 17.

81 **longtime slaves Harry and Peggy:** *Memoirs of Aaron Burr*, 403–4.

81 **at ease with classical languages:** Pidgin, *Theodosia*, 188.

81 **ponder composing a book:** Ibid., 222.

81 **Washington Irving was nurturing some affection:** Ibid., 223.

81 **"convince the world what neither sex appear":** Isenberg, *Fallen Founder*, 81.

81  **she had charmed a Mohawk chief:** Pidgin, *Theodosia*, 219.

81  **welcomed into the great reception hall:** Stone, *History of New York City*, 217. Stone quotes at length from Gulian Verplanck's "Reminiscences of New York," *Casket*, December 1829, 561–63. This unsigned and rather poignant account is of a visit to the old home by Verplanck; by the time he visited it in the 1820s, it had been converted into a rowdy entertainment hall.

81  **ranks of ancient oaks and basswood:** Stone, *History of New York City*, 216.

81  **a fine flower garden enclosed by hedges:** Pidgin, *Theodosia*, 212.

82  **an ancient boundary line . . . Bestaver's Killetje:** Ibid., 210.

82  **seized in 1776 as Washington's headquarters:** Isenberg, *Fallen Founder*, 32.

82  **doomed Battle of Quebec:** Ibid., 19.

82  **winter at Valley Forge with Washington, and . . . the Battle of Monmouth:** Isenberg, *Fallen Founder*, 85.

82  **"Pipes for the conveyance of Water":** Aaron Burr to Robert Livingston, 20 September 1799, in *Political Correspondence and Public Papers of Aaron Burr*, 1:406.

83  **"one of those Grecian temples":** Janvier, *In Old New York*, 204.

83  **"RICHMOND HILL. TO BE LET":** *GNDA*, 8 July 1799.

84  **to retrieve the ink bottles . . . and to lock up his papers:** Peggy Gartin to Aaron Burr, 3 December 1800, *Memoirs of Aaron Burr*, 1:403.

84  **"The extreme wrong I have suffer'd":** Henry Drinker to Aaron Burr, 15 January 1799, *Political Correspondence and Public Papers of Aaron Burr*, 1:379.

84  **"I do not as yet perceive any resource":** Aaron Burr to Pierpont Edwards, 14 December 1798, *Political Correspondence and Public Papers of Aaron Burr*, 1:359.

84  **promissory note for $1,500:** Promissory note to James and William Constable, 21 November 1799, Aaron Burr Papers, 1774–1836.

84  **The statesman was waiting outside:** *Extracts from the Journal of Elizabeth Drinker*, 356.

84  **Philadelphia entailed taking a ferry past:** Monaghan and Lowenthal, *This Was New York*, 1.

85  **three-story mansion on a double lot:** Ritter, *Philadelphia and Her Merchants*, 120.

85  **at the back of a chocolatier's shop . . . a cabinet workshop:** Ibid., 121.

85  **"Drinker's Big House":** *Extracts from the Journal of Elizabeth Drinker*, 27.

85  **walked in gingerly on his corns:** Maxey, "Union Farm," 611.

85 **the double chin of a successful Quaker merchant:** Ibid., 607.

85 **brought his young Theodosia for a visit once:** *Extracts from the Journal of Elizabeth Drinker*, 248.

85 **to purchase some eighty thousand acres:** Guide to the Pierpont Edwards Papers.

85 **"The Purchase if made will be with a View":** Aaron Burr to W. H. Drinker, 23 November 1795. This letter is not among the Henry Drinker Papers (1747–1867) at the Historical Society of Pennsylvania; it is owned by a private collector. The quote is drawn from a sales catalog transcription by the Gallery of History in Las Vegas, http://www.historyforsale.com/html/prodetails.asp?documentid=278468.

86 **property taxes had been accumulating:** Henry Drinker to Aaron Burr, 19 December 1799, *Political Correspondence and Public Papers of Aaron Burr*, 1:413.

86 **underwrote cargo ships from Britain and ran a busy iron mill:** Maxey, "Union Farm," 609.

86 **support the Revolutionary patriots . . . sell British tea:** Doerflinger, *Vigorous Spirit of Enterprise*, 167.

86 **holding the bag for immense debts:** Isenberg, *Fallen Founder*, 155.

86 **he was on the hook for at least $80,000:** Fleming, *Duel*, 98.

86 **"I am not aware of any cause of litigation":** Henry Drinker to Aaron Burr, 15 January 1799, *Political Correspondence and Public Papers of Aaron Burr*, 1:378.

87 **reputation for harrying foes with blizzards of appeals:** *Memoirs of Aaron Burr*, 2:14.

87 **"is whatever is boldly asserted and plausibly maintained":** Ibid.

87 **Burr pressed the merchant relentlessly:** *Political Correspondence and Public Papers of Aaron Burr*, 1:415f.

87 **missed his Sunday meeting at the Friends meetinghouse:** *Extracts from the Journal of Elizabeth Drinker*, 356.

87 **"I have had to pay a large demand":** Henry Drinker to Robert Bowne, 14 January 1800, *Political Correspondence and Public Papers of Aaron Burr*, 1:415ff.

87 **yet another $1,500 out of his local merchants:** Promissory note to James and William Constable, 23 January 1800, Aaron Burr Papers, 1774–1836.

87 **counterattack in the *New-York Mercantile Advertiser*:** *NYMA*, 13 January 1800.

88 **much of the state's legal talent was disbarred for Loyalism:** Isenberg, *Fallen Founder*, 88.

88 Their clientele tended to follow their political inclinations: Ibid., 89.

88 he accepted the job of New York's state attorney general: Ibid., 104.

88 a slave named Pompey for robbery: Indictment, *People [AB] v. Pompey and Tom*, 4 October 1791, NYSC Case 0397, Reel 16, Aaron Burr Papers, 1774–1836.

88 a rape suspect: Affidavit, *People [AB] v. Titus, Robert and Neilson, David*, 16 October 1791, NYSC Case 0395, Reel 16, Aaron Burr Papers, 1774–1836.

88 the hot-tempered proprietor of a glassworks: Indictment and Deposition, *People [AB] v. Moulter, Philip and Stalsenbergh, John*, 4 October 1791, NYSC Case 0396, Reel 16, Aaron Burr Papers, 1774–1836. There are few other records of these cases, but Philip Moulter's role as a glassworks owner in the town of Watervliet, New York, can be gleaned from a page 2 advertisement in the *Albany Gazette* of 13 October 1791. Placed immediately after his murder indictment, it seeks someone to run the glassworks for a while, as he understandably found himself "unable to carry on that important manufactory, which he views to be so very necessary in this new and flourishing country."

88 brother-in-law and an uncle both sat on the bench: *Memoirs of Aaron Burr*, 2:13.

88 a fine example of lawyer humor: *NYWM*, 2 November 1799.

89 he promptly and enthusiastically billed them: Rogow, *Fatal Friendship*, 99. To be fair, as Rogow points out, this reputation at least partly rests on the Le Guen settlement, and "by today's standards, [Burr's fees] were not excessive."

89 billed his client twice as much as had fellow counsel Alexander Hamilton: Ibid.

## 9. A PERFECT MONSTER

90 the office of Nicholas Cruger: *NYG*, 22 October 1799.

90 It abutted an icehouse: *NYDA*, 16 May 1800.

90 Cruger had personally hired: Chernow, *Alexander Hamilton*, 31.

90 36 Greenwich Street: *Longworth's American Almanack* (1800), 220.

90 "rather a shabby affair": Duras, "Alexander Hamilton's Place in History," 329.

90 *"These things are to be admitted"*: Alexander Hamilton to James Bayard, 16 January 1800 [i.e., 1801], *Works of Alexander Hamilton*, 6:420.

91 prone to furnishing a space with a plain pine desk: Chernow, *Alexander Hamilton*, 338.

91 **"Returned as being more than is proper"**: Allan McLane Hamilton, *Intimate Life of Alexander Hamilton*, 189.

91 **"He is far more *cunning*"**: Alexander Hamilton to James Bayard, 16 January 1800 [i.e., 1801], *Works of Alexander Hamilton*, 6:423.

91 *"The truth is, with great apparent coldness"*: Ibid.

91 **"Little Burr" . . . "We have always been opposed"**: *Papers of Alexander Hamilton*, 26:269.

92 **Ruddy and red-haired**: Fleming, *Duel*, 3.

92 **"rocking the cradle and studying"**: Allan McLane Hamilton, *Intimate Life of Alexander Hamilton*, 149.

92 **a job that, ironically, paid rather poorly**: Ibid., 163

92 **not Hamilton's usual line of work**: *Law Practice of Alexander Hamilton*, 1:687.

93 **a client accused in 1786 of dueling**: Ibid., 689

93 **a single murder case . . . a few shoplifting charges**: Ibid., 690

93 **"I remark as I go along everything"**: Chernow, *Alexander Hamilton*, 642.

93 **octagonal dining and parlor rooms**: *Papers of Alexander Hamilton*, 25:40.

93 **tens of thousands of dollars into debt**: Chernow, *Alexander Hamilton*, 724.

93 **"My country estate, though costly"**: Allan McLane Hamilton, *Intimate Life of Alexander Hamilton*, 419.

93 **fishing on the Harlem River**: Chernow, *Alexander Hamilton*, 584.

93 **nicknamed her house's tomcat Hamilton**: Rogow, *Fatal Friendship*, 55.

93 **questionable transactions with an embezzler**: Fleming, *Duel*, 15.

94 **"My real crime is an amorous connection"**: Chernow, *Alexander Hamilton*, 533.

94 **Burr's decision to serve as the mistress's divorce lawyer**: Isenberg, *Fallen Founder*, 121.

94 **save Hamilton from dueling with James Monroe**: Ibid., 163.

94 **"He has lately by a trick"**: Alexander Hamilton to James Bayard, 16 January 1800 [i.e., 1801], *Works of Alexander Hamilton*, 6:424.

94 **assembled every Monday and Thursday**: *Historic Buildings Now Standing*, 44.

94 **plumbing-supply outfit . . . "Lead Pipes to convey"**: *NYDA*, 25 January 1800.

95 **"five acres of putrid mud"**: *NYCA*, 19 April 1799.

95 **toll bridge . . . building one across Lake Cayuga**: *NYCA*, 30 September 1800.

95 **"a Tontine for raising Capital"**: Aaron Burr to Robert R. Livingston, 20 September 1799, *Political Correspondence and Public Papers of Aaron Burr*, 1:406.

95 **"suicide and the hands of justice always being excluded"**: *NYWM*, 18 March 1800.

96 **"We die reasonably fast"**: Chernow, *Alexander Hamilton*, 192.

96 **Hamilton's support for any Burr plan would come at a price**: Hammond, *Banks and Politics in America*, 151.

96 **not the bill Burr presented**: Ibid., 152.

96 **"begotten it on the body of the Legislature"**: Reubens, "Burr, Hamilton and the Manhattan Company," 603.

97 **"His object"** ... **"was a bank"**: *Memoirs of Aaron Burr*, 1:417.

97 **disenfranchised acquire property and qualify to vote**: Reubens, "Burr, Hamilton and the Manhattan Company," 579.

97 **"is now *totally* destroyed"**: Larson, *Magnificent Catastrophe*, 98.

97 **"All will depend on the city election"**: Ibid., 92.

97 **"The Collect is made the foundation of a Bank"**: *NYCA*, 29 April 1799.

98 **"a regular Roman triumph"**: Friedman and Israel, *Justices of the Supreme Court, 1789–1978*, 396.

98 **He'd gone to school with Hamilton**: Allan McLane Hamilton, *Intimate Life of Alexander Hamilton*, 154.

98 **to college with Burr**: Rogow, *Fatal Friendship*, 24.

98 **aide-de-camp to George Washington**: Livingston, *Livingstons of Livingston Manor*, 232.

98 **an explosive sense of humor and an equally unpredictable temper**: Friedman and Israel, *Justices of the Supreme Court, 1789–1978*, 396.

98 **an editorial of his made a mild if careless jest**: *NYCA*, 11 May 1798.

99 **The constable had refused even to arrest him**: Freeman, "Dueling as Politics," 301.

99 **"His best friends cannot lament his death"**: *NYCA*, 14 May 1798.

99 **Livingston had been held**: Chester and Williams, *Courts and Lawyers of New York*, 3:1364.

99 **John Young, a bassoonist**: Highfill, Burnim, and Langhans, *Biographical Dictionary of Actors*, 16:361.

99 **the musician panicked and shot**: De Voe, *Market Book*, 1:342.

99 **"an indecency"** ... **"which ought never to be tolerated"**: *NYDA*, 31 July 1797.

99 **"This shameful exposure was not through the wantonness"**: Quoted in De Voe, *Market Book*, 1:342.

## 10. The Silent Sleigh

101 At about nine o'clock that Friday: *Philadelphia Gazette*, 20 January 1800.

101 "entirely consumed" ... "the heavens illuminated": *NYCA*, 18 January 1800.

101 $70,000 worth of cargo: Ibid.

101 the *Olive*—went up as well: *Philadelphia Gazette*, 20 January 1800.

101 the work, it was murmured, of an arsonist: *NYMA*, 18 January 1800.

102 "Sworn, 18th day of January, 1800": *Law Practice of Alexander Hamilton*, 1:697.

102 she'd borne Ezra a daughter: *Paine Family Records*, 127. The daughter in question was Mary Ann Weeks [Paine] (1798–1852).

102 the young carpenter was released ... bail laws had been considerably loosened: *Law Practice of Alexander Hamilton*, 1:697.

102 New York's attorney general had been confined for a debt: Fleming, *Duel*, 99.

103 "Those who dared to suppose him innocent": Hardie, *Impartial Account of the Trial*, iv–v.

103 "Directly in the rear of Mr. McComb's houses": *NYCA*, 21 January 1800.

103 selling the $100,000 behemoth: *NYS*, 21 November 1801.

103 building a new City Hall: Burrows and Wallace, *Gotham*, 369.

104 Elias and Catherine Ring explained: William Coleman, *Report of the Trial of Levi Weeks*, 24.

104 *Elma told me that they were to be married*: Ibid., 29.

104 Levi's apprentice, came forward: Ibid., 46.

104 *I saw Elma and Levi in an indecent act*: Ibid., 43.

105 *another* murdered woman was found: *NYDA*, 6 December 1799.

105 Hoffman was Colden's brother-in-law: Alden, *Collection of American Epitaphs and Inscriptions*, 272.

105 a newspaper brought this thunderbolt: *NYCA*, 24 February 1800.

105 An act to pardon John Pastano: Hurd, *Institutional Care of the Insane*, 1:325.

106 no legal defense of insanity for a murder charge: Ordronaux, "Judicial Problems Relating to the Disposition of Insane Criminals," 594.

106 "Where is the magnanimous General Hamilton?": *GNDA*, 21 January 1800.

107 away in Albany for much of February: *Law Practice of Alexander Hamilton*, 1:699.

107 death of George Washington was already proving disastrous: Chernow, *Alexander Hamilton*, 600.

107 "If I should consent to the appointment of Hamilton": Ibid., 559.

107 justified by stoking fears of a French invasion: Larson, *Magnificent Catastrophe*, 97.

107 "volcano of atheism, depravity, and absurdity": *Papers of Alexander Hamilton*, 5:391.

107 "Speculations on a probable war in Europe have almost ceased": *NYCA*, 16 January 1800.

107 "The French will not have any cause to regret the loss of their naval power": Ibid., 8 February 1800.

108 more believable tale. It came from Susannah Broad: William Coleman, *Report of the Trial of Levi Weeks*, 46–47.

108 a basic courtesy of the road: *By-laws and Ordinances of the Mayor*, 205. By 1839, it was, in fact, illegal to drive a sleigh without "a sufficient number of bells," punishable by a ten-dollar fine. Similar laws were already in effect in Baltimore as early as 1797.

108 "When you hear sleigh bells jingling along the road": *United States Chronicle* (Providence, R.I.), 3 March 1796.

109 "I sent to take passage for to-morrow": Aaron Burr to Theodosia Burr, 5 March 1800, *Memoirs of Aaron Burr*, 2:144.

109 brought to them for appeal: *NYCA*, 3 March 1800.

109 stabbed a good Samaritan: *Albany Centinel*, 9 March 1798.

109 made a point of passing an act demanding it: *NYCA*, 3 March 1800.

109 counterfeiting Manhattan Bank currency: *NYWM*, 19 April 1800.

109 a $350 check drawn upon the Manhattan Bank account of Washington Irving's brother: *NYCA*, 21 March 1800.

109 *Yes,* said Arnetta Van Norden: William Coleman, *Report of the Trial of Levi Weeks*, 50.

110 one of the other cartmen: *Collections of the New-York Historical Society for the Year 1885*, 246.

110 *The Sunday before,* Matthew Musty recalled: William Coleman, *Report of the Trial of Levi Weeks*, 90. Although Coleman lists his name as "Mustee," this appears to be an error, as the name does not occur in any other documents; local directories repeatedly list a cartman named Matthew Musty.

110 Tea, ten shillings a pound: "Journal of Joshua Brookes" The various grocery prices in this section are from Brookes's notes from 1798 and 1802.

110 Many locals had been accustomed to using British currency: Monaghan and Lowenthal, *This Was New York*, 3.

110 He had lived and worked in his store . . . for years: *Argus and Green-leaf's New Daily Advertiser*, 11 December 1795.

111 name was prominent among Manhattan grocers: *Longworth's American Almanack* (1800), 192.

111 meetings of his professional brethren: *NYMA*, 23 January 1801.

111 ice shipped out from Philadelphia had yellow fever: *NYDA*, 5 February 1800.

111 Bonaparte had hired Thomas Paine: Ibid., 11 February 1800.

111 "His household is *French*": Ibid., 27 March 1800.

111 a duel between two bickering watchmakers: *NYCA*, 3 March 1800.

111 Benjamin Holmes was finally scheduled for hanging and dissection: Ibid.

111 city council session just having concluded the day before: *NYDA*, 26 March 1800.

111 circuit court was to commerce the following Tuesday: Ibid.

112 "Good morning, gentlemen": William Coleman, *Report of the Trial of Levi Weeks*, 82.

## 11. THE AMERICAN PHENOMENA

115 "a very clear day, but very blustery": Bleecker, Diary, 31 March 1800.

115 marrying one of his customers, the widow Mrs. Stackhaver: *Report on the Trial of Richard D. Croucher*, 6.

115 the widow's house on Ann Street: Ibid., 9. During Croucher's rape trial in July 1800, witness Abiel Brown mentions renting a residence in Croucher and Stackhaver's house. The *Longworth's Almanack* for 1800 (146) shows Brown at 10 Ann Street. The 1801 directory (126) shows Brown occupying both 8 and 10 Ann Street—perhaps having taken over the building after Croucher left to serve his prison sentence.

115 her teenaged daughter: Ibid., 5.

115 "Scarcely any thing else is spoken of": Bleecker, Diary, 31 March 1800.

116 "The American Phenomena": *NYMA*, 17 March 1800.

116 "the concourse of people was so great": Hardie, *Impartial Account of the Trial*, vi.

116 *"Crucify him!"*: Ibid.

116 Mr. Babb's shop . . . "to confine tame birds in a free country": Thorburn, *Fifty Years' Reminiscences of New-York*, 149.

116 the city's only hosiery shop: Ibid., 148

116 at the corner was an old buttonwood tree . . . for climbing: Ibid., 150.

117 a phalanx of constables and a citizen volunteer guard: Longworth, *Brief Narrative of the Trial*, 5.

117  "disposed to exercise it in its amplest extent": Ibid.

117  hawking door-to-door copies of . . . "Washington's Will": *NYDA*,
     13 February 1800.

118  "THE TRIAL OF LEVI WEEKS . . . BY JOHN FURMAN": *NYCA*, 31 March
     1800.

118  *Hear ye, hear ye*: Jenkins, *New Clerk's Assistant*, 133. This court procla-
     mation is italicized but not in quotation marks, as Coleman's transcript
     simply notes "Proclamation having been made in the usual form" (9).

118  he towered over most of the crowd . . . skated twenty miles up the
     Connecticut River: Bryant, *Reminiscences of the "Evening Post,"* 3.

118  *All manner of persons*: Jenkins, *New Clerk's Assistant*, 133.

118  an abandoned child at a Boston poorhouse: Pasley, *Tyranny of Printers*,
     240.

118  worked briefly as Aaron Burr's law partner . . . it was to Hamilton
     that the grateful and destitute Coleman owed: Chernow, *Alexander
     Hamilton*, 649.

119  he'd virtually walked out in disgust: Nannie Coleman, *Constitution and
     Its Framers*, 148.

119  publicly questioned the curious provisions buried in Burr's bill:
     Koeppel, *Water for Gotham*, 85.

119  he'd served as an aide to Hamilton's father-in-law: Gerlach, *Proud
     Patriot*, 312.

119  the general's former law partner: Fitch, *Encyclopedia of Biography of
     New York City*, 1:346.

119  now also a board member of Burr's new water company: Koeppel,
     *Water for Gotham*, 77.

120  *Approach the bar*: William Coleman, *Report of the Trial of Levi Weeks*, 9.

120  a respectable-enough-looking fellow: Longworth, *Brief Narrative of
     the Trial*, 5.

120  the custom to not let the accused testify: O'Neill, "Vindicating the
     Defendant's Constitutional Right to Testify at a Criminal Trial," 812.

120  didn't even have the right to counsel or to call witnesses: Ibid.,
     811.

120  "Levi Weeks, prisoner at the bar": William Coleman, *Report of the
     Trial of Levi Weeks*, 9.

120  local hacks took rapid notes: Hardie, *Impartial Account of the Trial*, vii.

121  "Hearken to what is said to you": William Coleman, *Report of the Trial
     of Levi Weeks*, 9.

121  Weeks immediately cut some of the jurors short: Ibid., 10.

121  "Juror, look upon the Prisoner": Ibid.

121  they'd served in the assembly together: *NYDA*, 2 June 1797.

121 So had the father of juror Garrit Storm: Barrett, *Old Merchants of New York City*, 4:323.

121 tobacco and beeswax merchant: *NYG*, 19 February 1799.

121 organizing local Irishmen for the Republicans: *NYDA*, 11 June 1794.

121 everything from shawls to gunpowder: Ibid., 23 November 1799.

121 "immense operations" in salt manufacturing: Barrett, *Old Merchants of New York City*, 1:354.

121 former president of the city's chamber of commerce ... "Prince of Merchants": Ibid., 104.

122 landowners holding property worth at least $250: Alschuler and Deiss, "Brief History of the Criminal Jury in the United States," 879. Alschuler and Deiss's account notes that although New York dropped its landowning requirement in 1821, it kept its $250 requirement until 1967.

122 nearly a year's wages for a common laborer: Lebergott, "Wage Trends, 1800–1900," 462.

122 Hunt and his fellow juror Jasper Ward had even run a grocery store together: *NYDA*, 19 April 1796.

122 "You shall well and truly try": William Coleman, *Report of the Trial of Levi Weeks*, 9.

122 It was his habit to divide his papers into two columns: Allan McLane Hamilton, *Intimate Life of Alexander Hamilton*, 195.

122 *Hale's Plea of the Crown*: William Coleman, *Report of the Trial of Levi Weeks*, 94.

123 "Gentlemen of the Jury": Ibid., 10.

123 *"The Jurors and the People of the State of New-York"*: Ibid., 10–11.

124 "Upon this indictment the prisoner at the bar hath been arraigned": Ibid., 11–12.

## 12. By the Hollow Stair

125 Colden had personally investigated: *NYG*, 5 December 1799.

125 Burr helped save Colden land: Coldengham History and Preservation Society, "The Colden Family of Early America," 12.

125 "The prisoner has thought it necessary for his defense": William Coleman, *Report of the Trial of Levi Weeks*, 12.

126 "His appearance interested us greatly in his favor": Longworth, *Brief Narrative of the Trial*, 5.

126 "He gained the affections of those who are now to appear": William Coleman, *Report of the Trial of Levi Weeks*, 12.

126 "The deceased was a young girl": Ibid., 13. The remainder of this section is drawn from this page in Coleman's trial transcript.

127 the defense was demanding that Elias Ring leave: Ibid., 18–19.

127 "You have a right to it, of course": Ibid., 19.

127 twenty-seven years old—just five years older than Elma: Ibid., 33.

127 "I regarded her as a sister": Ibid., 34.

127 "In July last, Levi Weeks came to board": Ibid., 19.

127 announce a whole series of legal precedents: Ibid. Specifically, according to Coleman's transcript, "4 *State Trials*, 487, 488, idem 291, 298; *Leeche's* [*sic*] *Cases* 399, idem 397, idem 437; 2 Bacon 563; *Skinner's Reports* 402."

127 Brockholst Livingston ... a copy of Leach's *Cases in Crown Law*: William Coleman, *Report of the Trial of Levi Weeks*, 19.

127 William Woodcock, accused in 1789 of beating his wife: Leach, *Cases in Crown Law*, 397–98.

127 "His Lordship" ... "then left it with the jury": Ibid., 401.

128 Aaron Burr leaped in: William Coleman, *Report of the Trial of Levi Weeks*, 20.

128 "Levi became very attentive to Elma": Ibid.

128 Elias Ring, who had crept back into the courtroom: Ibid., 21.

128 "I always thought her disposition rather too gay": Ibid., 33.

128 her niece seeming "much pleased": Ibid., 22.

129 "I heard the clock strike eight": Ibid., 23.

129 Colden dramatically unrolled an architect's plan: Ibid., 24.

129 "What kind of staircase is it?": Ibid., 25.

129 Levi seemed "pale and much agitated": Ibid., 26.

129 "I said, *Stop, Levi, this matter has become so serious*": Ibid., 30.

130 Mrs. Ring *also* heard Elma threaten to overdose: Ibid., 31.

130 "Why Levi! How can thee say so?": Ibid., 32. The remainder of this section is drawn from this page in Coleman's trial transcript.

130 he had visited the museum with Hope and Elma: Ibid., 38.

130 "After she was missing, he denied knowing any thing": Ibid., 37.

130 "I left my shoes at the bottom of them": Ibid., 36.

131 "He soon began to use all possible means to convince me": Ibid., 37.

131 Levi's Seventh Ward alderman: New York Common Council, *Minutes of the Common Council of the City of New York, 1784–1831*, 3:157.

131 assistant, the memorably named Mangle Minthorne: Ibid.

131 their tireless efforts to get local streets fixed: Ibid., 2:2. These duties are first noted with Furman in the 15 April 1793 entry on page 2, and he turns up in this capacity on numerous other occasions in the volume.

131 "he paid no more attention to Elma": William Coleman, *Report of the Trial of Levi Weeks*, 37.

131 "Levi, if I was to do it": Ibid., 38.

131 "Levi Weeks was a lodger in my house": Ibid., 39.

131 **Hamilton interrupted:** Ibid. The Coleman trial transcript is notable for, with a few exceptions, not specifying who on the defense team is speaking. It's a peculiar omission for such a careful chronicler—so peculiar, in fact, that it is worth asking whether Coleman thought that the speaker was *already obvious* to his readers.

In his account of the trial, Hamilton's grandson Allen McLane Hamilton explains that "Hamilton interrogated most of the witnesses" (186). In both Hardie's and Coleman's accounts, Hamilton is listed first among the defense team; what is more, when Coleman had his manuscript proofed after the trial, it was Alexander Hamilton that he showed it to (*NYAC*, 30 April 1800). My inference is that Hamilton was, in fact, the lead counsel.

On every occasion that we know Burr or Livingston to have spoken, they are clearly identified by name or as *"one* of the counsel." For instance, the defense's opening statement is attributed by Coleman to "one of the counsel" (64); both Longworth (10) and Hardie (21) identify this person as Burr.

Hamilton is never overtly identified as a speaker by Coleman—because, I believe, he is the default identity of the defense. Tellingly, the *NYDA*, 3 April 1800, identifies Hamilton as making the request to forgo the closing statement; Coleman identifies this simply as "counsel." My conclusion is that Hamilton, as the lead counsel, is speaking for the defense unless otherwise identified, and the courtroom dialogue in this book is rendered accordingly.

132 **"Did you ever know that the prisoner *and* Elma were in bed together?":** William Coleman, *Report of the Trial of Levi Weeks*, 40. The remainder of this section is drawn from this page in Coleman's trial transcript.

133 **"May it please the court and gentlemen of the jury":** Ibid., 43.

133 **his voice low and quick:** Ibid., 81.

133 **"I was satisfied, from what *I* saw":** Ibid., 43.

133 **As a newly married man:** *Report on the Trial of Richard D. Croucher*, 6.

133 **He'd gone to the coffeehouse and then to a birthday party:** William Coleman, *Report of the Trial of Levi Weeks*, 44.

133 **"I wish I had":** Ibid.

134 **"I believe I might have passed the glue manufactory":** Ibid., 45.

134 **"Ever had a quarrel with the prisoner?":** Ibid., 44.

134 **"She thought"** ... **"he was an *Adonis*":** Ibid., 45.

## 13. The Color of a Horse in the Night

135 **"Being in Greenwich Street"**: William Coleman, *Report of the Trial of Levi Weeks*, 47.

135 **"Did you see the face of Elma?"**: Ibid., 48.

136 **"aged and very infirm"**: Ibid., 46.

136 **"I live opposite Ezra Weeks's"**: Ibid.

136 **"When was this?"**: Ibid., 47.

136 **testified in the estate hearing of a late veteran**: Scisco, "Onondaga County Records—1793," 77. A May 4, 1793, deposition in an estate case "by Susannah Broad of New York City" is quoted under the entry for Henry Hawkey.

137 **"Her memory" . . . "was not very tenacious"**: Longworth, *Brief Narrative of the Trial*, 7.

137 **Sent by John Wesley in 1769**: Sprague, *Annals of the American Pulpit*, 5:266.

137 **"watch-night" services, some of which could stretch to midnight**: Baker, *From Wesley to Asbury*, 191.

137 **"I and my boy were coming home from Meeting"**: William Coleman, *Report of the Trial of Levi Weeks*, 48.

138 **A leather worker by trade**: *Longworth's American Almanack* (1800), 121. *Longworth's* lists his name as Berthrong Anderson, not "Buthrong," as listed in Coleman's trial transcript. The street address given in the directory and the transcript make it clear that this is same person, and while there are other examples of Berthrongs and, indeed, Berthrong Anderson on record, I find no others of "Buthrong Anderson." I have corrected Coleman's spelling accordingly.

138 **"I had been to Mr. Pilmore's church"**: William Coleman, *Report of the Trial of Levi Weeks*, 49.

138 **fellow parishioners dutifully confirmed his testimony**: Ibid., 50.

139 **Henry Orr was a cartman**: *Longworth's American Almanack* (1800), 293.

139 **"On the 22nd of December, after dark"**: William Coleman, *Report of the Trial of Levi Weeks*, 52.

139 **Union Furnace was a large iron smithy . . . "jambs, cog-wheels, gudgeons"**: *NYDA*, 22 September 1791.

139 **"I stayed there, I should judge, about an hour"**: William Coleman, *Report of the Trial of Levi Weeks*, 52.

139 **a doomed attempt a few years earlier . . . needed to sell three thousand one-dollar tickets**: *GNDA*, 27 June 1796.

139 **behemoth balloon sporting French and American flags**: "Balloon to Be Seen," *NYDA*, 27 August 1796.

139 **workshop was destroyed by a strong windstorm:** *Massachusetts Mercury* (Boston), 27 September 1796. The following spring, after bickering with his partner, museum promoter Gardiner Baker (see Baker's letter on page 2 of *NYDA*, 14 November 1796), aeronautical pioneer Jean-Pierre Blanchard did manage a Manhattan launch of a "miniature balloon" with live animals inside. According to the *Minerva* for 6 March 1797, "Blanchard's miniature balloon had a beautiful ascension; but the parachute, in its descention [*sic*], did not prove sufficiently strong to let the quadrupeds down with safety, for one of them was killed."

139 **a quiet spot for getting drunk:** *Minerva*, 26 December 1796. The ill-fated site on upper Broadway was known as the Balloon House for years afterward, and during this period there is reference to a "Balloon Tavern."

139 **"It was" . . . "the voice of a woman":** William Coleman, *Report of the Trial of Levi Weeks*, 52.

140 **"I got out of bed to see what I could":** Ibid., 51.

140 **whose property line ran near the well:** Ibid., 52. Orr's testimony on this page noted that "I got near Lewis's fence."

140 **"I discovered the track of a one-horse sleigh":** Ibid., 49.

140 **the prosecutor could, if he chose, call upon Levi's own attorney:** Jacob and Tomlins, "Evidence II.i," *Law-Dictionary*, vol. 1.

140 **"The sleigh drove so near the wall":** William Coleman, *Report of the Trial of Levi Weeks*, 49.

141 **Three young boys:** Ibid.

141 **"Eleven" . . . "Thirteen.":** Ibid.

141 **did not accept testimony from children under the age of discretion:** MacNally, *Rules of Evidence on Pleas of the Crown*, 149.

141 **Those unable to understand the spiritual import . . . were *incompetent witnesses*:** Ibid., 151.

141 **"Idiots, madmen, and children":** Jacob and Tomlins, "Evidence II.i," *Law-Dictionary*, vol. 1.

142 **Some children did not know their own exact ages:** Census of the United States, *Compendium of the Tenth Census*, Part 1, lxvii. As late as 1880, the U.S. Census found this persisted among many African Americans and poorer whites. A similar phenomenon was noted in Britain in the 1848 *Reports of the Commissioners of Inquiry into the State of Education in Wales* (32).

142 **"Thirteen?":** William Coleman, *Report of the Trial of Levi Weeks*, 52.

142 **led the boy through some crucial questions:** Ibid.

142 **"Pray, sir" . . . "What is your son's age?":** Ibid., 53.

142 **plea from Levi's table, *perhaps an adjournment*:** Ibid.

143 *It is ordered . . . that the jury empanelled have leave:* Chitty, *Reports*

*of Cases Principally on Practice and Pleading*, 1:403ff. The wording of the judge's order, rendered here in italics as a paraphrase, is taken almost exactly from this passage of Chitty, which contains the judge's 1796 impanelment order in the high treason case of *King v. Stone.*

143 **discretion in misdemeanor and felony trials to allow a jury to go home . . . "prisoners until they are discharged":** Chitty, *Reports of Cases Principally on Practice and Pleading*, 1:401.

143 **denied jurors "food, drink, or fire":** Ibid., 1:414.

143 **Finding accommodation for twelve men together was not easy:** "Hardy's Trial," 719.

143 **unroll mattresses in courthouses:** Ibid.

143 **told to go walk on the rooftop:** Sampson, *Trial of Robert M. Godwin*, 37.

143 **their makeshift quarters for the night:** Longworth, *Brief Narrative of the Trial*, 13.

144 **featured Trumbull's famed portrait of George Washington:** Howard, *Dr. Kimball and Mr. Jefferson*, 67.

## 14. Asleep, Seemingly

145 **in this very same courtroom in October 1793:** [Wyche], *Report of the Trial of Henry Bedlow*, 3.

145 **admitted the false name and the brothel visit:** Ibid., 20.

145 **she'd already *known* he was the infamous Henry Bedlow . . . "willing to be deceived":** Ibid., 23.

146 **"cloud of witnesses":** Ibid., 22.

146 **"Who are these witnesses?":** Ibid., 36–37.

146 **"Gentlemen, I stand here":** Ibid., 24–25.

146 **Angry mobs rampaged:** *New-York Diary*, 15 October 1793.

146 **menaced Livingston's far more respectable house:** Isenberg, *Fallen Founder*, 465.

146 **one man had been shot dead, and the mayor himself was injured:** *New-York Diary*, 15 October 1793.

146 **Lanah quickly sued Bedlow:** Hardie, *Impartial Account of the Trial*, 24.

146 **bankrupted the young man:** *NYDA*, 4 January 1796. *Daily Advertiser* notices announce Bedlow as an insolvent debtor on at least two other occasions as well, on 29 August 1815 and 27 June 1820.

146 **he landed in debtor's prison:** Hardie, *Impartial Account of the Trial*, 24.

146 **the former Miss Sawyer confessed:** *NYG*, 5 October 1798.

147 **Colden couldn't sleep:** William Coleman, *Report of the Trial of Levi Weeks*, 94.

147 **a false alarm:** Bleecker, Diary, 1 April 1800.

147 **a bailiff keeping watch:** Chitty, *Reports of Cases Principally on Practice and Pleading*, 1:404.

147 **prisoners and jurors could flee from a conflagration—but not, perhaps, from a windstorm:** Ibid., 1:402.

147 **local grocer James Lent:** Barrett, *Old Merchants of New York City*, 2:300. Coleman specifically identifies the witness as James W. Lent—that is, James Webber Lent, the subject of Barrett's account above.

147 **not contending with troublesome Federalists:** *Public Advertiser* (New York, N.Y.), 16 November 1810. The involvement of both Lent and his namesake son in Republican politics is mentioned in a number of sources, including in the above notice of his running as a Republican candidate for Sixth Ward assessor.

147 **"I, together with Mr. Page":** William Coleman, *Report of the Trial of Levi Weeks*, 56. Coleman's account (from pages 56 to 59) is the source of the remainder of the testimony in this section.

149 **a gold watch from Paris, a walking stick, and a scarlet cloak:** *NYCA*, 4 November 1802.

149 **"Dr. Skinner" . . . "are you not a surgeon":** William Coleman, *Report of the Trial of Levi Weeks*, 54.

149 **For years Skinner had been advertising . . . "the only operator in America that sets artificial eyes":** *NYCA*, 23 October 1797.

150 **install artificial ears, noses, and legs:** Ring, "Benjamin Franklin and the Dentist," 64.

150 **"I am a dentist":** William Coleman, *Report of the Trial of Levi Weeks*, 54.

150 **hitting up Benjamin Franklin for a twenty-dollar loan:** Ring, "Benjamin Franklin and the Dentist," 64.

150 **picking a fight with George Washington's dentist:** Kirk, "Pioneer Dentistry in New York," 990.

150 **selling gold teeth at four dollars apiece:** *NYCA*, 23 October 1797.

150 **dental tincture for a half guinea per bottle:** *NYDA*, 20 April 1797.

150 **yanking out teeth at four shillings:** *NYCA*, 23 October 1797.

150 **"I *have* made the subject of surgery":** William Coleman, *Report of the Trial of Levi Weeks*, 54. Coleman's account (54–56) is the source of the remainder of the testimony in this section.

152 **Dr. James Snedeker, a young doctor with a practice on Barley Street:** Ibid., 59.

152 **"There were many discolorations":** Ibid. The grammar is from the rendering in this original court transcript; the mixing of "was" and "were" appears common throughout.

153 **Hosack had only narrowly avoided a law career:** Robbins, *David Hosack*, 18.

153 **friend of Aaron Burr's . . . Hamilton's friend and family physician:** Hosack, *Memoir of the Late David Hosack, M.D.*, 300.

153 **he'd awoken to find Hamilton kneeling by his bedside:** Ibid., 307–8.

153 **"Upon looking at the neck":** William Coleman, *Report of the Trial of Levi Weeks*, 60. Coleman's account (60–61) is the source of the remainder of the testimony in this section.

154 **hiring a man to ride a horse:** Ibid., 62.

155 **"Circumstantial evidence is all that can be expected":** Ibid. Please note that Colden's quotation from Morgan is taken from Coleman's transcript of the trial, not from Morgan directly. An important discrepancy between the two versions is discussed in my notes for chapter 16.

155 **"The prejudice entertained against receiving circumstantial evidence":** Ibid., 63.

## 15. The Devil's Advocate

156 **"Gentlemen of the jury":** William Coleman, *Report of the Trial of Levi Weeks*, 64.

156 **Colonel Burr's duty to begin the defense's counterattack:** Longworth, *Brief Narrative of the Trial*, 10. Coleman's transcript of the trial does not note Burr specifically here (though he does distinguish him from Hamilton as *"one of* the prisoner's counsel"), but Longworth's trial account does; so does a newspaper account immediately afterward (*NYDA,* 3 April 1800).

156 **Burr was known for speaking slowly and precisely:** *Memoirs of Aaron Burr,* 2:21.

156 **"Extraordinary means have been adopted":** William Coleman, *Report of the Trial of Levi Weeks,* 64.

157 **"Notwithstanding testimony of an intimacy":** Ibid., 65.

157 **"The story, you will see":** Ibid., 66.

157 **"Even in this city a case had occurred":** Ibid., 67.

157 **"it was one of the most eloquent speeches we have ever heard":** Longworth, *Brief Narrative of the Trial,* 10.

157 **"*Now* it comes out that the accusation":** William Coleman, *Report of the Trial of Levi Weeks,* 67.

158 **"We shall show you":** Ibid., 65.

158 **"Demas Mead" . . . "Do you live with Ezra Weeks":** Ibid., 86. Coleman's transcript renders his last name as "Meed"; as is often the case with William Coleman, he appears to have misspelled the name. I find no "Meed" in local records. However, there are later records for

a Demas *Mead*—listed as a carpenter, which makes sense given his apprenticeship with Weeks: for example, *Minutes of the Common Council of the City of New York, 1784–1831*, 17:413; and *Longworth's American Almanac* (1837), 428.

159 **his own recollection of the evening matched:** William Coleman, *Report of the Trial of Levi Weeks*, 86–87. The remainder of this section is drawn from this passage in Coleman.

160 **Mrs. Forrest quickly confirmed where Levi had heard about the muff:** Ibid., 70.

160 **"In cases depending on a chain of circumstances":** Ibid., 67.

161 **"I was called upon by a constable":** Ibid., 77.

161 **"I was called together with Dr. Prince":** Ibid.

162 *scarf skin* **was a term:** Hooper, *Compendious Medical Dictionary*, n.p.

162 **"Near the instep there was a small spot":** William Coleman, *Report of the Trial of Levi Weeks*, 77–78.

163 **Formerly a trustee of Columbia:** Stookey, "Nicholas Romayne," 580.

163 **he had completed his training in Britain:** Ibid., 578.

164 **died in convulsions on his genteel estate in Warwickshire in 1780:** *Trial of John Donnellan, Esq.*, 7–8.

164 **to the horror of medical professors around the country:** Davis, "George Edward Male M.D.," 117.

165 **Dr. Hosack had once been among Romayne's most promising students:** Hosack, *Memoir of the Late David Hosack, M.D.*, 292.

165 **"are chiefly discovered by the facts":** Farr, *Elements of Medical Jurisprudence*, 87.

165 **"Is there any way"** ... **"in which the testimony":** William Coleman, *Report of the Trial of Levi Weeks*, 79. The remainder of this section is drawn from Coleman's account. Hosack's testimony also goes on to briefly touch upon the work of "Coleman"—not the court clerk, but rather Dr. Edward William Coleman, an English surgeon who authored *A Dissertation on Suspended Respiration, from Drowning, Hanging, and Suffocation* (London: J. Johnson, 1791). Coleman's experiments make for grim reading; many of its chapters commence with the words "A cat was drowned" or "A dog was suspended by the neck." But his work was highly regarded, and sustained experimentation in the postmortem effects of drowning was still a relatively new area of medical research.

## 16. Look upon the Prisoner

169 **"at the bar he is more remarkable for ingenuity":** Chernow, *Alexander Hamilton*, 193.

169 "He delighted in surprising his opponents": *Memoirs of Aaron Burr*, 2:15.

169 hammering nails and tongs for New Yorkers for years: *NYWM*, 28 May 1791.

169 "Do you remember" . . . "any thing in the conduct of *Mr. Ring*": William Coleman, *Report of the Trial of Levi Weeks*, 71. In Coleman's transcript, Watkins says that Elma's bed stood "within four inches of the partition"; after being corrected by James Hardie, Coleman retracted this particular phrase in his letter to the *NYAC* of 30 April 1800. Apparently it was the partition itself that was four inches thick, but as Coleman did not indicate the revised quote's exact wording in his correction, I have left it out of the quotation.

170 "rustling of beds, such as might be occasioned": Hardie, *Impartial Account of the Trial*, 27–28.

170 "It continued some time": William Coleman, *Report of the Trial of Levi Weeks*, 72.

170 an affidavit from Watkins's ailing wife: Ibid., 74.

171 "I heard her say" . . . "the Thursday after she was missing": Ibid., 73.

171 Betsy, had heard similar sentiments: Ibid., 76.

171 one of Levi's own coworkers—had heard by that fourth day: Ibid., 83.

171 "Did you ever speak of this noise": Ibid., 73.

171 "When did you first mention to Croucher": Ibid., 74.

172 Hugh McDougall, a Broadway glazier and sign painter: *NYCA*, 27 October 1800. *Longworth's American Almanack* for 1800 (265) also notes McDougall as running an oil and paint store at the same 92 Broadway address.

172 "I have been acquainted with this *Mr. Croucher*": William Coleman, *Report of the Trial of Levi Weeks*, 82.

172 "I told him I thought it was *wrong*": Ibid., 83.

172 a Greenwich Street grocery: *Longworth's American Almanack* (1800), 203.

173 "On Friday last, Croucher came running to the store": William Coleman, *Report of the Trial of Levi Weeks*, 80–81.

173 Alexander Hamilton snatched up a candle from the table: Ibid., 82.

173 "Did you ever publish the handbills about apparitions?": Ibid., 93.

174 "I saw a young man, the week before the girl was missing": Ibid., 90.

174 she had lost her husband to yellow fever back in the outbreak of '98: Hardie, *Account of the Malignant Fever*, 83.

175 **"On the 22nd of December" . . . "being my little boy's birthday":** William Coleman, *Report of the Trial of Levi Weeks*, 92.

175 **Several others . . . were not witnesses of great public reputation:** Ibid., 93. Specifically, of the four other witnesses noted by name in Coleman's transcript, three are not even listed in any edition of *Longworth's American Almanack*. The only witness at the Ashmore party with any public profile, Jacob Hopper, does not exactly speak to the moral character of the gathering. He is listed on page 233 of the 1800 edition as a cartman, but later went on to become well-known indeed—as a swindler who absconded with substantial sums of money from Manhattan banks and merchants. He was to be captured soon afterward in Cuba. *Essex Register* (Salem, Mass.), 26 November 1807.

175 **Colden had used an impressive quote . . . "Circumstantial evidence is all that can be expected":** William Coleman, *Report of the Trial of Levi Weeks*, 62.

176 **"Positive and direct proof of fraud is not to be expected":** Morgan, *Essays*, 1:208.

176 **the fraudulent policy on a £110 cargo of oats:** Park, *System of the Law of Marine Insurances*, 238. The Morgan quotation is itself drawn from this passage in Park.

176 **testimonials by local worthies:** William Coleman, *Report of the Trial of Levi Weeks*, 90.

176 **"In some cases, presumptive evidences go far":** Ibid., 93.

177 **It was now 2:30 A.M.:** Ibid.

177 **"sinking under the fatigues he had suffered":** Longworth, *Brief Narrative of the Trial*, 13.

177 **"Really" . . . "he had not the strength to proceed":** William Coleman, *Report of the Trial of Levi Weeks*, 94.

177 **"was obliged to at five or six in the morning to enter a reply":** Longworth, *Brief Narrative of the Trial*, 13.

177 **at least one was quietly teetering on the edge of insolvency:** *NYG*, 8 August 1801. The reference is to a notice of insolvency for juror Richard Ellis. He had also been listed as insolvent on at least one previous occasion, in *Diary; or, Loudon's Register* (New York, N.Y.), 27 September 1797.

177 *Two nights passed in this manner might make some of them sick*: Longworth, *Brief Narrative of the Trial*, 13.

177 **"The examinations of the paintings must doubtless be very edifying":** Ibid.

177 *we relinquish our closing argument*: William Coleman, *Report of the Trial of Levi Weeks*, 94. In one newspaper account (*NYDA*, 3 April 1800), Hamilton is specifically noted as the counsel making this statement.

178 *The question involves considerations of great moment*: Ibid., 95.

178 *You must find the prisoner guilty*: Ibid., 97.

179 **"beyond a *reasonable* doubt" had started to gain currency as a legal concept**: Langbein, *Origins of Adversary Criminal Trial*, 33.

179 **ten minutes**: *NYMA*, 3 April 1800.

179 **four**: Hardie, *Impartial Account of the Trial*, 34.

179 **or five**: William Coleman, *Report of the Trial of Levi Weeks*, 98.

179 **"less than two"**: Longworth, *Brief Narrative of the Trial*, 14.

179 **called a final roll**: Ibid.

179 **Simon Schermerhorn . . . foreman**: Hardie, *Impartial Account of the Trial*, 34.

179 **He raised his right hand**: Longworth, *Brief Narrative of the Trial*, 14.

180 *Look upon the prisoner*: Jacob and Tomlins, "Trial," *Law-Dictionary*. This wording by the clerk is alluded to as "universally" used in courts in a discussion during, ironically enough, Aaron Burr's trial for treason in 1807 (Robertson, *Trial of Aaron Burr for Treason*, 550).

180 **"Not guilty"**: William Coleman, *Report of the Trial of Levi Weeks*, 98.

180 **shouts and applause as the judge gaveled loudly for order**: *NYDA*, 3 April 1800.

## 17. THE CATCHPENNY CONTRIVANCE

181 **"many hundreds, perhaps thousands"**: *NYMA*, 14 April 1800. Specifically, this was a letter sent to the paper by Monteath McFarlane, the printer of James Hardie's account of the trial.

181 **four years of hard labor for stealing a black mourning cloth**: *NYAC*, 10 April 1800.

181 **"Although some circumstances point to him"**: Letter by Abraham Bancker, 12 January 1800, Bancker Papers.

181 **"Mr. Burr opened the defense with perspicuity"**: *NYDA*, 3 April 1800.

182 **Within hours of the acquittal**: William Coleman, *Report of the Trial of Levi Weeks*, ii.

182 **David Longworth was known for publishing plays**: Remer, *Printers and Men of Capital*, 91.

182 **sentimental prints of the late General Washington**: *NYCA*, 25 January 1800.

182 **now this hastily assembled account**: *NYDA*, 16 April 1800. Although the pamphlet itself lists no publisher, Longworth takes credit for it in this public response to William Coleman.

182 set the type even as his "Gentleman" wrote it: Longworth, *Brief Narrative of the Trial*, 16.

183 "The narrative I published was too hastily written": *NYDA*, 16 April 1800.

183 "The careless and inelegant style": Longworth, *Brief Narrative of the Trial*, 15.

183 "he had procured the clerk of the circuit court": *NYDA*, 5 April 1800.

183 "The miserable shift of trying to put off this catch-penny": *NYCA*, 4 April 1800. Though the ad is not initially identified as Coleman's, when it ran again the following day in the *New-York Mercantile Advertiser*, it included his byline.

183 "gratify the public curiosity": *NYCA*, 4 April 1800.

183 "By what privilege does this man insult me": *NYDA*, 16 April 1800. Coleman should have known better, as New York printers could be ruthless. In just the previous few months, one printer had accused another of stealing a set of translations right off its press (*NYCA*, 14 December 1799); another claimed an imposter had strolled into its office to steal copy (*NYDA*, 18 March 1800); and still another press saw its proprietor grab up an iron rod to chase a rival out of his shop (*NYS*, 12 March 1800). The assailant, as it happens, was the radical journalist and gadfly William Cobbett; he turns up as a character in my book *The Trouble with Tom: The Strange Afterlife and Times of Thomas Paine* (New York: Bloomsbury, 2005).

184 As a brilliant young Scottish scholar, Hardie came to New York: Ross, *Scot in America*, 285–86.

184 "Greek, Latin and English languages grammatically": *NYDA*, 8 May 1798.

184 running a Literary and Intelligence Office: *NYG*, 22 July 1799.

184 "Not being acquainted with the art": Hardie, *Impartial Account of the Trial*, vii.

185 thirty-seven and a half cents: *Impartial Register* (Salem, Mass.), 14 July 1800.

185 "When it was promised at an earlier day": William Coleman, *Report of the Trial of Levi Weeks*, i.

185 before the adversarial system . . . confessions and dying words on the scaffold: Halttunen, *Murder Most Foul*, 94.

186 stenographic systems had been around for two centuries: *Diary of Samuel Pepys*, lxxxvii. Samuel Pepys and Isaac Newton, among others, were enthusiastic early users.

186 Coleman favored—known as Byrom's New Universal Shorthand: Gillogly, "Breaking an Eighteenth Century Shorthand System,"

93. Specifically, this article identifies Byrom shorthand in a 1796 letter of Coleman's.

186  **developed by a brilliantly deceitful courtier:** King-Hele and Hancox, "Man of Many Mysteries," 250.

186  **Full transcripts were published of Henry Bedlow's rape trial:** *Report of the Trial of Henry Bedlow.*

186  **Pennsylvania trial of four murderous conspirators against one Francis Shitz:** *A Correct Account of the Trials of Charles M'Manus.*

187  **"Let me ask":** *NYAC,* 26 April 1800.

187  **builder had quietly tried to bribe the author . . . Coleman rebuffed him:** Willard, *Willard's History of Greenfield,* 163. As Coleman was a former resident of Greenfield, this account goes into substantial detail about both the man and his subsequent friendship with Ezra Weeks, particularly their patronage of the arts.

187  **in a response to his critics, Coleman revealed:** *NYAC,* 30 April 1800. Coleman quickly published (*NYCA,* 29 April 1800) official filings of copyright in New York newspapers, a formality so unusual in that piratical era that most readers could have been forgiven for not even knowing what the newspaper notice meant. It was an unmistakable shot across the bow of any competitor, and a necessary one—for another printer in town, William Davis, was about to bring a *fourth* trial account to press (*NYMA,* 14 April 1800). Curiously, this newest trial manuscript vanished from the historical record, never to be heard of again. It's unclear whether Davis was put off by the number of competitors or by Coleman's saber rattling over copyright, or whether Ezra Weeks found Davis more open to being bribed.

188  **the launch of a new frigate:** *NYAC,* 11 April 1800.

188  **"Huzza for the President":** Ibid., 10 April 1800.

188  *Ground & Lofty Tumbling*: Ibid., 11 April 1800.

188  **Livingston and Hamilton were on one side of an insurance suit:** *Law Practice of Alexander Hamilton,* 591.

188  **Livingston and Burr:** NYSC Case 0452, *Arnold & Ramsey v. United Insurance Company,* 1800, Aaron Burr Papers, 1774–1836.

188  **Burr took out another $1,500 loan:** Promissory note to William and James Constable, 29 April 1800, Aaron Burr Papers, 1774–1836.

188  **"account, by the former ones":** Charles Wilkes (Bank of New York cashier) to Alexander Hamilton, 22 April 1800, *Papers of Alexander Hamilton,* 24:420.

188  **"It is universally acknowledged":** *NYS,* 23 April 1800.

188  **pen name of . . . John Quincy Adams:** Nagel, *John Quincy Adams,* 75.

189 **caucused in the Tontine City Hotel on April 15, 1800:** *NYDA*, 17 April 1800.

189 **they were weakened by the party's:** Chernow, *Alexander Hamilton*, 607.

189 **"two grocers, a ship chandler":** Matthew Davis, quoted in Wills, *"Negro President,"* 70.

189 **"Now I have him all hollow":** John Adams to James Lloyd, 17 February 1815, *Works of John Adams*, 10:125.

189 **"What means these gigantic figures?":** *NYDA*, 28 April 1800.

189 **"Committees were in session day and night":** Isenberg, *Fallen Founder*, 199.

190 **Burr had virtually invented modern electioneering:** Chernow, *Alexander Hamilton*, 607.

190 **"Many people wonder that the ex-Senator":** *NYDA*, 28 April 1800.

190 **"The leaders of the aristocratic faction bewailed":** *NYAC*, 28 April 1800.

## 18. EVERY MARK OF A VILLAIN

191 **precipitating a neighbor's baby into a well:** *NYS*, 8 March 1800.

191 **"We swept near Rhinelander's Battery":** William Coleman, *Report of the Trial of Levi Weeks*, 89.

192 **"in a little time the cries stopped":** Ibid., 51.

193 **within the *Proceedings of the Old Bailey*:** *Proceedings of the Old Bailey*, 20 September 1797, case reference t17970920-59. No previous account of the Elma Sands murder has noted this *previous* criminal record of Croucher's; it may the first new lead in the case since 1800.

193 **a woman sentenced to whipping:** *Proceedings of the Old Bailey*, 20 September 1797, case reference t17970920-58.

193 **a young mute caught stealing silver buttons:** Ibid., case reference t17970920-57.

193 **a shoemaker's shop by St. Paul's:** Ibid., case reference t17970920-59.

194 **birthday party at the house of Ann Ashmore:** William Coleman, *Report of the Trial of Levi Weeks*, 93.

194 **a brandy-making firm in her house:** *Longworth's American Almanack* (1800), 125.

194 **"I have seen him very often in liquor":** *Proceedings of the Old Bailey*, 20 September 1797, case reference t17970920-59.

194 **Burr claimed that Elma was known to sneak out at night:** William Coleman, *Report of the Trial of Levi Weeks*, 65.

195 "those who have been instrumental and active": *NYDA*, 3 April 1800.

195 *Come help me scrub my old room clean*: *Report of the Trial of Richard D. Croucher*, 4.

195 **A forty-year-old man such as Croucher**: *Philadelphia Gazette*, 10 July 1800.

195 **a slight, slender girl like Margaret**: *Report of the Trial of Richard D. Croucher*, 10. Witness Abiel Brown notes that the victim was not substantial in "shape or age"; on page 25, the prosecutor similarly notes that "her age—her size—her sufferings" warranted particular protection.

195 **Her mother had already been upbraiding her**: *Report of the Trial of Richard D. Croucher*, 13.

195 **others hardly discerned much impertinence**: Ibid., 10.

195 FALSE SHAME!: *NYAC*, 23 April 1800.

195 **Peter Schermerhorn . . . announced his withdrawal**: *NYDA*, 23 April 1800.

195 *I was there—at the trial*: *Report of the Trial of Richard D. Croucher*, 23.

195 **Margaret had been learning her lessons at school**: Ibid., 8.

196 *We shall pack and clean in the morning*: Ibid., 5.

196 **the same witness stand . . . the very man . . . another familiar face**: Ibid., 3.

196 **"Thirteen"**: Ibid., 5. Unusually for trial transcripts, this one makes a particular and repeated note of the witness's distress and crying on the stand. Newspaper accounts of the trial show other observers were also particularly struck by the girl's suffering.

197 **"every mark on his face"**: *Philadelphia Gazette*, 10 July 1800.

197 **"He used force"**: *Report of the Trial of Richard D. Croucher*, 5.

197 **"He whipped me, and turned me out of doors"**: Ibid., 7.

197 **just like the Henry Bedlow rape trial**: Ibid., 18.

197 **"If any thing of an improper nature has passed"**: Ibid., 15.

197 **"It is said, her youth renders it impossible"**: Ibid., 18.

197 **"our ill-judged mode of educating"**: Ibid., 19.

197 **"She *knew* that a young woman had been cruelly murdered"**: Ibid., 23.

198 **five minutes to find Croucher guilty**: Ibid., 27.

198 A MONSTER: *Impartial Register* (Salem, Mass.), 14 July 1800.

198 **"Every one must rejoice"**: *Philadelphia Gazette*, 10 July 1800.

## 19. Duel at Dawn

201 "AARON BURR . . . is using every wicked art": *NYAC*, 23 April 1804.

201 "upwards of twenty women of ill-fame": Chernow, *Alexander Hamilton*, 675.

201 spurned by President Jefferson: Fleming, *Duel*, 145.

201 He'd run to the middle: Ibid., 163.

202 "I had rather seen Lansing governor": Alexander Hamilton to Robert G. Harper, 19 February 1804, *Papers of Alexander Hamilton*, 26:192. Lansing almost instantly dropped out of the race, and the Republicans instead ran a weaker candidate, Morgan Lewis. Thanks in part to Hamilton's efforts, they still managed to vanquish Burr in the election.

202 Burr lost the resulting election by a crushing margin: Isenberg, *Fallen Founder*, 255.

202 "I send for your perusal a letter": William Coleman, *Collection of the Facts and Documents*, 1.

202 "Tis evident that the phrase": Ibid., 2.

202 "The question is not . . . grammatical accuracy": Ibid., 5.

202 "I should not think it right in the midst of a Circuit Court": Ibid., 15.

203 expression of apology flickering momentarily: Ibid., 17.

203 "This is a mortal wound, Doctor": Ibid., 19.

203 "The streets were lined with people": Ibid., 42.

204 a city funeral procession: Ibid., 36.

204 "their Indignation amounts almost to a frenzy already": Fleming, *Duel*, 337.

204 "The last hours of Genl H": Ibid., 344.

204 "throw away my first fire": William Coleman, *Collection of the Facts and Documents*, 26.

204 Hamilton had been in far more duels: Fleming, *Duel*, 287.

204 "the shocking catastrophe which deprived America": William Coleman, *Collection of the Facts and Documents*, 1.

205 "got the paper out in good style": Allan McLane Hamilton, *Intimate Life of Alexander Hamilton*, 72.

205 "Dueling" . . . "is now looked upon": William Coleman, *Collection of the Facts and Documents*, 181.

205 the vice president fled the state: Fleming, *Duel*, 347.

205 "If thee dies a natural death": "The Manhattan Well Murder," 929. The myth originated from an 1870 fact-based novel, Keturah Connah's anonymously authored *Guilty, or Not Guilty: The True Story of the Manhattan Well*. (See my notes for chapter 20.) Though the myth has often been

repeated since then, this unsigned article in *Harper's* appears to be the first instance of its being repeated as alleged fact.

205 **left nearly destitute by his chaotic personal finances:** Fleming, *Duel*, 360.

205 **a stateless and bankrupt shadow of a man:** Chernow, *Alexander Hamilton*, 719.

205 **the strange fate reserved for the trial judge:** Barnes, *Life of Thurlow Weed*, 33.

206 **lost his home within a year . . . and work as a mechanic:** *Longworth's American Almanack* (1801), 161. In this edition Elias Ring is listed as a mechanic living on Lower Catherine Street.

206 **debtor and bankrupt notices:** *NYDA*, 20 June 1803; and *American* (New York, N.Y.), 9 September 1820.

206 **"for the continued intemperate use of intoxicating spirits":** Kleiger, *Trial of Levi Weeks*, 199.

206 **mown down by yellow fever:** Ibid., 198.

206 **Croucher was granted a pardon:** *NYCA*, 18 February 1803.

206 **mingling among Richmond merchants:** *NYAC*, 12 June 1803.

206 **promptly robbed them:** Ibid., 4 July 1803.

206 **Virginia bounty notices . . . "R. D. CROUCHER, about six feet high":** *Alexandria (Va.) Expositor*, 22 July 1803.

207 **"he was executed for a heinous crime":** Lodge, *Alexander Hamilton*, 243. Croucher's dark deeds outlived the man. His rape victim, Margaret Miller, never even made it to the age of twenty. Neighbors recalled a girl who simply cried and drank; then she married a brutal German sailor, who declared she was a whore and slit her throat. Asked afterward if he'd done it, he replied: "Yes, and I would kill a dozen like her, for she was a damn'd bitch." See *Only Correct Account of the Life, Character, and Conduct of John Banks*, 8.

207 **"the generalissimo of Federal editors":** *NYAC*, 23 November 1801.

207 **sworn enemy of pigs:** Muller, *William Cullen Bryant*, 62.

207 **"The stranger that walks through this street":** Ibid., 66.

207 **He became one of the city's great hoteliers:** *NYS*, 21 November 1801.

207 **he served without incident on an 1806 jury:** *Connecticut Journal*, 31 July 1806.

207 **defense counsel to a man charged with aiding Alexander Hamilton:** *NYG*, 12 January 1805.

207 **mayor of New York in 1818:** Biographical Dictionary of the United States Congress, http://bioguide.congress.gov/scripts/biodisplay.pl?index =C000604.

208 Colden helped found the state's first formally chartered scientific society: Harris, "New York's First Scientific Body," 329.

208 founding officers of the Literary and Philosophical Society: *Transactions of the Literary and Philosophical Society of New-York*, 1:17.

208 rose to the state supreme court and . . . to the U.S. Supreme Court: Hall, *Oxford Companion to the Supreme Court of the United States*, 587.

208 helping to found Bellevue Hospital: Sherk, "David Hosack, M.D., and Rutgers," 23.

208 leading vaccination drives across the city: Hosack, *Memoir of the Late David Hosack, M.D.*, 319.

208 Their first meeting was in the Portrait Room: Lamb, *History of the City of New York*, 3:505.

208 moved back to Deerfield: Willard, *Willard's History of Greenfield*, 164. The area he moved to is now known as South Deerfield, Massachusetts.

208 work in selling liquor and dry goods: Kleiger, *Trial of Levi Weeks*, 202.

209 "Son" . . . "I wish I knew": Ibid.

209 In 1805, he ended his dry goods partnership: *Republican Spy* (Springfield, Mass.), 3 September 1805.

209 "they were brought up among slaves": Levi Weeks to Epaphras Hoyt, 27 September 1812, Kleiger, *Trial of Levi Weeks*, 221.

209 recording his travels in a diary: Kleiger, *Trial of Levi Weeks*, 215.

209 Levi and his belongings went toppling into the water: Ibid.

209 "Ultimately" . . . "he became a vagabond": Willard, *Willard's History of Greenfield*, 164.

## 20. A Complicated Evil

210 a decade since the last Spanish garrison: McLeMore, *History of Mississippi*, 1:171.

210 "Its vicinity is very uneven": Kleiger, *Trial of Levi Weeks*, 210.

210 fashionable Georgian and Federalist neoclassical design: Black, *Art in Mississippi, 1720–1980*, 36.

210 "The brick house I am now building": Kleiger, *Trial of Levi Weeks*, 211.

211 fellow Massachusetts native, Lyman Harding: Ibid.

211 trusted army friend of Aaron Burr's: Beveridge, *Life of John Marshall*, 3:364.

211 Ionic columns along the front of the house, topped by Corinthian entablature: Kleiger, *Trial of Levi Weeks*, 211.

211 the inspiration for other grand mansions in the region: Black, *Art in Mississippi, 1720–1980*, 36.

211 **commissions for Natchez's new city hall and college building:**
      Ibid., 35.

211 **"Colonel Burr has been here":** Kleiger, *Trial of Levi Weeks*, 202.

212 **a ten-by-ten rented room:** *Private Journal of Aaron Burr*, 2:102.

212 **dodging petty debts to Parisian shopkeepers:** Ibid., 2:108.

212 **"Had one sous left":** Ibid., 2:103.

212 **"I must, infallibly, have been taken":** Ibid., 2:101.

212 **"I can sit in my chair":** Ibid., 2:105.

212 **a volume containing "abuse and libels":** Ibid., 2:108.

212 **"You are a scoundrel, sir!":** Fleming, *Duel*, 404.

212 **military pension denied by a Congress:** Isenberg, *Fallen Founder*, 399.

212 **"very thin and straight, dressed in black":** Morhouse, "Boy's Remi-
      niscences," 340.

212 **one of America's first specialists in family law:** Isenberg, *Fallen
      Founder*, 389.

212 **almost never heard him speak again of Alexander Hamilton:**
      Ibid., 406.

213 **sometimes mused over: the death of Miss Elma Sands:** Parton, *Life
      and Times of Aaron Burr*, 148.

213 **friend of William Coleman's:** Slawinski, "Tale of Two Murders," 368. I
      am indebted to Slawinski's article for drawing my attention to Brown's use
      of the Weeks trial in this story.

213 **"A recent instance has occurred":** Brown, "Trials of Arden," 19.

213 **"Of all men his lot was most disastrous":** Ibid., 20.

213 **reviews of both Coleman's trial transcript *and* the newly published
      transcript of Croucher's:** Slawinski, "Tale of Two Murders," 398.

213 **riot and attack Arden and then even the jury:** Brown, "Trials of
      Arden," 26.

213 **"Europe had been for a long time the theatre of his crimes":**
      Ibid., 27.

213 **an old Princeton classmate of Burr's:** Isenberg, *Fallen Founder*, 418.

213 **"Gulielma Sands—the unfortunate event":** Freneau, *Collection of
      Poems*, 1:113.

214 **the city filled in and platted out Lispenard's Meadow:** *NYDA*,
      29 June 1804. Specifically, this was an ad seeking cartmen to bid on a con-
      tract "for filling up to the level of the street, a number of Lots, situated on
      Spring-street, near the Manhattan Well."

214 **bought by John Jacob Astor:** *Southern Portrait* (Charleston, S.C.),
      8 April 1848.

214 **modern descendant:** Bank of the Manhattan Company, *Early New-York
      and the Bank of the Manhattan Company*, n.p.

214 **the author was Keturah Connah:** *Orange County Times-Press* (Middletown, N.Y.), 26 April 1910. Her authorship was revealed in this obituary placed by her family after her death in 1910 at the age of ninety.

214 **"our story, or rather, *history*":** Connah, *Guilty, or Not Guilty*, 155.

214 **originating the popular story of Mrs. Ring's curse:** Ibid., 374.

214 **Hope Sands, a witness in the trial—was *still alive*:** Ibid., v.

214 **"an abundance of light auburn hair"** . . . **"small, piercing, black eyes":** Ibid., 47.

215 **"He was tall, and well formed":** Ibid., 153.

215 **"the little mountain maid":** Ibid., 34.

215 **"she had been always a delicate child":** Ibid., 10.

215 **listening to the piano:** Ibid., 68.

215 **"The eyes were dark":** Ibid., 10.

215 **"Were you to ask me now to give you the exact location":** Ibid., 332.

215 **"Since the above was written":** Ibid., 333.

216 **"The old well, known as the Manhattan Well":** *New York Times*, 18 April 1869.

216 **129 Spring Street:** Stone, *History of New York City*, 342. The 1869 *Times* article misprints the address as 115 Spring Street. Subsequent accounts, for example, an 1872 *Harper's* article and later newspaper articles (including in the *Times* itself), identify the location as either 129 Spring Street or 89½ Greene Street, which is the alleyway behind 129 Spring. Stone might be the first key identification, though, because while he does not give a street address, he identifies the well's location as "just above the present line of Spring Street between Greene and Wooster Streets." This description fits for 129 Spring, but not 115 Spring. It was indeed at 129 Spring Street that a well was rediscovered a century later.

That the well was near Spring Street—something that some later commentators were not even sure of—is clearly indicated by the aforementioned advertisement seeking landfill (*NYDA*, 29 June 1804), which identified "lots, situated on Spring-street, near the Manhattan Well."

216 **a pawnbroker:** *New-York Herald*, 11 May 1856.

216 **"O. Spotswood's Antidote for Tobacco":** *Farmer's Cabinet* (Amherst, N.H.), 25 December 1862.

216 **a German beer hall:** *Der Zeitgeist* (Egg Harbor City, N.J.), 12 November 1870.

216 **a Communist meeting elected Victorian firebrand Victoria Woodhull:** "Crinoline in Communist Councils," *New-York Herald*, 10 March 1873.

216 **"on the anniversary of her murder":** *Brooklyn Daily Eagle*, 21 July 1889.

216 **"a sturdy German carpenter":** *Pittsburg Dispatch*, 16 June 1889. The alternate spelling of *Pittsburgh* is per the original newspaper.

217 **"Winds stir sooty papers in it":** "About New York," *New York Times*, 23 October 1957.

217 **the owner of the Manhattan Bistro set about excavating:** *Ghost Stories:* "The Ghost of Elma Sands," Travel Channel, 18 June 2010. There is otherwise very little accurate information in this production.

217 **the owners and employees like to trade stories:** Ibid.

217 **it was said that Levi's defense counsel:** Parton, *Life and Times of Aaron Burr*, 148.

217 **"He used to say":** Ibid.

218 **When Hamilton's son recounted it:** John C. Hamilton, *History of the Republic of the United States of America*, 746.

# [ SOURCES ]

Adams, John. *Works of John Adams, Second President of the United States: With a Life of the Author, Notes, and Illustrations, by His Grandson Charles Francis Adams.* 10 vols. Boston: Little, Brown, 1850–56.

Alden, Timothy. *A Collection of American Epitaphs and Inscriptions: With Occasional Notes.* 5 vols. New York: S. Marks, 1814.

Alschuler, Albert W., and Andrew G. Deiss. "A Brief History of the Criminal Jury in the United States." *University of Chicago Law Review* 61, no. 3 (1994): 867–928.

*Aristotle's Master-Piece: Completed in Two Parts.* New York: Company of Flying Stationers, 1798.

Arnebeck, Bob. "Yellow Fever in New York City, 1791–1799." Presented at the 26th Conference on New York State History, June 9–11, 2005, Syracuse, New York. Archived at http://bobarnebeck.com/yfinnyc.html.

Baker, Frank. *From Wesley to Asbury: Studies in American Methodism.* Durham, N.C.: Duke University Press, 1976.

Bancker, Abraham. Papers, ca. 1774–1815. New-York Historical Society.

Bank of the Manhattan Company. *The Act of Incorporation of the Manhattan Company: Passed April 2, 1799.* New York, 1833.

———. *Early New-York and the Bank of the Manhattan Company.* New York, 1920.

Barnes, Thurlow Weed. *The Life of Thurlow Weed, Including His Autobiography and a Memoir.* Boston: Houghton Mifflin, 1884.

Barrett, Walter. *The Old Merchants of New York City.* 5 vols. New York: Carleton, 1863.

Bartley, O. W. *A Treatise on Forensic Medicine; or, Medical Jurisprudence.* Bristol, England: Barry and Son, 1815.

Berger, Meyer. *Meyer Berger's New York.* New York: Fordham University Press, 2004.

Beveridge, Albert. *The Life of John Marshall.* Boston: Houghton Mifflin, 1919

Black, Patti Carr. *Art in Mississippi, 1720–1980.* Jackson: University Press of Mississippi, 1998.

Blackmar, Elizabeth. *Manhattan for Rent, 1785–1850.* Ithaca, N.Y.: Cornell University Press, 1989.

Bleecker, Elizabeth de Hart. Diary, 1799–1806. New York Public Library.

Blumberg, Phillip. *Repressive Jurisprudence in the Early American Republic: The First Amendment and the Legacy of English Law.* New York: Cambridge University Press, 2010.

Brookes, Joshua. "The Journal of Joshua Brookes, 1798–1803." Typed manuscript. New-York Historical Society.

Brown, Charles Brockden. "The Trials of Arden." *Monthly Magazine* 2 (July 1800): 19–36.

Bryant, William Cullen. *Reminiscences of the "Evening Post."* New York: W. C. Bryant, 1851.

Bullough, Vern L. "An Early American Sex Manual; or, Aristotle Who?" *Early American Literature* 7, no. 3 (1973): 236–46.

Burney, William. *A New Universal Dictionary of the Marine.* London: T. Cadell et al., 1830.

Burr, Aaron. *Memoirs of Aaron Burr: With Miscellaneous Selections from His Correspondence.* Edited by Matthew L. Davis. 2 vols. New York: Harper and Brothers, 1836.

———. Papers, 1774–1836. New-York Historical Society.

———. *Political Correspondence and Public Papers of Aaron Burr.* Edited by Mary-Jo Kline. 2 vols. Princeton, N.J.: Princeton University Press, 1983.

———. *The Private Journal of Aaron Burr During His Residence of Four Years in Europe.* Edited by Matthew Livingston Davis. New York: Harper and Brothers, 1838.

Burrows, Edwin G., and Mike Wallace. *Gotham: A History of New York City to 1898.* New York: Oxford University Press, 1998.

*By-laws and Ordinances of the Mayor, Aldermen and Commonalty of the City of New York.* New York: William B. Townsend, 1839.

Census of the United States. *Compendium of the Tenth Census,* Part 1. Washington, D.C.: Government Printing Office, 1880.

Chernow, Ron. *Alexander Hamilton.* New York: Penguin Press, 2004.

Chester, Alden, and Edwin Melvin Williams. *Courts and Lawyers of New York: A History, 1609–1925.* 3 vols. New York: American Historical Society, 1925.

Chitty, Joseph. *Reports of Cases Principally on Practice and Pleading, Determined in the Court of the King's Bench . . . with Copious Notes of Other Important Decisions.* 2 vols. London: Henry Butterworth, 1820.

"Christmas in America." *The Living Age* 64, no. 816 (January 1860): 171.

Clarkson, Thomas. *A Portraiture of Quakerism: Taken from a View of the Education and Discipline, Social Manners, Civil and Political Economy, Religious*

*Principles and Character, of the Society of Friends.* New York: Samuel Stansbury, 1806.

Coldengham History and Preservation Society. "The Colden Family of Early America." http://www.coldenpreservation.org/ColdenDescendents January2011.pdf.

Coleman, Nannie McCormack. *The Constitution and Its Framers.* Chicago: Scott Foresman, 1904.

Coleman, William. *A Collection of the Facts and Documents, Relative to the Death of Major-General Alexander Hamilton, with Comments.* New York: I. Riley, 1804.

———. *Report of the Trial of Levi Weeks: On an Indictment for the Murder of Gulielma Sands, on Monday the Thirty-First Day of March, and Tuesday the First Day of April, 1800. Taken in Short Hand by a Clerk of the Court.* New York: John Furman, 1800.

[Connah, Keturah.] *Guilty, or Not Guilty: The True Story of the Manhattan Well.* New York: G. W. Carleton, 1870.

*A Correct Account of the Trials of Charles M'Manus, John Hauer, Elizabeth Hauer, Patrick Donagan, Francis Cox, and Others; at Harrisburgh June Oyer and Terminer, 1798. For the Murder of Francis Shitz, on the Night of the 28th December, 1797, at Heidelberg Township, Dauphin County, in the Commonwealth of Pennsylvania: Containing, the Whole Evidence, and the Substance of All the Law Arguments in Those Celebrated Trials.* Harrisburg, Pa.: John Wyeth, 1798.

Costello, Augustine E. *Our Police Protectors: History of the New York Police from the Earliest Period to the Present Time.* New York: Cadmus Press, 1885.

Davis, B. T. "George Edward Male M.D., the Father of English Medical Jurisprudence." *Proceedings of the Royal Society of Medicine* 67, no. 2 (1974): 117–20.

De Voe, Thomas. *The Market Book: Containing a Historical Account of the Public Markets in the City of New York, Boston, Philadelphia and Brooklyn.* New York: Printed for the author, 1862.

Diamond, Beatrice. *An Episode in American Journalism: A History of David Frothingham and His "Long Island Herald."* Port Washington, New York: Kennikat Press, 1964.

Dietz, Robert E., and Fred Dietz. *1913: A Leaf from the Past, Then and Now; Origin of the Late Robert Edwin Dietz—His Business Career, and Some Interesting Facts About New York.* New York: R. E. Dietz, 1914.

Doerflinger, Thomas A. *A Vigorous Spirit of Enterprise: Merchants and Economic Development in Revolutionary Philadelphia.* Chapel Hill: University of North Carolina Press, 1986.

Drinker, Elizabeth. *Extracts from the Journal of Elizabeth Drinker, from 1759–1807.* Philadelphia: J. B. Lippincott, 1889.

Duras, Victor Hugo. "Alexander Hamilton's Place in History." *Americana* 6 (April 1911): 325–30.

Dwight, Timothy. *Travels in New-England and New-York*. Vol. 3. New Haven, Conn.: S. Converse, 1822.

Eddy, Thomas. *A Report of a Committee of the Humane Society: Appointed to Inquire into the Number of Tavern Licenses; the Manner of Granting Them; Their Effects upon the Community . . . and to Visit Bridewell*. New York: Collins and Perkins, 1810.

Farr, Samuel. *Elements of Medical Jurisprudence; or, A Succinct and Compendious Description of Such Tokens in the Human Body as Are Requisite to Determine the Judgment of a Coroner*. London: J. Callow, 1814.

"Fatal Accidents: How Far Preventable." *Edinburgh Review* 94 (July 1851): 98–127.

Fawcett, Edgar. "New Year's Day in Old New-York." *Lippincott's Magazine*, January 1895, 136–38.

*Fifteenth Annual Report, 1910, of the American Scenic and Historic Preservation Society*. Albany, N.Y.: J. B. Lyon, 1910.

Fitch, Charles Elliott. *Encyclopedia of Biography of New York City*. New York: American Historical Society, 1916.

Fleming, Thomas. *Duel: Alexander Hamilton, Aaron Burr, and the Future of America*. New York: Basic Books, 1999.

Freeman, Joanne B. "Dueling as Politics: Reinterpreting the Burr-Hamilton Duel." *William and Mary Quarterly* 53, no. 2 (1996): 289–318.

Freneau, Philip. *A Collection of Poems, on American Affairs, and a Variety of Other Subjects*. New York: David Longworth, 1815.

Friedman, Leon, and Fred Israel, eds. *The Justices of the Supreme Court, 1789–1978: Their Lives and Major Opinions*. 5 vols. New York: Chelsea House, 1980.

Gerlach, Don. *Proud Patriot: Philip Schuyler and the War of Independence, 1775–1783*. Syracuse, N.Y.: Syracuse University Press, 1987.

Gillogly, James J. "Breaking an Eighteenth Century Shorthand System." *Cryptologia* 11, no. 2 (1987): 93–98.

Guide to the Pierpont Edwards Papers, MS 1357. Yale University Library.

Hall, Kermit, ed. *Oxford Companion to the Supreme Court of the United States*. New York: Oxford University Press, 2005.

Halttunen, Karen. *Murder Most Foul: The Killer and the American Gothic Imagination*. New York: Harvard University Press, 1998.

Hamilton, Alexander. *The Law Practice of Alexander Hamilton: Documents and Commentary*. Edited by Julius Goebel, Jr. 5 vols. New York: Columbia University Press, 1964–81.

———. *The Papers of Alexander Hamilton*. Edited by Harold C. Syrett. 27 vols. New York: Columbia University Press, 1979.

————. *The Works of Alexander Hamilton: Containing His Correspondence, and His Political and Official Writings, Exclusive of the Federalist, Civil and Military.* Edited by John C. Hamilton. 7 vols. New York: J. F. Trow, Printer, 1850–51.

Hamilton, Allan McLane. *The Intimate Life of Alexander Hamilton: Based Chiefly upon Original Family Letters and Other Documents, Many of Which Have Never Been Published.* New York: Charles Scribner's Sons, 1910.

Hamilton, John C. *The History of the Republic of the United States of America: As Traced in the Writings of Alexander Hamilton and of His Contemporaries.* Vol. 7. Philadelphia: J. B. Lippincott, 1864.

Hammond, Bray. *Banks and Politics in America, from the Revolution to the Civil War.* Princeton: Princeton University Press, 1957.

Hardie, James. *An Account of the Malignant Fever, Lately [sic] Prevalent in the City of New-York.* New York: Hurtin and M'Farland, 1799.

————. *An Account of the Yellow Fever, Which Occurred in the City of New-York, in the Year 1822: To Which Is Prefixed a Brief Sketch of the Different Pestilential Diseases, with Which This City Was Afflicted, in the Years 1798, 1799, 1803, and 1805.* New York: Samuel Marks, 1822.

————. *An Impartial Account of the Trial of Mr. Levi Weeks, for the Supposed Murder of Miss Julianna Elmore Sands: At a Court Held in the City of New-York, March 31, 1800.* New York: M. M'Farlane, 1800.

"Hardy's Trial." *Scots Magazine* 56 (November 1794): 715–26.

Harris, J. "New York's First Scientific Body: The Literary and Philosophical Society, 1814–1834." *Annals of the New York Academy of Sciences* 196, no. 7 (1972): 329–37.

Highfill, Philip H., Jr., Kalman A. Burnim, and Edward A. Langhans, eds. *A Biographical Dictionary of Actors, Actresses, Musicians, Dancers, Managers, and Other Stage Personnel in London: 1660–1800.* 16 vols. Carbondale: Southern Illinois University Press, 1993.

*Historic Buildings Now Standing in New York Which Were Erected Prior to Eighteen Hundred.* New York: Bank of the Manhattan Company, 1914.

Hooper, Robert. *A Compendious Medical Dictionary: Containing an Explanation of the Terms in Anatomy, Physiology, Surgery, Materia Medica, Chemistry, and Practice of Physic.* 2nd ed. London: Murray and Highley, 1801.

Hosack, Alexander Eddy. *A Memoir of the Late David Hosack, M.D . . . by His Son.* Privately printed.

Howard, Hugh. *Dr. Kimball and Mr. Jefferson: Rediscovering the Founding Fathers of American Architecture.* New York: Bloomsbury, 2006.

Hudson, Mrs., and Mrs. Donat. *The New Practice of Cookery, Pastry, Baking, and Preserving: Being the Country Housewife's Best Friend.* Edinburgh: J. Moir, 1804.

Hurd, Henry Mill, et al. *The Institutional Care of the Insane in the United States and Canada.* 4 vols. Baltimore: Johns Hopkins Press, 1916.

Isenberg, Nancy. *Fallen Founder: The Life of Aaron Burr.* New York: Viking, 2007.

Jacob, Giles, and T. E. Tomlins. *The Law-Dictionary: Explaining the Rise, Progress, and Present State, of the English Law, in Theory and Practice.* 2 vols. London: Andrew Strahan, 1797.

Janvier, Thomas A. *In Old New York.* New York: Harper and Brothers, 1894.

Jenkins, John Stilwell. *The New Clerk's Assistant; or, Book of Practical Forms.* Auburn, N.Y.: Derby and Miller, 1851.

King-Hele, Desmond, and Joy Hancox. "Man of Many Mysteries." *Notes and Records of the Royal Society of London* 50, no. 2 (1996): 256–58.

Kirk, Edward C. "Pioneer Dentistry in New York: An Historical Study." *Dental Cosmos* 48, no. 10 (October 1906): 990.

Kleiger, Estelle Fox. *The Trial of Levi Weeks; or, The Manhattan Well Mystery.* Chicago: Academy Chicago, 1989.

Koeppel, Gerald. *Water for Gotham: A History.* Princeton, N.J.: Princeton University Press, 2001.

Laight, Henry. Diaries, 1795–1803, 1816–1822. New-York Historical Society.

Lamb, Martha J. *History of the City of New York: Its Origin, Rise, and Progress.* 3 vols. New York: A. S. Barnes, 1877.

Langbein, John. *The Origins of Adversary Criminal Trial.* New York: Oxford University Press, 2003.

Larson, Edward J. *A Magnificent Catastrophe: The Tumultuous Election of 1800, America's First Presidential Campaign.* New York: Free Press, 2007.

Law, John. *The New York Directory, and Register, for the Year 1796.* New York: John Buel, 1796.

Leach, Thomas. *Cases in Crown Law, Determined by the Twelve Judges.* 2nd ed. London: T. Cadell, 1792.

Lebergott, Stanley. "Wage Trends, 1800–1900," in *Trends in the American Economy in the Nineteenth Century: A Report of the National Bureau of Economic Research,* 449–98. Princeton, N.J.: Princeton University Press, 1960.

Livingston, Edwin Brockholst. *The Livingstons of Livingston Manor: Being the History of That Branch of the Scottish House of Callendar Which Settled in the English Province of New York During the Reign of Charles the Second.* New York: Knickerbocker Press, 1910.

Lodge, Henry Cabot. *Alexander Hamilton.* Boston: Houghton Mifflin, 1883.

Longworth, David. *Longworth's American Almanack, New-York Register, and City Directory: For the Twenty-Third Year of American Independence.* New York: T. and J. Swords, 1798.

————. *Longworth's American Almanack, New-York Register, and City Directory: For the Twenty-Fourth Year of American Independence.* New York: John C. Totten, 1799.

————. *Longworth's American Almanack, New-York Register, and City Directory: For the Twenty-Fifth Year of American Independence.* New York: D. Longworth, 1800.

————. *Longworth's American Almanack, New-York Register, and City Directory: For the Twenty-Sixth Year of American Independence.* New York: D. Longworth, 1801.

Longworth, David, [ed]. *A Brief Narrative of the Trial for the Bloody and Mysterious Murder of the Unfortunate Young Woman in the Famous Manhattan Well.* New York: David Longworth (attrib.), 1800.

MacNally, Leonard. *The Rules of Evidence on Pleas of the Crown, Illustrated from Printed and Manuscript Trials and Cases.* London: J. Butterworth, 1802.

"The Manhattan Well Murder." *Harper's New Monthly* 44 (May 1872): 924–29.

Maude, John. *Visit to the Falls of Niagara in 1800.* London: Longmans et al., 1826.

Maxey, David W. "The Union Farm: Henry Drinker's Experiment in Deriving Profit from Virtue." *Pennsylvania Magazine of History and Biography* 107, no. 4 (1983): 607–29.

McLeMore, Richard. *A History of Mississippi.* 2 vols. Hattiesburg: University and College Press of Mississippi, 1981.

Mines, John F. *A Tour Around New York, and My Summer Acre: Being the Recreations of Mr. Felix Oldboy.* New York: Harper and Brothers, 1893.

*The Minutes of the Common Council of the City of New York, 1784–1831.* 19 vols. New York: City of New York, 1917.

Mohl, Raymond A. *Poverty in New York, 1783–1825.* New York: Oxford University Press, 1971.

Monaghan, Frank, and Marvin Lowenthal. *This Was New York: The Nation's Capital in 1789.* Garden City, N.Y.: Doubleday, 1943.

Morgan, John. *Essays: Upon 1. The Law of Evidence. II. New Trials. III. Special Verdicts. IV. Trials at Bar. And V. Repleaders.* 3 vols. Dublin: E. Lynch et al., 1789.

Morhouse, Oliver. "A Boy's Reminiscences." *Old New York* 1, no. 5 (December 1889): 332–44.

Moulton, Alphonso, Howard L. Sampson, and Granville Fernald, eds. *Centennial History of Harrison, Maine: Containing the Centennial Celebration of 1905, and Historical and Biographical Matter.* Portland, Maine: Southworth, 1909.

Muller, Gilbert. *William Cullen Bryant: Author of America.* Albany: State University of New York Press, 2008.

Myers, Gustavus. *The History of Tammany Hall*. 2nd ed. New York: Boni and Liveright, 1917.

Nagel, Paul. *John Quincy Adams: A Public Life, a Private Life*. New York: Knopf, 1997.

New York Common Council. *Manual of the Corporation of the City of New York, for the Years 1845–46*. New York: Council, 1846.

Nolosco, Marynita Anderson. *Physician Heal Thyself: Medical Practitioners of Eighteenth-Century New York*. New York: Peter Lang, 2004.

"The Olden Time." *Old New York* 1, no. 6 (January 1890): 422–40.

Oliver, Wes. "The Modern History of Probable Cause." Widener Law School Legal Studies Research Paper No. 10–12, April 22, 2010. http://ssrn.com/abstract=1594261.

O'Neill, Timothy P. "Vindicating the Defendant's Constitutional Right to Testify at a Criminal Trial." *University of Pittsburgh Law Review* 51, no. 4 (1990). http://ssrn.com/abstract=1008143.

*The Only Correct Account of the Life, Character, and Conduct of John Banks, Who Was Executed on the 11th Day of July, 1806 for the Wilful Murder of His Wife [with] Correct Copy of His Trial*. New York, 1806.

Ordronaux, John. *Commentaries on the Lunacy Laws of New York State: And on the Judicial Aspects of Insanity at Common Law and in Equity, Including Procedure, as Expounded in England and the United States*. Albany, N.Y.: John D. Parsons, 1878.

———. "Judicial Problems Relating to the Disposition of Insane Criminals." *Criminal Law Magazine* 2, no. 5 (1881): 591–618.

*Paine Family Records: A Journal of Genealogical and Biographical Information Respecting the American Families of Payne, Paine, Payn, etc.* New York, 1880.

Paris, John, and John Fonblanque. *Medical Jurisprudence*. London: W. Phillips, 1823.

Park, James Allan. *A System of the Law of Marine Insurances: With Three Chapters on Bottomry; on Insurances of Lives; and on Insurances Against Fire*. London: T. Whieldon, 1787.

Parton, James. *The Life and Times of Aaron Burr: Lieutenant-Colonel in the Army of the Revolution, United States Senator, Vice-President of the United States, etc.* New York: Mason Brothers, 1857.

Pasley, Jeffrey. *The Tyranny of Printers: Newspaper Politics in the Early American Republic*. Charlottesville: University of Virginia Press, 2002.

Pelletreau, William Smith. *A History of Long Island: From Its Earliest Settlement to the Present Time*. 3 vols. New York: Lewis, 1905.

Pepys, Samuel. *The Diary of Samuel Pepys*. Boston: C. C. Brainard, 1892.

Pidgin, Charles Felton. *Theodosia, the First Gentlewoman of Her Time: The Story of Her Life, and the History of Persons and Events Connected Therewith*. Boston: C. M. Clark, 1907.

Powell, John Harvey. *Bring Out Your Dead: The Great Plague of Yellow Fever in Philadelphia in 1793*. Philadelphia: University of Pennsylvania Press, 1949.

*Proceedings of the Old Bailey*, 20 September 1797. http://www.oldbaileyonline .org/browse.jsp?path=sessionsPapers%2F17970920.xml.

Rapalje, Stewart, and Robert L. Lawrence, *A Dictionary of American and English Law: With Definitions of the Technical Terms of the Canon and Civil Laws*. 2 vols. Jersey City, N.J.: Frederick D. Linn, 1888.

Remer, Rosalind. *Printers and Men of Capital: Philadelphia Book Publishers in the New Republic*. Philadelphia: University of Pennsylvania Press, 1996.

*Report of the Manhattan Company*. New York: John Furman, 1799.

*Report of the Trial of Henry Bedlow, for Committing a Rape on Lanah Sawyer: Final Arguments of the Counsel on Each Side: In a Court of Oyer and Terminer, and Gaol Delivery for the City and County of New-York, held 8th October, 1793*. New York, 1793.

*Report on the Trial of Richard D. Croucher: On an Indictment for Rape on Margaret Miller; on Tuesday, the 8th Day of July 1800*. New York: George Forman, 1800.

*Reports of the Commissioners of Inquiry into the State of Education in Wales*. London: William Clowes and Sons, 1848.

*The Reprobate's Reward; or, A Looking-Glass for Disobedient Children*. Philadelphia, 1793.

Reubens, Beatrice G. "Burr, Hamilton and the Manhattan Company: Part I: Gaining the Charter." *Political Science Quarterly* 72, no. 4 (December 1957): 578–607.

Ring, Malvin. "Benjamin Franklin and the Dentist: The Story of R. C. Skinner." *Journal of the History of Dentistry* 54, no. 2 (2006): 64–68.

Ritter, Abraham. *Philadelphia and Her Merchants: As Constituted Fifty–Seventy Years Ago*. Philadelphia: Abraham Ritter, 1860.

Robbins, Christine. *David Hosack, Citizen of New York*. Philadelphia: American Philosophical Society, 1964.

Robertson, David. *The Trial of Aaron Burr for Treason: Printed from the Report Taken in Short Hand*. 2 vols. New York: James Cockcroft, 1875.

Rogow, Arnold. *A Fatal Friendship: Alexander Hamilton and Aaron Burr*. New York: Hill and Wang, 1998.

Ross, Peter. *The Scot in America*. New York: Raeburn, 1896.

Sabine, Lorenzo. *Notes on Duels and Duelling: Alphabetically Arranged with a Preliminary Historical Essay*. Boston: Crosby, Nichols, 1855.

*Sacred Music, to Be Performed in St. Paul's Church, on Tuesday the 31st December,*

*1799, by the Anacreontic and Philharmonic Societies, at the Funeral Ceremonies in Honor of the Memory of the Late General Washington.* New York, 1799.

Sampson, William. *Trial of Robert M. Godwin, on an Indictment of Manslaughter for Killing James Stoughton, Esq.* New York: G. L. Birch, 1819.

Scisco, L. D. "Onondaga County Records—1793," *New York Genealogical and Biographical Record* 33, no. 2 (April 1902): 76–79.

"Seal Stalking in the Orkneys," *Fishing, Fish Culture, and the Aquarium,* 21 December 1889, 585–86.

Sherk, H. H. "David Hosack, M.D., and Rutgers: The Politics of Medical Education in the Nineteenth Century." *New Jersey Medicine: The Journal of the Medical Society of New Jersey* 99 (2002): 17–22.

Simonhoff, Harry. *Jewish Notables in America, 1776–1865.* New York: Greenberg, 1956.

Slawinski, Scott. "A Tale of Two Murders: The Manhattan Well Case as Source Material for Charles Brockden Brown's 'The Trials of Arden.'" *Early American Literature* 44, no. 2 (2009): 365–98.

Sprague, William. *Annals of the American Pulpit; or, Commemorative Notices of Distinguished American Clergymen of Various Denominations, from the Early Settlement of the Country to the Close of the Year Eighteen Hundred and Fifty-Two.* 9 vols. New York: Robert Carter and Brothers, 1857–[1869].

Stone, William L. *History of New York City: From the Discovery to the Present Day.* New York: Virtue and Yorston, 1872.

Stookey, Byron. "Nicholas Romayne: First President of the College of Physicians and Surgeons, New York City." *Bulletin of the New York Academy of Medicine* 43, no. 7 (July 1967): 576–97.

Stoutenburgh, Isaac. *Report of the Inspectors of the State-Prison.* Albany, N.Y.: Loring Andrews, 1799.

Thorburn, Grant. *Fifty Years' Reminiscences of New-York; or, Flowers from the Garden of Laurie Todd.* New York: Daniel Fanshaw, 1845.

Tiedemann, Joseph, and Eugene R. Fingerhut. *The Other New York: The American Revolution Beyond New York City, 1763–1787.* Albany: State University of New York Press, 2006.

Tomlins, Thomas. *The Law Dictionary: Defining and Interpreting the Terms or Words of Art and Explaining the Rise, Progress, and Present State of the English Law.* London: C. and R. Baldwin, 1810.

*The Trial of John Donnellan, Esq., . . . for the Wilful Murder of Sir Theodosius Boughton, Bart.* London: T. Brewman, 1781.

Ukers, William Harrison. *All About Coffee.* New York: Tea and Coffee Trade Journal Company, 1922.

Washington, George. *Washington's Political Legacies: To Which Is Annexed an Appendix, Containing an Account of His Illness, Death, and the National*

*Tributes of Respect Paid to His Memory, with a Biographical Outline of His Life and Character.* Boston: John Russell and John West, 1800.

Watson, John F. *Annals and Occurrences of New York City and State in the Olden Time: Being a Collection of Memoirs, Anecdotes, and Incidents Concerning the City, Country, and Inhabitants, from the Days of the Founders.* Philadelphia: H. F. Anners, 1846.

———. *Historic Tales of Olden Time: Concerning the Early Settlement and Advancement of New-York City and State.* New York: Collins and Hannay, 1832.

Webster, Noah. *A Brief History of Epidemic and Pestilential Diseases; with the Principal Phenomena of the Physical World, Which Precede and Accompany Them, and Observations Deduced from the Facts Stated.* 2 vols. Hartford, Conn.: Hudson and Goodwin, 1799.

Wharton, Francis. *State Trials of the United States During the Administrations of Washington and Adams: With References, Historical and Professional, and Preliminary Notes on the Politics of the Times.* Philadelphia: Carey and Hart, 1849.

Wharton, Francis, and Moreton Stillé. *A Treatise on Medical Jurisprudence.* Philadelphia: Kay and Brother, 1855.

Willard, David. *Willard's History of Greenfield.* Greenfield, Mass.: Kneeland and Eastman, 1838.

Wills, Garry. *"Negro President": Jefferson and the Slave Power.* New York: Houghton Mifflin, 2003.

Young, James Harvey. *The Toadstool Millionaires: A Social History of Patent Medicines in America Before Federal Regulation.* Princeton N.J.: Princeton University Press, 1961.

# [ Index ]

# [ ABOUT THE AUTHOR ]

PAUL COLLINS is an associate professor at Portland State University and the author of seven previous books. His work has also appeared in the *New York Times*, *New Scientist*, and *Slate*. He edits the Collins Library imprint of McSweeney's Books and appears on NPR's *Weekend Edition* as the show's resident literary detective.